The First Americans
Race, Evolution, and the Origin of Native Americans

Who were the first Americans? What is their relationship to living
native peoples in the Americas? What do their remains tell us of the
current concepts of racial variation, and short-term evolutionary
change and adaptation? The recent discoveries in the Americas of the
9000–12 000-year-old skeletons such as "Kennewick Man" in
Washington State, "Luzia" in Brazil, and "Prince of Wales Island Man"
in Alaska, have begun to challenge our understanding of who first
entered the Americas at the end of the last ice age. New archaeological
and geological research is beginning to change the hypothesis of land
bridge crossings and the extinction of ancient animals. *The First
Americans* explores these questions by using racial classifications and
microevolutionary techniques to understand better who colonized the
Americas and how. It will be required reading for all those interested in
anthropology, and the history and archaeology of the earliest
Americans.

JOSEPH POWELL is Associate Professor in the Department of
Anthropology at the University of New Mexico. He has published
extensively on the skeletal and dental remains of Paleoindian peoples,
and was a lead scientist for the US Federal Government investigation of
the "Kennewick Man" skeleton.

The First
Americans

Race, Evolution, and the Origin of Native Americans

JOSEPH F. POWELL
University of New Mexico

CAMBRIDGE UNIVERSITY PRESS

PUBLISHED BY THE PRESS SYNDICATE OF THE UNIVERSITY OF CAMBRIDGE
The Pitt Building, Trumpington Street, Cambridge, United Kingdom

CAMBRIDGE UNIVERSITY PRESS
The Edinburgh Building, Cambridge CB2 2RU, UK
40 West 20th Street, New York, NY 10011-4211, USA
477 Williamstown Road, Port Melbourne, VIC 3207, Australia
Ruiz de Alarcón 13, 28014 Madrid, Spain
Dock House, The Waterfront, Cape Town 8001, South Africa

http://www.cambridge.org

First published 2005

Printed in the United Kingdom at the University Press, Cambridge

Typeface Swift 9/13pt.   *System* Advent 3B2 8.07f [PND]

A catalog record for this book is available from the British Library

Library of Congress Cataloging in Publication data

ISBN 0 521 82350 1 hardback
ISBN 0 521 53035 0 paperback

Dedication

To Gentry, who pointed out the path,
And to Leah, who has been at my side while I traveled along it.

Contents

Acknowledgments   *page*   viii

Prologue   The Kennewick controversy   1

PART I
Race and variation

1   Debating the origins of Native Americans   17
2   A brief history of race   29
3   Evolutionary approaches to human variation   58
4   Recent population variation in the Americas   85

PART II
The Pleistocene peopling of the Americas

5   The Pleistocene and ice-age environments   103
6   Ancient cultures and migration to the Americas   114
7   Kennewick Man and his contemporaries   128
8   Human variation in the Pleistocene   169

PART III
The First Americans, race and evolution

9   Racial models of Native American origins   187
10   Evolutionary models of Native American origins   214
11   The First Americans: Native American origins   229

References   237
Index   265

Acknowledgments

Several people helped to bring this book into being. My thanks to Dr. Tracey Sanderson and the rest of the Cambridge University Press Staff for their editorial skills and patience, through the many incarnations of the text and figures. Many thanks to Chris Millington and Tom Windes, for their help in making and re-making many of the illustrations. Chris's hard work and dedication to the pre-production process was critical for the completion of the final text and figures. His help was invaluable and is much appreciated. I was fortunate to have the support and help of my wonderful wife Leah, our families, friends, and colleagues, who have offered advice and love in innumerable ways.

Thanks to my colleagues in Brazil, especially Drs. Walter Neves and André Prous, who have graciously involved me in their research on the oldest South American remains. I thank Dr. James Chatter for access to the cast and photographs of the Kennewick Man skull, as well as Dr. Frank McManamon and the US Department of the Interior for providing access to the original Kennewick Man skeleton. Thanks also to my colleagues who were a part of the government analysis team(s) for the Kennewick remains and to the tribal leaders and elders who allowed our study to be carried out after the consultation process. I also appreciate the funding and support of the Fundacão de Amparo à Perquisa do Estado de São Paulo, Brasil, the Wenner-Gren Foundation for Anthropological Research (Grant No. 5666), the L. S. B. Leakey Foundation and the University of New Mexico, for continued research support. Several of my students have been involved in this work. While many people and institutions provided support and encouragement, I alone am responsible for any errors in this book.

Prologue   The Kennewick controversy

As the curator of biological anthropology at the Maxwell Museum, I often passed through the exhibits in the biological anthropology area, on my way to the Museum office. One day, I encountered a group of second graders examining the displays of fossil hominids. I noticed that one group of kids was gathered around a display, a reproduction of a 17 000-year-old human burial from a Pleistocene site in France. Our replica had been arranged in the exact state of repose that the original skeleton held for nearly 18 000 years: legs and arms flexed as if asleep, and surrounded by grave goods, including stone tools and shell beads from a necklace. I approached the kids and asked what they could tell about this person. Most smiled and shrugged.

"He's dead," one boy said in a flat voice.

I asked, "Are you sure it's a 'he'?" after the giggles died down.

"How can you tell?" another kid looked to me and asked.

That was my opening to explain the differences in male and female skeletal anatomy and show them the features used to determine sex from a skeleton. Several hands went up, and I called on a girl who seemed particularly interested in the burial display.

"What was her name?" the girl asked.

"We don't know – we can't tell that from the bones," I said.

I went on to use the well-worn "book analogy," explaining how a skeleton was like a book, containing different kinds of information about the person to whom it belonged, provided you could read the information correctly. A boy raised his hand,

"But you don't know who she was?" he asked.

As I thought about how better to explain this, I realized that these kids, like most Americans, were *less* interested in the *what* and *why* questions and simply wanted answers to the *who* questions. *Who* was this person? *Who* were her relatives?

In 1996, the *who* questions were so important that a skeleton was dragged into federal court. American Indians (Native Americans) requested that a 9000-year-old skeleton be returned to them under federal law, while scholars demanded access to it for research purposes. For the first time since its inception, NAGPRA became a (nearly) household word in the USA.

THE NATIVE AMERICAN GRAVES PROTECTION AND REPATRIATION ACT

On November 16, 1990, the 101st US Congress passed Public Law 101–601 (HR 5237; 104 STAT.3050), a piece of human rights legislation better known as the *Native American Graves Protection and Repatriation Act (NAGPRA).*[1] A coalition of lawmakers, Native American activists, tribal elders, and leaders from the museum, archaeology and physical anthropology communities wrote to NAGPRA, to regulate the disposition of Native American remains and associated grave goods.

Many museums contained large skeletal and artifact collections derived from Work Progress Administration[2] (WPA)-era and other excavations of prehistoric and historic archaeological sites in the USA. In addition to human remains, NAGPRA also pertained to "associated funerary objects," "sacred objects," as well as "objects of cultural patrimony." What constituted an "object of cultural patrimony" was open to broader interpretation, despite the two pages-worth of circuitous definitions within the document.

Institutions, such as publicly funded museums, universities, and federal agencies, were required by NAGPRA to create a summary of human remains and artifacts and send it to culturally affiliated Native American tribes, no later than November 2, 1993. The institutions were required to make complete and detailed inventories of human remains, associated funerary objects, and items of cultural patrimony by this date, and then to send the summaries to federally recognized Native American tribes or Native Hawaiian organizations to which these collections were *culturally affiliated.*

It is stated in NAGPRA that, for purposes of repatriation, "cultural affiliation" could be proved by tribes using a

> preponderance of the evidence based on geographical, kinship,
> biological, archaeological, anthropological, linguistic, folkloric, and oral
> traditional, historical or other relevant information or expert opinion.
> (PL101–601; USC 3005. Sec. 7)

The problem was that the law incorporated geographic proximity to the source of a collection or set of remains as a means of determining their cultural affiliation. This was much to the consternation of some biological anthropologists and archaeologists. Geographic proximity has been perhaps the strongest rule used for some prehistoric archaeological collections.

In NAGPRA, museums, institutions, and federal agencies were required to produce summaries of their affected holdings by November 2, 1993, and completed inventories by November 2, 1995. Punishment for those who failed to do so was severe: civil penalties and damages for each offense – each artifact or skeleton was one offense – so that penalties for non-compliance could potentially be in the millions of dollars, in the case of a large collection. Some museums feared loss of federal funding, something not specified in the damages portion of the law. Complicating matters was a concern that museums could be sued over their repatriation decisions. A few last-minute changes to NAGPRA cleared that up.

Complying with NAGPRA was a nightmare for some museums, many of which held extensive archaeological collections. For example, prior to NAGPRA, the Peabody Museum at Harvard University contained a mere 8 million artifacts and other items from North America alone (Lawson, 1999). The situation was no easier for the 771 federally recognized Native American nations, tribes, and bands that were buried in a deluge of NAGPRA-generated paperwork from the 700 or so museums around the country (Lawson, 1999). This meant that tribes often had the burden of responding to numerous NAGPRA requests for consultation from museums that were hundreds or even thousands of miles away. This was especially true in the case of tribes or native organizations in Alaska and Hawaii.

Another difficulty for both museums and tribes in complying with the consultation mandate in NAGPRA relates to the shameful history of forced relocation of Native Americans from their traditional tribal lands. The question for museums was in the case of collections from areas no longer occupied by a tribe (the result of expatriation during the early nineteenth century), such as those tribes relocated to reservations in the Oklahoma and Kansas Territories, during the 1838 "trail of tears." Those tribes would need to prove their cultural affiliation by means other than geographic proximity. That was the tricky part. NAGPRA allowed historical, cultural, archaeological, biological, folkloric, and oral traditional evidence to determine cultural affiliation with artifacts or human remains. However, the law gave no indication of which criterion should have the greatest weight in determining cultural affiliation. This aspect of NAGPRA caused a great deal of consternation for those trying to comply with the law. Some anthropologists felt that mere geographic proximity was not a valid rule for tribes to make affiliation claims for some museum collections, given the history of fluidity of prehistoric peoples across the landscape of North America, especially during the earliest occupation of the Americas by prehistoric peoples known as Paleoindians.[3]

The other problem – how to resolve competing claims – was also dealt with in the details of the law (NAGPRA Sec. 7). The latter is a sore point for some tribal representatives and elders with whom I consulted during the Maxwell Museum's NAGPRA inventory process. Some of the elders distrusted NAGPRA and felt that the law was intended to create inter-tribal conflict over sacred items, which in fact did happen in a few instances, although inter-tribal difficulties were resolved through compromise and discussion.

One repatriation case in which I took part involved over two thousand human remains and their associated grave goods from the site of Pecos Pueblo, New Mexico. Several museums (Peabody Harvard, Peabody Andover, and Maxwell museums) with skeletal collections from the prehistoric Pecos Pueblo and the associated Spanish mission participated in the repatriation process. The museums and tribes coordinated their inventory and consultation process over a period of two years. Ultimately, many of the initial claimant tribes bowed out to allow the Pecos descendants, now living at Jemez Pueblo, to take the lead in accepting the repatriation and in conducting a mass reburial ceremony near the original site. For many museums the inventory process was painful, because of the significant role Pecos collections played in A. V. Kidder's reconstruction of southwestern prehistory, and because of the role the Pecos skeletons played in early attempts to understand *temporal* changes in skeletal variation (Hooton, 1930). Despite some anthropologists' misgivings, the repatriation proved meaningful in terms of understanding and incorporating the tribal views regarding handling the remains and their concerns over accidental inclusion of European burials along with their honored dead. The latter almost occurred at Pecos, as the inventory identified one non-native person (probably a Spanish priest serving at the Pecos mission), whose remains were subsequently returned to the Museum and excluded from the repatriation and reburial ceremony, after consultation with the claimant pueblos and Pecos Pueblo Governor Ruben Sando. Cases of mistaken identity can, and do, happen (Owsley, 1999) but are less frequent in prehistoric collections than those from more recent times.

Many anthropology professors and their graduate students were concerned that their ongoing research would be devastated as skeletal material was repatriated and reburied. But lawmakers included provisions in NAGPRA for that situation, with a catch: the repatriation process and deadline could be delayed if the studies would be of "major benefit to the United States" (PL 101–601 Sec. 7: 5b). Other scientists feared that NAGPRA was the death-knell of scientific archaeology and bioarchaeology in America. This fear resulted from the fact that scientific studies require replication and confirmation of results by independent researchers. Repatriation with subsequent reburial makes confirmation of results impossible. Those fears appear to be unfounded because, as of 2000, only a small proportion (9.5%) of the nearly 200 000 individual Native American skeletons then in museum collections have been repatriated and reburied (Lawson, 1999). NAGPRA's requirement of consultation has led to new research questions and has encouraged improved relationships between anthropologists and the people whose ancestors they study.

Finally, NAGPRA has prompted biological anthropologists to consider the implications of their work and its impact on Native peoples, which has been useful for most of us. On the museum side, the inventories have become very useful, since some collections had not been examined, because of a lack of funding and interest, nor inventoried in great detail since the day they were removed from the ground – with, of course, the exception of Kidder and Hooton's studies.

Speaking of a lack of funding, NAGPRA was, and remains, an unfunded mandate for the institutions, as well as for the tribes. It was a source of financial burden at a time when funds for tribal economic initiatives and public museums were at a low. Ironically, the three- and five-year limits for summaries and inventories pushed institutions to update their collection records and made collections of human remains more accessible for research than they had been at any point over the past 50 years. The inventory process provided information needed by anthropologists to formulate new research questions about American prehistory.

The NAGPRA legislation addressed many issues of concern to Native Americans, as well as those of concern to anthropologists. The legislation was fairly clear on what to do with existing archaeological collections; it was a bit more muddied as far as new and inadvertent discoveries were concerned.

THE KENNEWICK SAGA

July 28, 1996, Columbia River near Kennewick, Washington DC:[4] two college students wading along the Benton county shore of the Columbia River in search of a better vantage point to watch for the start of the annual hydroplane race stumble across a "rock with teeth," which turned out to be a human skull. After the race, they took the sodden skull, now secured in a bucket, to Kennewick police officers patrolling the area.

The officers, students, Benton County Coroner Floyd Johnson, and Deputy Coroner James C. Chatters went back to the recovery site to look for more of the skeletal remains. Once the search was completed and all the bones were collected, a nearly complete skeleton emerged from bones collected along a 60-foot stretch of the river's shoreline. The coroner turned over the bones to Chatters for reconstruction and analysis. Chatters determined that the bones were the remains of a 5-foot-9 (1.75 m)- or 5-foot-10 (1.76 m)-inch tall, somewhat gracile, 40- to 50-year-old male, who had subsisted on a diet of soft foods with a lot of meat. More importantly, after analyzing the reconstructed skull, he reported that the biological heritage of the individual was "Caucasoid," owing to the skull's European morphological features, such as a long, low, cranial vault, and large projecting nose.

Historic-period artifacts were recovered at the discovery site, including an old metal knife. The historic artifacts, combined with the "Caucasoid morphology" of the skull, suggested that this man might have been a deceased trapper. Chatters knew that the first incursion of Europeans into the mid-Columbia plateau was the 1805 Lewis and Clark expedition. His examination of the post-cranial skeleton revealed a temporal inconsistency. Chatters had earlier noted something stone imbedded in the right ilium of the pelvis. He had the bone X-rayed, and when the object did not show up clearly on the X-ray film, as would a piece of metal, Chatters ordered a CAT scan.

The CAT scan revealed the object to be a 2-inch-long stone spear point similar to a Cascade point, a projectile point type common to the area about 4500 to 9000 years ago. Obviously, this was no recent homicide case, nor a lost trapper. This revelation suggested to Chatters and Johnson that an exact date for the skeleton might be in order before they could proceed further. They sent a small piece of bone (about 3 g) to a radiocarbon laboratory. While they waited, Chatters made a set of plastic casts of the odd skull and contacted sculptor Tom McClelland, who often assisted Chatters and the

Coroner's Office in making facial reproductions of unknown persons using skull casts and markers of tissue depths at certain locations.

On August 28, 1996, Chatters and Johnson received the results from the bone sample they had sent to the University of California–Riverside radiocarbon laboratory. The radiocarbon (^{14}C) age[5] confirmed their suspicions, based on the embedded projectile point, about the skeleton's age. The Kennewick skeleton was between 9200 and 9600 years before present (yr BP), with an average ^{14}C age of 9400 yr BP, thus placing him among the limited number of human skeletons older than 8000 yr BP in North and South America. It was also one of the most complete skeletons dating to the time just after the Pleistocene (the Early Holocene), known archaeologically in some areas as the Late Paleoindian period or the Early Archaic period in others.

Not long thereafter, Johnson and Chatters held a press conference to announce the exciting discovery of a 9400-year-old "Caucasoid" man, then dubbed the "Kennewick Man," in the Pacific Northwest. The announcement created a media frenzy, with coverage in national magazines, newspapers, and television programs:

> The cover of *The New Yorker* asked, "Was someone here before the Native Americans?" The tabloid-style headline in *Discover* magazine trumpeted "Europeans Invade America, 20 000 BC." A cover story in *US News & World Report* featured Kennewick Man as evidence for "An America Before the Indians." An article in the *Santa Fe New Mexican* began this way, "When Columbus came to the New World in 1492 and set into motion the chain of events that led to the decimation of Native Americans, was he unknowingly getting revenge for what was done to his ancestor thousands of years before?" (Thomas, 2000: xxi)

All of the fevered speculation about re-writing American pre-history based on just one odd-looking skeleton revealed the public's, and some scientists', very skewed view of human population variation in both the present and past.

On September 13, 1996, a mere five days after the announcement by the Coroner's Office, the US Army Corps of Engineers (COE) Walla Walla District (the federal agency that controls the Columbia River and its shoreline, including the Kennewick Man discovery site) announced its intention to turn the skeleton over to a coalition of five Native American tribes in the area, led by the Confederated Tribes of the Umatilla Indian Reservation, but also including the Colville and Nez Perce tribes, the Wanapum bands, and the Yakima Nation. Under NAGPRA's "inadvertent discoveries" provision (104 Stat.

3051d). After the Corps's notification, "scientists across the country screamed 'foul'" (Thomas, 2000: xxii). Some anthropologists were alarmed about the Corps's decision, and felt that more than mere geographic proximity or oral tradition should be used in assigning cultural affiliation to such an ancient skeleton without detailed study. The provisions of NAGPRA stated that a "preponderance of the evidence" should be used to establish cultural affiliation. However, the COE's decision was based entirely on oral tradition and geographic proximity of the five tribes, and had not considered any possible archaeological, biological, and genetic evidence that could only be provided through a more intensive study of the Kennewick remains. Some anthropologists and other scientists felt that attempts to trace cultural affiliation back 9000 years would be difficult, if not impossible, to support – because the bones were "... so ancient, they rightfully belong to the American public, rather than any special-interest group" (Thomas, 2000: xxii). The media and plaintiffs continued to question how an ancient "Caucasoid" like the Kennewick skeleton might fit into the previously accepted anthropological view of Native American origins, in which Pleistocene-age north Asian people migrated from Siberia to Alaska using the so-called "Bering Land Bridge" and traveled south through an "ice-free" corridor between the Laurentide and Cordilleran glacial masses, subsequently exiting in what is now southern Saskatchewan Province in Canada.

Within weeks, the Kennewick Man became the most famous and controversial deceased person in America, with coverage of the furor in the worldwide media. One late-night television comedian quipped that more Americans could name "a 9000-year-old dead guy in Washington" than could name the Vice-President of the United States. Washington State's congressional delegation tried to pursuade the Walla Walla District COE to allow detailed study by qualified scientists. But the COE had conducted a preliminary NAGPRA summary and a general inventory of the bones, and had locked the skeleton in a secure area of their Battelle facility to secure the remains (Thomas, 2000: xxii–xxiii).

The news of the impending repatriation and possible reburial of the Kennewick remains prompted a group of scientists to intervene in the COE repatriation plans. Led by archaeologist Robson Bonnichsen (Director of Oregon State University's Center for the Study of the First Americans), six other scientists specializing in Paleoindian archaeology and biology filed an injunction in federal court to stop the repatriation process for Kennewick, which they argued was not legal under NAGPRA.

The seven *Bonnichsen* plaintiffs were a very impressive group of scholars. In addition to Bonnichsen (a well-respected leader in Paleoindian-period archaeology), the others involved in the suit included Dr. Douglas Owsley (Smithsonian Institution, physical anthropologist), Dr. Dennis J. Stanford (Smithsonian Institution, archaeologist), Dr. D. Gentry Steele (Texas A&M University, physical anthropologist), Dr. Richard Jantz (University of Tennessee, physical anthropologist), Dr. George Gill (University of Wyoming, physical anthropologist), Dr. C Loring Brace (University of Michigan, physical anthropologist), and Dr. C. Vance Haynes, Jr. (University of Arizona, geoarchaeologist). Bonnichsen also contacted a Portland attorney and archaeology advocate, Alan Schneider, to represent the seven scientists. The case of *Bonnichsen et al.* v. *United States of America* began on October 16, 1996 (Shafer and Stang, 1996).

When the story appeared in the press, it refueled the debate over the origins of Native Americans (see Chapter 1 for a discussion of the scholarly debates regarding Native American origins that began with de Acosta and Garcia in the sixteenth century). The Kennewick case continued in federal court, with federal magistrate John Jelderks reviewing the evidence provided by the defendants, the Army Corp of Engineers. After nearly a year of court arguments, Judge Jelderks issued a criticism of the COE decision to return the Kennewick remains to the tribal coalition without better evidence of cultural affiliation (McManamon, 1997).

On July 30, 1997, the Corps admitted in court that it had not limited access to the Kennewick remains, but had allowed members of the tribal coalition to observe the Corps's handling and storage of the bones. The COE had also permitted tribal elders and spiritual leaders to perform religious ceremonies where the bones were securely housed at Walla Walla District headquarters.

A month later, the Kennewick case took a rather unexpected turn, when another claimant group, the Asatru Folk Assembly, attempted to join the Kennewick fracas. The Asatru are a northern California neo-Pagan religious group who went to the Kennewick discovery site to perform ceremonies and rituals to worship the pre-Christian, northern European (Viking) god Odin. The Asatru Folk Assembly members' feelings of cultural affiliation appear to have been driven solely by the description of the Kennewick remains as "Caucasoid." Exploring this further, Chapter 2 presents past and present views on the concept of *race,* and its use in modern scientific studies of human diversity. The public and scientific confusion over *race* in the case of Kennewick and other ancient skeletons has had a major impact in studies of Native American origins and research regarding the peopling of the Americas.

As the *Bonnichsen et al.* case wound on, several additional controversies arose. First was the release of Chatters' and McClelland's facial reproduction based on the cast of the Kennewick skull. Although facial reproduction can be quite accurate, many tell-tale features critical for identification of a deceased person depend on an assessment of race to determine the size and shape of unpreserved soft tissue features such as the eyes, nose, ears, and lips (Ubelaker, 1989). These features are critical for positive identification in forensic cases, and are the choice of the artist. Chatters' and McClelland's Kennewick bust was beautiful. It depicted an average 40-year-old "Caucasoid" male (based on the initial assessment of the prehistoric skull) that was strikingly similar to English actor Patrick Stewart, of *Star Trek* fame. As noted by Vine Deloria, Jr. (Thomas, 2000: xxv), the bust was also similar to an 1833 portrait of the captive Sauk (Sac) Chief Ma-ka-tai-me-she-kia-kiah, also known as "Black Hawk." The Kennewick facial reproduction also kept the media frenzy going, prompting interviews with both Stewart and Chatters.

The second controversial event was the Corps's burial of the discovery site in April, 1998, during which they dumped several tons of rock and gravel on the bank and adjacent areas, then planted trees to "stabilize" the embankment against erosion. The Bonnichsen plaintiffs charged that the site was more than protected from erosion; it was also protected from any further scientific study. By April, 1998, the Corps had relinquished control of the Kennewick remains to the US Department of the Interior (DOI).

After an out-of-court mediation with all involved parties, the DOI began plans for a more detailed study of the skeleton which they hoped would resolve the question of cultural affiliation by providing geological, archaeological, and biological evidence of affiliation as stipulated in NAGPRA. In September, 1998, Judge Jelderks ordered the relocation of the skeleton to the University of Washington's Burke Museum, as agreed during the mediation, followed by implementation of the DOI's study plan.

In February, 1999 Dr. Jerome Rose (a physical anthropologist at the University of Arkansas), Dr. Julie Stein (a geoarchaeologist at the University of Washington), Dr. Gary Huckleberry (a geoarchaeologist at Washington State University), Dr. Vance Haynes (a geoarchaeologist at the University of Arizona), and I began a week-long inventory and analysis to help determine the cultural affiliation of the skeleton, using cranial measurements and complex statistical analyses to determine his "biological affinity." During the examination, Haynes collected a set of samples for new radiocarbon dates to confirm the age of the skeleton. The radiocarbon tests ultimately confirmed the 9200-year age obtained by Chatters and Johnson. In the biological analyses, we found several interesting pathological and other features in the bones that indicated that Kennewick probably had a difficult and painful life, as Dr. Chatters had first noted. We also found that many of the pathological features noted in the report to the Coroner's Office could not be verified in our analysis. This confirms the Bonnichsen plaintiffs' point, that science proceeds by testing and confirmation (or rejection) of previous studies. Later, in court affidavits, plaintiffs Owsley and Jantz were able to find faults[6] in the DOI team's analyses. The DOI research team found that while a few morphological features were more common in European "Caucasoids," our statistical analyses found a greater probability that the skeleton was most similar to East Asian populations, especially those in Polynesia or from prehistoric Japan, sometimes referred to as Eurasians (Brace *et al.*, 2002; Birdsell, 1951; see also Chapter 3). The Kennewick Man's teeth and skull were not like any Native American sample for which we had cranial or dental data. In fact, like most other ancient skeletons from North and South America, the "Ancient One"[7] looked nothing like someone from a prehistoric, historic, or living Native American population. Such a finding means very little, unless one presumes that all skeletal features are fixed and immutable over time, the main assumption of racial categorizations (also called racial–typological assessments, discussed in Chapter 5).

The basis and methods of racial–typological and evolutionary analyses provide scientists with quite different views of the First Americans, as in the case the initial (Chatters, 1998) and DOI analyses of Kennewick Man. The remainder of this book details the theories, assumptions, data, and results of these conflicting methodologies.

Chapters 5 through 10 examine the possible reasons why Kennewick Man and his ancient contemporaries, from Alaska to Tierra del Fuego have a cranial, facial, and dental morphology that differs so significantly from contemporary Native American peoples who are thought to be the direct descendants of the ancients, and what this pattern means in terms of prehistoric migrations to the Americas, *in situ* population structuring (e.g. microevolution), and response to environmental and dietary change. The final chapter summarizes my findings, views, and thoughts on future research, and contains an attempt to dissuade my anthropological colleagues from using simplified racial and migrationist models typical in research during the first half of the twentieth century. I also present the problem of constructing fanciful interpretations and models from a limited data set, a crime of which I too have been guilty in the past.

KENNEWICK REVISITED?

As I write these words, a new issue over repatriation with respect to ancient American burials is taking place. This is the impending reburial of over 80 skeletons from the Buckeye Knoll (41 VT 105) Cemetery in Victoria County, Texas. The site is located on a diversion channel of the Inter-coastal waterway on the Gulf coastal plain near Victoria, Texas. In this case, many of the 80+ burials are dated in excess of 8000 yr BP (12 000–8000) majority of the burials of just 1000 years younger than Kennewick but approximately the same age as the well-preserved burials from Florida's Windover site. The closest tribes are the Isleta del Sur Pueblo, a mere 700 miles west of Buckeye Knoll in El Paso, Texas, and the Caddo nation of East Texas and Louisiana. This situation has yet to go to court, although the Kennewick plaintiffs and other anthropologists are watching it carefully. The final outcome of the Kennewick case is briefly discussed in Chapter 10.

NOTES

1 The full text of NAGPRA is available at: http://www.web2.cast.uark.edu/other/nps/nagpra/nagpra.dat/lgm003.html.
2 The WPA was established in the 1930s by President Franklin Delano Roosevelt (FDR) as a federal program to keep post-depression unemployed people working, rather than giving them hand-outs or welfare payments. WPA workers built most of the roads into, and buildings inside, the extensive National Parks and forests. WPA workers created bridges, railways and schools, state and federal highways, and other public works still in use across the United States. Much of the excavation of US archaeological sites was accomplished by the men and women of the WPA, under the direction of federal archaeologists.
3 The term Paleoindian is used here to refer to late-Pleistocene (12 500–10 000 yr BP) and early Holocene (11 000–8000 yr BP) (Goodyear, 1999: 434) human skeletons. Most of these skeletons are archaeologically associated with artifacts and deposits from the "Paleoindian period" in a region. However, several of my colleagues have begun to use the term "Paleoamerican," in part to avoid giving the impression that remains so old could be linked to any Native American tribes, and also to indicate that many of these bodies are actually

not clearly associated with *true* Paleoindian culture complexes, such as Clovis or Folsom, but are instead associated with the emergence of early Archaic tools and lifeways (broad-spectrum foraging). For this book, I choose to buck the trend and will use the term Paleoindian to refer to people in the Americas older than 9000 yr BP.

4 The information and chronology concerning the Kennewick Man controversy are drawn from my own recollection as well as from conversations with Jim Chatters and Frank McManamon, and from news accounts by *Tri-City Herald* reporter Mike Lee, made available at the *Herald*'s Kennewick Man Interpretive Center (http://www.tri-cityherald.com). I also verified my ordering of events using D. H. Thomas' excellent book on the history of anthropological studies of Native Americans (Thomas, 2000: xii–xix). These sources are not responsible for any errors contained in my account of the Kennewick Man case.

5 Radiocarbon dating uses the clock-like decay of a radioactive isotope of the carbon atom, which is incorporated into all living organic matter. The clock starts ticking when the organism dies. Carbon-14 has a half-life of about 5730 years, so that the amount left at the time of analysis can be used to estimate the time at which the organism died. See Taylor (1994) for a more detailed account of modern radiocarbon dating methods.

6 What else were they going to say? If the DOI research team did a perfect job, then their case would be moot. But as plaintiff D. G. Steele (personal communication) pointed out: the issue was not the quality of the DOI team's data but the scientific process of independent testing and verification; just as the DOI team confirmed the skeleton's ^{14}C age and verified or refuted some of the findings in the Deputy Coroner's report. This is the way science *should* work. See Goodman's example of forensic mistakes in the Oklahoma City bombing (1998), cited in Thomas (2000: 113).

7 The Umatilla words for the Kennewick Man are Oid-p'ma Natitayt, which roughly translate to the English term "Ancient One."

PART I Race and variation

1

Debating the origins of Native Americans

But in the Southe parte of that contrey,
The people go nakyed always,
The lande is of so great hete!
In the North parte all the clothes
That they were is but bestes skynnes,
They have no nother fete;
But howe the people furst began
In that contrey, or whens they cam,
For clerkes it is questyon

John Rastell, *Interlude of the Four Elements* (1520)
(in Huddleston, 1967: 110)

1.1 EARLY EUROPEAN THOUGHT ON NATIVE AMERICAN ORIGINS

Some of the most perplexing questions in American prehistory concern how and when humans first colonized the New World. Since the sixteenth century, Americanist scholars have debated the origin of Native American peoples. In 1492, most scholars felt that Columbus had sailed to islands just off the coast of Cathay (Asia), so there was no need to question the origin of people he met in Hispañola: it was clear that they were Asians. However, by 1503, "[Amerigo] Vespucci had seen so much of the coastline of America (from Argentina to North Carolina) … that he became convinced it could not be Asia." (Huddleston, 1967: 5). This prompted European speculation that the inhabitants were not therefore Asians. So who were they? How did humans get to the "New World"?

In the sixteenth century, putative answers came fast and furious, based on scanty evidence. The suggestions ranged from refugees from

Plato's sunken Atlantis, to one of the ten lost tribes of Israel (the latter concept found today in the Book of Mormon), to Alejo Vangas' theory that the progenitors of native people in the Americas were lost Carthaginians.

1.2   SCHOLARLY THOUGHT 1492–1729

Acosta's views (1590/1940)

Perhaps the best scholarly work on Native American origins before the nineteenth century was by a Jesuit Missionary named Joseph de Acosta, who, unlike most of his fellow theorists, had actually visited the Americas and had spent time among native peoples there. Acosta went to Peru as part of Viceroy Toledo's entourage in 1570, and began an extensive history of the New World in 1584. He also traveled to Mexico in 1586 to add new information on the Aztecs and Mixtecs to that collected by Juan de Tovar, and returned to Spain in 1587 with extensive notes on the natives that he and others had encountered.

Ultimately, this information was compiled and published as *Historia natural y moral de las Indias* (Acosta, 1590/1940). In *Historia,* Acosta rejected the popular idea that word comparisons from Peruvian languages indicated a Hebraic origin for Native Americans. Acosta felt that language comparisons proved "too weak as arguments to sustain such grand conclusions" (Acosta, 1590/1940: 52). He further argued that because all humans are descended from a single source (i.e. Adam), they must have come from Europe, Africa, or Asia. This view is similar to our current scientific understanding of modern human origins (Stringer, 1985), despite the fact that Acosta was simply trying to fit his observations to the biblical origin story. He rejected the ideas of a second Eden or a second Ark, two of the ideas initially proposed by some Spanish clerics, based on supposed similarities of selected characteristics of dress or custom between the ancient Jews and some Native American groups. Of the theory involving Plato's story of Atlantis, Acosta stated that "only children and old women" would find the theory credible (Acosta, 1590/1940: 84). He refuted the ten lost Jewish tribes model, reasoning that the Jews were commanded to preserve their laws and rituals (such as circumcision) when they left their homeland (Huddleston, 1967: 51), and that the natives of the Indies gave no evidence of practicing the rites of Judaism. Acosta broke with biblical tradition by criticizing the model of Noah and the Ark, pointing out that the Old and New Worlds both had wolves and other aggressive carnivores and that "it was more than enough for men to escape with their lives, driven against their will by the tempest, without carrying foxes and wolves and feeding them at sea" (Acosta, 1590/1940: 76). Acosta then rejected the idea that men carried these animals in ships or that the beasts swam across the broad oceans, or that angelic intervention or a second ark had brought them to the New World. Based on these observations, he postulated, "that the new world we call the Indies is not completely divided and separated from the other [Old] World" (Acosta, 1590/1940: 8990). Acosta presciently conjectured that somewhere in the undiscovered north or south, the Old and New Worlds had a land connection, or at worst a narrow strait between them (Acosta, 1590/1940: 77–81).

García's views (1607)

In the period between 1589 and 1607, two schools of thought dominated scholarly discussions of the origin of New World humans: Acosta's and another, represented by Gregário García (1589–1607). García, like Acosta, spent considerable time in the New World, but proposed a less heretical view in which the biblical flood was an unshakable and fundamental axiom for making conclusions about the origin of American natives (Fé humana).

García used inductive reasoning to support his ideas, and admitted only four types of evidence regarding the origins of American natives: Ciencia, Opinión, Fé divina (divine faith), and Fé humana. Based on these four lines of proof, he examined competing views in a massive volume entitled: Origen de los Indios de el Nuevo Mundo, e Indias Occidentales (1607, reprinted 1729). García presented 11 theories of Native American origins, along with the supporting evidence for each and the reasoning behind them. He covered several views in great detail, including the lost-tribes-of-Israel theory and the Atlantean/Carthaginian/Phoenician models.

García also discussed a little-known idea proposed by Gonzalo Fernández de Oviedo y Valdez: that American natives originated in Spain or Portugal. This concept was ultimately traced to historian López de Gámara's view that there was a pre-Columbian Spanish incursion into the Americas by King Rodrigo after his defeat by the Moors in AD 711 (Huddleston, 1967: 73).

European progenitors?

In the twentieth century, a few scholars (Nelson, 1933; Stanford, 1999) revived and modified Oviedo's European origin model, and have suggested that Native Americans were derived not from King Rodrigo, but from Solutrean peoples in northern Europe – Upper Paleolithic hunter-gatherers of France and Spain. Some of these European models are based on the observation of superficial morphological and functional similarity between Clovis projectile points (11 500 yr BP) in the Americas and 20 000–14 000 yr BP Solutrean points from western Europe, but the Solutrean origins model is not without its critics (Straus, 2000).

García's *Origen* also included an east Asian origin theory in which Chinese, Tatars (Tartars), and Scythians were linked to natives of the Americas based on the similarity of physical features (hair color and type, eye shape, facial shape).

García's final conclusion was that all 11 views were correct, or that some combination of the theories was the best explanation of Native American origins (Huddleston, 1967: 74):

> [Native Americans] proceed neither from one Nation or people, nor went to those parts from one [part] of the Old World. Nor did the first settlers walk or sail by the same road or voyage, nor in the same time, nor in the same manner. But actually they proceed from various nations. (García, 1729: 315, cited in Huddleston, 1967: 74)

Asian origins and connections (1729–1790)

Both Acosta and García presented the concept that Native Americans had their biological and cultural roots in Asia and this was adopted by many eighteenth-century naturalists, including Georges Louis LeClerc Buffon (1788), and Johannes Blumenbach. Blumenbach's (1775) *De generis humani variate nativa* used differences in morphological features between major geographic populations to derive four human varieties or "races" that included the "Mongoloids," "Negroids," "Caucasoids," and "American Indians." In Blumenbach's later (1795) work, Native Americans were placed into the "Mongoloid" variety, thus creating the now ubiquitous tri-racial classification of modern humans. According to Crawford, Blumenbach " ... further hypothesized that several migrations [to the New World] occurred at different times and that the Eskimos more closely resembled the Asian Mongoloids" (Crawford, 1998: 3). The concept of biological races will be discussed at length in Chapter 3.

Thought on Native American origins during the eighteenth and early nineteenth centuries hinged on the timing of entry for an Asian

"Mongoloid" founder population. The year 1859 produced remarkable advances in archaeology and biology (Meltzer, 1993b). First, the 1858–9 excavations at Brixham Cave, England, proved that there were humans in existence with extinct glacial-age (Pleistocene) animals and thus a human prehistory, before recorded history, which they dubbed the *Paleolithic*. The discovery upset the traditional biblical account of human existence on the Earth and the presumed timing of the appearance of humankind from the biblical creation (Genesis 1: 26–8).

The other fundamental advance in this area was the 1859 publication of Charles Darwin's *On the Origin of Species by Means of Natural Selection, or the Preservation of Favoured Races in the Struggle for Life*. Darwin's theory, as applied to humans, depended on the discovery of a prehistoric human antiquity. Darwin himself remarked that "The high antiquity of Man has recently been demonstrated ... and this is an indispensable basis for understanding [human] origins" (quoted in Meltzer, 1993b: 44).

1.3   THE AMERICAN PALEOLITHIC (1892–1927)

The discovery of a prehistoric period in Europe set several scholars searching for an American equivalent. Charles Conrad Abbott, a Trenton, NJ physician, was one such proponent of an American Paleolithic. Abbott had discovered "rude paleoliths" mixed among what he thought were Pleistocene-age gravels. Based on his finds, Abbott contacted Harvard University to request assistance in dating the gravels. In early 1877, Harvard dispatched geologist Nathaniel Shaler to the Trenton gravels, who verified their antiquity. This was such an amazing discovery that Abbott's fellow supporter of an American Paleolithic, Frederick Ward Putnam, a Harvard anthropologist and archaeologist, hired a man to walk along the Trenton gravels to look for bones or artifacts.

Abbott himself took action by publishing a description of the Trenton discoveries in a paper for the journal *Science*: "Recent archaeological explorations." Much like the recent discovery of Kennewick Man, Abbott's announcement sparked newspaper articles, scientific symposia, and books about the discovery of an American Paleolithic.

However, Abbott, Putnam, and their supporters had critics. One, the Smithsonian Institution's William Henry Holmes, had shown through his own studies along the Delaware River that the Trenton gravel "Paleoliths" were "rude" in form because they were manufacturing failures – recent artifacts damaged during the production process – and that their appearance was not evidence for their antiquity but was evidence of the manufacturing process of stone tools. In his view, this established that the Trenton finds were recent artifacts that had become stratigraphically mixed with Pleistocene deposits – the reverse of the Kennewick situation, where an ancient skeleton was mixed with historic artifacts.

Of Abbott's paper, Holmes (1892) wrote to a colleague, "I am inclined to think you ought not mention it by name. It contains such a mass of errors, geologic, archeologic and otherwise, that it cannot be mentioned by name." Holmes also referred to the now prestigious journal *Science* as "the trough into which the slops are thrown" (Holmes, 1892). Such vitriolic statements were typical of the American Paleolithic debate and of the government scientist's disdain for amateurs in the field. Abbott and colleagues doggedly pursued evidence for an American Paleolithic, despite being referred to as "bestinselled charlatans" and "harpies." In 1899, their perseverance was rewarded.

That December, Putnam's man inspecting the Trenton gravels made a discovery of a human femur well situated in the gravels. Looking for verification, Putnam took the bone to Holmes' colleague and fellow critic at the Smithsonian Institution, physical anthropologist Ales Hrdlička.[1] After his examination, Hrdlička dismissed the bones as those of a modern Native American and not at all like the robust bones of Neanderthals from the European Paleolithic. Over a period of 25 years, the Trenton gravels would produce a number of human bones, including several skulls. Each time Hrdlička, Holmes, and geologist T. C. Chamberlin would dismiss them, citing poor stratigraphic controls or a lack of Archaic human skeletal features (Hrdlička, 1902).

Other potential Pleistocene human remains known in the early twentieth century include Lansing, Kansas (1902); Gilder Mound, Nebraska (1906); the Rancho La Brea, California tar pits (1914); the bodies at Vero Beach, Florida (1916), and a discovery at Melbourne, Florida (1918). In each case, Hrdlička or his colleagues and others would perform site visits to confirm the Pleistocene age of the remains. Although many of the above skeletons were confirmed as being situated in Pleistocene geological context by some of the visiting geologists, Holmes and Hrdlička held fast to their denial of an American Paleolithic (Hrdlička, 1902, 1907, 1913, 1918, 1920, 1923).

Abbott died in 1919, followed by Putnam in 1920, but they would be vindicated in 1926 by Jesse Figgins' and Harold Cook's investigation of the 1908 discovery of stone spear points and bones of extinct bison (*Bison antiquus*) in Wild Horse Arroyo, near Taos, New Mexico, by George McJunkin.[2]

For most of the twentieth century, researchers have been unable to agree on the ultimate origin of Amerindians.[3] Only recently have biological anthropologists carefully examined ancient American skeletons in a systematic way (see Neves and Pucciarelli, 1991; Steele and Powell, 1992) with the goal of understanding how ancient human remains are related to modern peoples in both the New World and across the globe, and the processes by which any differences between them may have occurred. Since the publication of analyses of ancient skeletons in the Americas by Hrdlička (1917, 1928), Jenks (1936), Neves and Pucciarelli (1989, 1991), and Steele and Powell (1992), there has, however, been little in the way of consensus among Paleoindian bioarchaeology specialists regarding *how* and *when* humans colonized the New World, and *who* exactly these ancient people were, despite nearly a century of research on the subject.

Unfortunately, archaeological models of the peopling of the New World are of little help because of uncertainties and disagreements over critical points such as:

1. the timing of New World colonization (Dillehay, 1999; Goebel *et al.*, 1991; Lynch, 1990; Meltzer, 1993a,b; Mochanov, 1978, 1992; Waters, 1985);
2. the route and pattern of migration taken (Dixon, 1999; Fladmark, 1983; Gruhn, 1988, 1994);
3. subsistence modes of the migrants (Kelley and Todd, 1998; Martin, 1984; Meltzer and Smith, 1986; and
4. how the process of population dispersal took place and subsequently impacted late Pleistocene hunter-gatherer biology and behavior (see Dillehay and Meltzer, 1991 for a notable exception).

Yet another problem is that the same set of archaeological data can be employed to paint contradictory pictures of how humans entered the New World and spread through it. This lack of agreement is due in part to competing schools of thought, parochialism, and reliance on inadequate data to support various models (Dillehay and Meltzer, 1991).

In response to this impasse, anthropologists have examined genotypic and phenotypic variation among past and present Native American populations. Their hope is that the biological data might provide more direct evidence, and better resolution of prehistoric population dispersal and migration than is possible using archaeological information alone, and that the biological data may provide support for one of the competing models of the peopling of the New World.

From these various lines of evidence, a consensus is slowly emerging regarding the process of New World colonization by humans. The current debate, centered on issues of data interpretation and opposing theoretical standpoints, however, has a rich and deep history in American biological anthropology.

1.4   PATTERN AND PROCESS IN THE PEOPLING OF THE NEW WORLD

In the nineteenth and twentieth centuries, the heart of the debate over the peopling of the Americas had mostly to do with Native American (specifically, Amerindian) biological, linguistic, and cultural homogeneity, and how any observed variation should be interpreted in either a racial or evolutionary context (Genovés, 1967). The observation of limited biological variation among Amerindians prompted speculation that such shared characteristics as hair type and skin color reflected their common ancestry, and that Native Americans "constituted a major isolate that was homogeneous, both phenotypically and genotypically" (Stewart, 1960: 269). Other researchers observed biological heterogeneity among Native American groups, and recognized that in addition to migration, other evolutionary forces such as genetic drift, natural selection, or *in situ* gene flow helped to explain the observed patterns of variation (Lahr, 1996; Powell, 1995; Spuhler, 1979; Szathmary, 1994: 127). These alternative interpretations of both *variation* in selected biological characteristics and the *processes* by which this variation arose have their roots in earlier discussions of Native American origins and relationships.

Native American biological homogeneity: migrationist views

One of the earliest and most influential European assessments of Native American biological and cultural variation was that of Christopher Columbus (Cristobal Colón), who wrote in 1492 that "In all these islands, I saw no great diversity in the appearance of the people or in their manners and language. On the contrary they all understood one another" (Colón, 1969: 196–7).

Stewart and Newman (1951), in their important historical overview of the concept, traced the European view of Native American biological homogeneity not to Columbus, but to the writings of the eighteenth-century Spanish traveler Antonio de Ulloa, who said "Visto un Indio de qualquier región, se puede decir que se han visto todos en quanto al colór y contextura" (Ulloa, 1944: 242 [cited in Stewart and Newman, 1951]), which literally means "If you have seen an Indian of whichever region, you can say that you have seen all in color and context (behavior)." This off-hand remark has taken form in English as the invective: "If you've seen one Indian, you've seen them all."

This statement had become an unshakable axiom in scientific circles by the nineteenth century, principally because it was supported by observations on phenotypic traits that exhibited relatively little between-group variation. These features included hair type and color, the presence of epicanthic folds, and skin color (Stewart and Newman, 1951). Ulloa's observations of Native American biological homogeneity were further supported in Samuel Morton's (1839) *Crania Americana*, in which he reiterated Ulloa's statement and made an attempt to justify this view using craniometric data of dubious quality (Gould, 1981). The influential Ales Hrdlička, while recognizing a certain degree of variability among Native American populations, generally supported the concept of Native American biological homogeneity:

> [T]he more substantial differences which exist between the tribes are everywhere underlaid by fundamental similarities and identities that outweigh them and that speak strongly not only against any plurality of race on the American continent, taking the term *race* in its fullest meaning, but for the general original unity of the Indians. (Hrdlička, 1923: 481; italics in original)

Much like the cultural and linguistic data suggesting the uniformity of Native Americans, the biological data were interpreted as the result of migrations from the Old World. Similarities in speech, behavior, or biology could not have arisen through *in situ* processes because, according to the view accepted as late as the 1920s, Native Americans had been in the New World only a few thousand years and therefore constituted one distinct racial "type" unified by descent from a single ancestral migrant population. Many anthropologists and biologists not only lumped various Native American populations together, but assumed that natural selection and other evolutionary processes, while playing a role in shaping other species, did not affect anatomically modern[4] humans over short time-spans. Thus, any differences between populations were felt to reflect *independent* migrations of people from the Old World to the New (Stewart and Newman, 1951: 29). Most biological anthropologists "disavowed the possibility that physical changes could have occurred among New World peoples" (Stewart and Newman, 1951: 21). Such views were well suited to classification schemes and racial typologies, which tended to view populations as "internally static, changing if at all, primarily as a result of gene flow and, to a lesser extent, genetic drift" (Schindler, 1985: 475). In his later writing, even Hrdlička criticized the racial–typological, migrationist approach to Native American cranial morphology (Hrdlička, 1935):

> One of the greatest faults and impediments of anthropology has always been and is largely to this day, in spite of ever-growing evidence to the contrary, the notion of the permanence of skull types and of their changeability only through racial mixtures or replacements. It is time that this attitude be replaced by more modern and rational on the subject, based on the steadily increasing knowledge of biological laws and processes together with such powerful factors as segregation and isolation. (Hrdlička, 1935)

Amerindian heterogeneity: *in situ* evolution

The concept of Native American biological unity gained widespread popularity in the nineteenth and early twentieth centuries, owing, in part, to the influence of S. G. Morton (1839) and Hrdlička. However, this view did have some opposition. Several nineteenth-century writers and naturalists such as d'Orbigny (1839) and von Humboldt (1811) felt that there was tremendous biological diversity among living Native Americans, despite the obvious but superficial phenotypic similarities of skin color or hair type (Hooton, 1946: 649). Some scholars examining the biology of Native Americans also observed extensive intra- and inter-tribal biological diversity and generally dismissed the idea of Native Americans as a unified biological group (Boas, 1912a; Hooton, 1930; Virchow, 1888; Wilson, 1857).

These alternative conclusions were supported by the recognition that biological variation appeared to be correlated with cultural or environmental conditions, suggesting that biological differences among Native Americans might be due to normal evolutionary processes, such as natural selection or physiological adaptation, rather than being solely the result of past migrations (Stewart and Newman, 1951: 31–2). Some researchers, including Boas at Columbia University (1912), attempted to reconcile the migrationist approach with models of *in situ* biological change resulting from natural selection or genetic drift. Boas thought that Native Americans originated through one or more migrations that introduced some variation to the New World (Boas, 1912a). However, once these populations settled in the Americas:

> The isolation and small number of individuals in each community gave
> rise to long-continued inbreeding, and with it, to a sharp
> individualization of local types. This was emphasized by subtle influences
> of natural and social environment. With the slow increase in numbers,
> these types came into contact; and through mixture and migration a new
> distribution of typical forms developed. (Boas, 1912a: 14)

This viewpoint was at odds with the traditional interpretation of biological variation in Native Americans. Although Boas recognized that migration and founder effect played a role in shaping the appearance of native populations, he also allowed that other evolutionary forces and environmental differences could additionally bring about divergence. Most importantly, Boas (1912a) recognized that population growth and gene flow could also lead to homogeneity over time.

In later chapters I present the migrationist models – ranging from Harold Gladwin's (1947) six migration model to Greenberg *et al.*'s (1986) tripartite model – as well as those that rely on microevolutionary theory to explain Native American biological diversity. As we will see in the next chapter, the migrationist views tend to be somewhat typological in their approach to human variation.

NOTES

1 Ales Hrdlička (1869–1943) was the first physical anthropologist (then called a *somatologist*) at the Smithsonian Institution's National Museum of Natural History in Washington, DC. A Czech-born, French-trained physician and anthropologist, Hrdlička is considered by most to be the father of American physical anthropology (Spencer, 1982). He styled himself academically after France's Paul Broca and was an ardent supporter of W. H. Holmes' view on the (lack of) human antiquity in America.

2 George McJunkin (1851–1922), a former slave, was the foreman of the Crowfoot Ranch near Folsom, New Mexico. On August 27, 1908, while checking fence lines along Wild Horse Arroyo, McJunkin made one of the most significant archaeological discoveries of the twentieth century. He found clear evidence of human-manufactured tools mixed among a bed of fossil bison (*Bison antiquus*) bones. The direct association of the stone tool with extinct fauna was scientifically proven by Figgins and Cook's (Colorado Museum of Natural History) excavation at the site in 1926, which provided clear, verifiable documentation of tool–fauna association (Meltzer, 2001; Meltzer, *et al.*, 1997).

3 In order to distinguish arctic and sub-arctic Native American populations (Aleuts, Eskimos, and Na-Dene peoples of the Pacific Northwest and the southwest deserts of North America, e.g. the Navajo) from other Native American populations of North and South America, the term *Amerindian* will be used to designate the latter group only. Although this division generally

follows that of Greenberg *et al.* (1986), it is used here as a matter of convenience rather than as indicative of historical or phylogenetic relationships.

4 By "modern," a term that appears throughout this book, I refer to human populations within the past 500 years, including living peoples seen around the world today.

2

A brief history of race

"There are no races, only clines"

F. B. Livingston (1962)

"The biological concept of race ... has no basis in science."

A. Goodman (1998)

"Slightly over half of all biological/physical anthropologists today believe in the traditional view that human races are biologically valid and real. Furthermore, they tend to see nothing wrong in defining and naming the different populations of *Homo sapiens*."

G. W. Gill (2000)

2.1 THE FOUNDATIONS OF RACE

Higher primates, including humans, appear to have the capacity for identifying those who are part of a group and those who are not (Goodall *et al.*, 1996) – in other words, detecting who are a part of "us" and who are a part of "them." Most cultures have strong notions about who are "us" and what defines "them." These markers of "us" vs. "them" are primarily based on dress, custom, and language. Here, I focus on European views that (arguably) have had the greatest impact on how western cultures view worldwide human variation, especially that seen among the native peoples of the Americas.

Roman scholar Plinius, also known as "Pliny the Elder" (AD 62–113), produced one of the earliest classifications of humans into subgroups. Following Aristotelian tradition, Pliny divided the world's people into the *civilized peoples* (classical Greeks and Romans), the *barbarians* (those

Portions of this chapter are modified from Powell (1995: chapter IV) with permission.

tribal peoples outside the immediate Greco-Roman sphere of influence), and the *monstrous* (deviants from the classical human form, including the Cyclops, dog-faced people, giants, and dwarfs). Monstrous peoples lived in the unexplored regions well beyond the lands of the barbarians. This view dominated western thought about human variation for centuries.

Swedish botanist and systematist Karl von Linnaé, better known as Linnaeus, created the binomial system of taxonomic nomenclature,[1] which is still used in modern biology, biological anthropology,[2] and systematics. Linnaeus' 1735 publication of *Systema naturae* set the course for scientific thinking about human "racial" variation for the following 200 years (Morton, 1839; Coon, 1968). Linnaeus used common-alties or differences in outward morphology (the phenotype) in classifying different geographical groups of humanity. In *Systema naturae* he arranged humans into four subspecies of *Homo sapiens: H. sapiens americanus* (Native Americans),[3] *H. sapiens europaeus* (Europeans, including the Turks), *H. sapiens asiaticus* (east Asians), and *H. sapiens afer* (Africans). Linnaeus' taxonomic descriptions of the races were also laden with derogatory comments about the behavior and personalities of foreign peoples. So that: *Homo sapiens europaeus* was "white, gracious, and governed by reason"; *Homo sapiens asiaticus* was "pallid, dour, and governed by opinion"; *Homo sapiens americanus* was "reddish, single-minded, and guided by tradition"; and *Homo sapiens afer* was "black, wily, and ruled by whimsy" (Linnaeus, 1735).

Race, variety, and species

In the nineteenth century in the United States (and in some states as recently as the 1950s), laws were in place that were intended to prevent persons of different races from intermarrying and hopefully, therefore, from reproducing. These laws arose out of a mistaken belief that the so-called races belonged to different subspecies, or in some cases species, and through the mistaken fear that offspring from such a union would suffer the effects of "miscegenation" such as birth defects and thus become kin to Pliny's "monstrous people."

At this point, we should carefully consider what we mean by various terms such as "race." The following terms are important to my further discussion of *race*:

Race a group of individuals determined geographically (and for humans, culturally[4]) who share a common gene pool and varying combinations of distinguishing characteristics (Wolpoff, 1997: 407).

Variety   a group of similar populations within a species that differ in one or a few characteristics from other populations of the species. An ambiguous category, but one that is still allowed in plant and fungal taxonomy. If there is a significant geographic component to such variation, then "subspecies" is the more appropriate term.

(Biological) species   in living organisms, a group of populations that can actually or potentially interbreed and produce fertile offspring, and are reproductively isolated from other such species. This may also include other species concepts such as phylogenetic, crypto-, genealogical, and morpho-species (Mayr, 1963; Wolpoff and Caspari, 1997: 408).

Subspecies   an aggregate of populations inhabiting a geographical subdivision of the species range that is consistently different in phenotype from other populations of the species.

The Linnaean approach to race was, in large part, based on the philosophy of essentialism. This worldview is derived from Plato's concept of *eide*,[5] the unchanging essence of all forms making up the physical world. Essentialism is the basis for typological thinking relative to human variation, since it holds that the essence of each race is unique and unchanging, as well as internally static (Wolpoff and Caspari, 1997: 61).

In the late eighteenth century, scholars such as J. F. Blumenbach continued Linnaeus' efforts to classify living humans. The nineteenth century embodiment of the essentialist view is "descriptive-historicism" (Armelagos *et al.*, 1982), which attributes any change in the "types" used to describe variation (i.e. "races") to historical events such as colonization and migration (see Greenberg *et al.*, 1986). A modern example of descriptive historicism (see Armelagos *et al.*, 1982: 306–8) is found in popular press accounts of both the Luzia skeleton in Brazil and the Kennewick skeleton from Washington State (e.g. "Vikings Invade America, 10 000 BC").

2.2   EIGHTEENTH-CENTURY RACIAL CLASSIFICATION

In 1775, Johann Blumenbach,[6] anatomist at the University of Göttingen (Germany), began working with a sample of 82 human skulls from around the world to build a Linnaean-type taxonomy of human races. In that year, he published *De generis humani variate nativa*, in which he proposed an essentialist view of human racial variation. "[In] his early writing he defined the races geographically... later, though he turned them into taxonomically ranked entities" (Wolpoff and Caspari, 1997: 63). The three major races he included were: (1) *Caucasoids* from the Caucasus mountain region of the republic of Georgia; (2) east Asian *Mongoloids* (Tungus of Mongolia); and (3) *Ethiopians* (Africans), along with two less broadly defined *minor races*: Native Americans (Carib Indians) and Malays (Tahitians), which were gradations between the three major races (Wolpoff and Caspari, 1997: 61).

Blumenbach set the European "Caucasoids" as the ideal[7] or original major race, with the Asians (Mongoloids) and Africans (Ethiopians) being the most divergent in ideal cranial morphology from this. The link between the Caucasoids and Asian Mongoloids were the Native Americans; likewise, the "Tahitian Malays" (Negritos and Polynesians) linked the Caucasoids to the Ethiopians.

While Blumenbach (1775) lumped most human populations into major and minor races, he also realized that individual members of a race exhibited some morphological differences among themselves for certain characteristics. Furthermore, this inter-racial variation developed as humans moved into and exploited new territories with new climates, further away from the homeland of the Caucasoid archetype (Wolpoff and Caspari, 1997: 62).[8]

He also stated that, "The Caucasian must, on every physiological principle, be considered as the primary or intermediary of these five principal Races. The two extremes from which it has deviated are, on the one hand the Mongolian, on the other the Ethiopian" (Blumenbach 1775, quoted in Wolpoff and Caspari, 1997: 62).

One great irony is that Blumenbach was not only an essentialist, but was also a biblical monogenist, believing that all humans have a common source of origin after the great biblical flood (Genesis 8: 18).[9] Given the contradictory nature of these viewpoints, it is hard to under-stand how Blumenbach could find differences between the races, as they should have sprung from the same divine source. Such differ-ences, he suspected, were due to movements of the Caucasoids to areas with climates different from the Caucasus. Another irony is that Blumenbach was not a racist; he felt that all races had the same potential for advancement and achievement, owing to their common origin. He also believed that differences in intelligence were negligible, and that racial differences in behavior were learned and not innate. The impact of Blumenbach's views and scientific attempt to prove his view of human racial variation was to have an enormous impact on later scholars specializing in the classification of human phenotypic variation. Some physical anthropologists (see Brace, 1982: 15) consider Blumenbach to be the true father of scientific craniometry,[10] as he was the first to use craniometric techniques (Wolpoff and Caspari, 1997: 64). Those of us who use cranial measurements to assess individual and population variation in prehistoric or modern humans feel his influence even today.

Samuel George Morton and American views of race

By the nineteenth century, Blumenbach's work spurred racial scholars to find supporting data for their claims. One such person was Samuel George Morton (1830–51), a physician from Philadelphia. Morton worked on racial typologies based on craniometry.

In *Crania Americana* (1839), Morton took ten basic measurements of human skulls to compute statistical values such as cranial index and cranial capacity. The latter was recorded by measuring the volume of a cranium using mustard seeds, which were poured in, shaken or compacted,[11] then poured out and their volume measured to obtain an estimate of brain case volume as a proxy measure of brain size, and thus of intelligence. Morton used these measurements to rank races by brain size (see Gould, 1981).

Morton's *Crania Americana* is perhaps the more notorious of his two major works because of his apparent racist motives for fabricating his data (Gould, 1981). His data collection methods are suspected to be faulty, irreproducible, and used specifically for the Native American samples to obtain his desired result of smaller cranial capacity to prove his hypothesis of their racial inferiority (see Gould, 1981).

As perhaps the best-known "scientific racist," Morton has been vilified by Harvard biologist Stephen J. Gould (Gould, 1981) in the book, *The Mismeasure of Man*. Gould proved that Morton's data could not be verified by re-measuring the same skulls that Morton had clearly skewed or fabricated the data to achieve a result that supported his views on the link between race and intelligence.

Morton, like Blumenbach, created a hierarchical classification of skull shapes to demonstrate that Caucasian[12] crania were more "beautiful and had larger brain cases"(neurocrania), at an average of 1425 cm^3 (87 in^3), than Native Americans (1344 cm^3; 82 in^3) or African Blacks (1278 cm^3; 78 cu in^3) (Morton, 1839, cited in Gould, 1981). In Morton's study, the skulls of African Blacks[13] had consistently smaller brain cases than White Europeans, which in his opinion meant, therefore, that African Blacks had smaller brains and were less intelligent than Whites. He felt that the connection of cranial/brain size and intelligence was a primary "logical principle." Morton's measurements were used to prove his views of a divine human hierarchy, with Caucasians as the superior race, containing subsets of ranked white populations: "Anglo-Saxons and Teutonics were at the pinnacle, just above Jews (in the middle), with Hindus below in the lowest rank" (Thomas, 2000: 41). It is no coincidence that the lowest ranked Caucasians have the darkest skin and eyes (non-Dravidians from southern India), while the highest ranked have the lightest skin and eyes. Morton followed Linnaeus in attributing certain negative behavioral characteristics to other races. As Thomas observes:

> He [Morton] found the "Esquimaux" of Greenland to be "crafty, sensual, ungrateful, obstinate, and unfeeling ... their mental faculties, from infancy to old age present a continued childhood." The Chinese were almost as bad, "a monkey race," and black Hottentots were "like the lower animals." To Morton these racial differences reflected a Divine master plan. The Caucasian type had been, and always would be supreme – God's will expressed as a natural order and verified by empirical science. (Thomas, 2000: 41)

It is unlikely that Morton had ever encountered living "Esquimaux," Chinese, or Hottentot persons, so his character assassinations were probably reflective of nineteenth-century prejudice based only on limited experience with other cultures.

In *Crania Ægyptica* (1844), Morton presented the idea that some groups of people (African Blacks) were "natural" slaves. Views of this sort have been described by Wolpoff and Caspari (1997) as a form of "romantic racism" in which the "lesser races" must be cared for like children (Brace, 1982). Romantic racism was used to justify enslavement of west African tribes and to provide justification for the expatriation of Native American tribes. Morton's *Crania Ægyptica* and *Crania Americana* volumes espoused a polygenic[14] view of human variation, and were later used by southern US racists to "prove" that the Africans had a "natural propensity" to be slaves as they had been in ancient Egypt for hundreds, if not thousands, of years.

Romantic racism was also used to justify placing Native Americans in the custodial care of the American federal government, whose actions were, in fact, more like those of an abusive parent (see Thomas, 2000 for examples throughout). Theories about such racial differences in intelligence are founded upon the false assumption that brain size is a correlate of behavior and intelligence – a view later repudiated by twentieth-century research.

Craniometry (but not the phrenological use thereof)[15] continues to this day – in a highly modified form. Some modern day craniometrists have been criticized (e.g. by Swedlund and Anderson, 1999) as having racist motives similar to those of Morton and his contemporaries, simply because craniometric techniques were employed in scientific racism like that of Morton (1839, 1844) and British anatomist Sir Arthur Keith (1911).

The Smithsonian Institution's Ales Hrdlička

Ales Hrdlička's heavy emphasis on the use of craniometry in assessments of Native American cranial variation, and his research on Native American origins, easily eclipsed that of Morton (1839) (Brace, 1982: 15–23). In the early twentieth century, Hrdlička published a series of papers on the racial affinities of the American natives (Hrdlička, 1902, 1907, 1913, 1918, 1920, 1923, 1937). The 1920 publication was perhaps one of his most important, in which he defined a dental trait, shovel-shaped incisors, that linked Native Americans to east Asians (Hrdlička, 1920). This trait was later redefined and scaled by Dahlberg (1968), Carbonell (1963), Mizoguchi (1985), and Turner *et al.* (1991). These authors have used dental variation to propose two phenotypic sub-divisions within the "Mongoloid" racial group: the *Sinodonts* of northeast Asia and *Sundadonts*[16] of southeast Asia and Australasia. Native Americans were linked to an east Asian homeland based on this proposed common dental trait[17] – a view which has been challenged by several authors (Haydenblit, 1993, 1996; Lahr, 1996; Powell, 1993, 1995; Powell and Neves, 1999).

2.3   RACE IN EARLY-TWENTIETH-CENTURY BIOLOGICAL ANTHROPOLOGY

Hooton and the races of Pecos Pueblo

Harvard University's Earnest Albert Hooton was a former student of confirmed racial determinist Sir Arthur Keith. Not only were Hooton's publications blatantly racist, but his ideas extended into the social realm in his paper "Noses, knowledge and nostalgia: the marks of a chosen people" (Hooton, 1933). He comments on the solution to the "Jewish Problem," noting the difficulties experienced by Jews worldwide, especially in Nazi Germany, and explaining that it was the Jews' own fault because of the Judaic "traditional policy and propensity to be socially isolated and toward inbreeding." Hooton's solution was that the Jews (as a socially isolated and "inbred" people) needed to "interbreed" and be assimilated by other cultural groups in Europe (Hooton, 1939, as described by Thomas, 2000: 109). He also stated in *Crime and Man* that: "The primary cause of crime is biological inferiority" (Hooton, 1933: 130).

Hooton is best known in American anthropology for his assessment of "racial variation" within the Native American skeletal series from Pecos Pueblo. He used 129 well-preserved skulls from this archaeological site in New Mexico[18] to create a series of racial "types" within a series of nearly 2000 prehistoric individuals buried during the site's long occupation by Puebloan people. Within the series, Hooton found "pseudo-Alpine" types with long, low, narrow crania (dolichocranics), and "pseudo-Negroids" with broad noses and rounded neurocrania. Ultimately, however, many of the long-faced pseudo-Alpines were found to belong to the historic mission at Pecos Pueblo and were likely to have been European priests, and Christianized and/or admixed native individuals interred under the church floor. Hooton analyzed his data temporally following A. V. Kidder's pottery chronology (Thomas, 2000: 109), to look for short-term changes in craniofacial morphology during the occupation of Pecos Pueblo. The possibility of such short-term changes was held by Hrdlička and his student to result from genetic (not evolutionary) change resulting from historical events such as population replacement, rather than by adaptation to changing environment, as was proposed by Franz Boas and his students.

Franz Boas and the New York immigrants

After witnessing the negative consequences of racial determinism in Europe, Columbia University professor Franz Boas began a long-term (1908–11) research project on first-generation children of Russian, Jewish, and Sicilian immigrants to America. Boas found that these American-raised offspring differed significantly in head shape from their Old World counterparts. Boas' intention was to challenge the essentialist and descriptive historical view of variation, which included the concept that racial fixity was hereditary, and to see what role, if any, the environment had on the human craniofacial phenotype. In his research, Boas employed Morton's measurements of head shape and cephalic index (determined by the ratio of breadth to length of the head).[19] The cephalic index can be applied to dry skulls and is then referred to as the "cranial index."

Unlike Morton's use of the cranial index, Boas' analysis was not an attempt to demonstrate that different races had differences in intelligence because of their differences in skull/head shape. Boas questioned the degree of fixity in skull size and shape and the underlying causes of the observed differences in head and facial shape, because he had noted that the then-recognized races were internally variable. Boas' Worchester study was not motivated by scientific racism but by the desire to understand the roles of heredity and environment in the creation of population and racial "types." Boas had, in an earlier paper, supported the use of craniometry and auxology[20] as descriptive tools for the study of human phenotypes. By 1910, he found that the cranial index was useless and unstable in racial analyses, as first-generation Russian and Sicilian immigrant children were significantly different from similar, non-immigrant children in Russia and Sicily. These results were proof that the fixity of racial characteristics was a myth not supported by scientific analysis, as head shape could be shown to differ between children who presumably had similar genetic backgrounds but who grew up in different environments (diet, temperature humidity, sanitation, better health, etc.).

Boas' results should have destroyed the essentialist view of human races, but they did not. Critics felt that because Boas did not personally measure all 6000+ immigrant children in the study, and despite his efforts to carefully train all of his students and assistants in collecting the data, this negated the study's results. The sample size was also described as "too small" (Radosavljevich, 1911). Boas wrote of his attempts to prove the stronger effects of environment over heredity in head form and racial "types," saying that he was: "struggling along – so far practically alone" (Boas, 1969; letter in Thomas, 2000: 105). Unfortunately, this was to be the case until the 1950s, when most human biologists and geneticists came to reject the idea of races as valid characterizations of human variation. A few American physical anthropologists refused to accept the Boasian view of environmental effect on human craniofacial variation (Coon, 1965; Gill and Rhine, 1990; Jantz and Owsley, 2001). Of these authors, the most influential on public perception of race and human variation was Coon (1965).

2.4 COON'S RACES AND ECO-GEOGRAPHIC VARIATION

Of modern physical anthropologists dealing with worldwide phenotypic variation, the works of Carlton S. Coon (1954, 1957, 1962, 1965), a
student of Hooton, are the most well known and accessible to the
American public. In *The Origin of Races* (1962) and subsequent work
(1965), Coon divides modern humanity into seven subspecies of *Homo
sapiens*: Caucasoids, Mongoloids, Australoids, Negritos (e.g. 'dwarfed
Australoids'), Congoids, Pygmies ('dwarfed Congoids'), and Capoids
(South African Khoisan peoples). Each of these groups will be briefly
described below, following Coon (1965: 11–14). Coon *et al.* (1950)
addressed the geographic component of human variation by describing
what they termed "local races," which contain subunits by tribe, and
villages that they called "*micro-races*" (equivalent in some ways to the
"breeding population").

The following major races are presented in the same order as
Coon's original (Coon, 1965: 11–14). Please note that these are Coon's
(1965: 11–14) descriptions, which I have *paraphrased* or quoted
(as indicated typographically). These descriptions also include arbitrary
labels for color and type of some phenotypic features. I have also
used the traits listed by Rhine (1990) for assessing race from dry
skulls.

Mongoloids

General location: Asia (north and south), the Americas (Figure 2.1).

Phenotypic features

Coon described the skin color of the Mongoloid race as varying regionally with latitude in all areas, ranging from "sallow brunette" in east
Asia to "reddish-brown" in west central Asia and in the Americas.
He also noted that "... the eyes of Mongoloids are brown with an
epicanthic fold ... Their hair is black, with red undertones, as well as
straight and coarse, and grows long on the head, but is sparse on body
and beard". Mongoloids rarely become bald, and do not turn gray until
an advanced age. Their noses range from flat to beaked. Flat noses are
usual in southern China, southeast Asia, Siberia, and Alaska, as well as
among Amazon basin groups, while beaked noses are seen among
many tribes of American Indians and some Asiatic tribal people, such

(a)

(b)

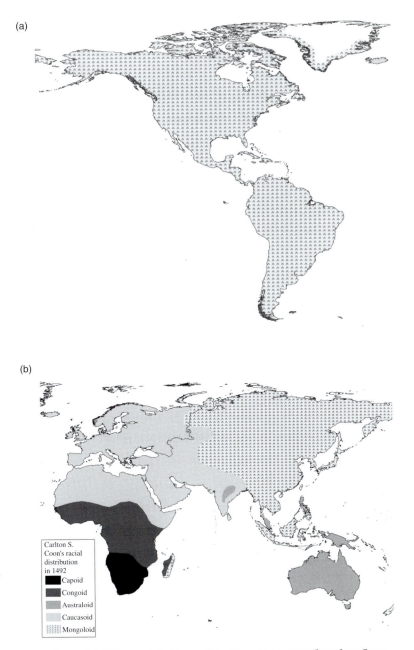

Figure 2.1 Global distributions of human races, *c.* 1492 (based on Coon, 1965).

as the Nagas of Assam. Faces are usually flat (orthognathic) looking, with alveolar prognathism and receding chins in some groups. Skulls range from *Brachycranic* to *Mesocranic;* the body build is variable but tends toward a long trunk and short limbs.

Cranial features

Rhine (1990) described the crania of members of the Mongoloid race as often possessing the following craniofacial features in varying combinations: an inion hook (especially in Native Americans), a "keeled skull," along with short base chord, high base angle, and complex sutures (especially coronal and lambdoidal sutures), with wormian bones and other ossicles, rounded orbits, gracile supraorbital region, "flared" base of nasal aperture, slight nasal depression with some nasal overgrowth, blurred nasal sill, "tented" nasal bones, small nasal spine, projecting zygomatics, large malar tubercle, posterior zygomatic tubercle, moderate prognathism, shovel-shaped upper and lower incisors, and enamel extensions on molars, as well as buccal pits. They also have an elliptical dental arcade, elliptical external auditory meatus, oval window not visible, straight palatine suture, and angled zygomaxillary suture, and moderate mastoid process (more robust in males) (Rhine, 1990: 11). These features are more pronounced in northeast Asians and Native Americans, while southeast Asians tend to be less extreme, more gracile, with more dolichocranic vaults, and (in this author's opinion) more like Australian populations in mid-facial features and dental morphology.

Congoids (full-sized)[21]

General location: sub-Saharan Africa (see Figure 2.1), southern United States, Caribbean islands, and some areas of Brazil.

Phenotypic features

"Skin is glossy black to dark brown; their eyes are black with flecks of pigment in the sclera" (Coon, 1965: 12). Congoid hair is dark brown to black and tightly curled. Congoids have moderate to sparse beards and body hair. Mid-facial prognathism is apparent, as well as are broad noses. The skull is rounded in all planes, with a protruding occiput (Coon, 1965; Rhine, 1990). Their bodies tend to be mesomorphic to endomorphic. Skulls are often mesocranic to dolichocranic, depending on the region from which they are originally derived.

Cranial features

Congoids may have some or all of the following in varying combinations: post-bregmatic depression, long basal chord, low base angle,
slight nasal depression, "guttered" lower nasal border, small nasal
spine, vertical zygoma, square orbits, robust supraorbital torus, simple
major sutures, hyperbolic dental arcade, oval window visible, nasal
bones in "quonset hut" shape, "bulging" palatine suture, rounded
external auditory meatus, mid-facial prognathism, and "S-shaped"
zygomatocomaxillary suture (Rhine, 1990: 11–12).

Pygmies ("dwarfed Congoids")

General location: better known as "Pygmies," dwarfed Congoids
occupy the Ituri Forest in west central Africa, including Rwanda,
Burundi, and parts of Cameroon.

Phenotypic features

Skin is "a reddish-brown to dark brown (mahogany-colored, according
to Gates), with tightly curled hair and more abundant beards and body
hair than is found in Negroes" (Coon, 1965: 13). They have also been
described as having bulbous foreheads, broader noses, and protruding
eyeballs to a greater degree than most Negroes. "Some look infantile,
others achondroplastic; that is they have the 'bulldog syndrome'[22]
of big head, short face, and short lower legs and forearms seen in
comparable dwarfs of all human races and many other animal species"
(Coon, 1965: 13). He goes on to claim: " They may represent more than
one independent line of dwarfing in noncontiguous populations"
(Coon, 1965: 13). The dwarfed Congoid body type (somatotype) can
be attributed to a mutation resulting in a defect in the gene producing insulin-like growth factor-I (IGF-I) (i.e. somatomedin-C), similar to those persons with achondroplasia (R. Malina, personal
communication, 1984).

Cranial features

Dwarfed Congoids may have some or all of the following in varying
combinations: like most Congoids, the skull is rounded in all planes,
occiput is usually protruding, and the nasal aperture is broad. Orbits
are rectangular to square (Coon, 1965).

Capoids

General location: "Reduced to no more than 100 000 individuals [by 1965] even if one includes the recent mixtures, the Capoids inhabit marginal areas of south and east Africa (Kalahari Desert and adjacent areas), [see Figure 2.1] and were once more numerous and full-sized. They are the atypical remnants of a former major division of mankind"[23] (Coon, 1965: 13–14). Khoi (Hottentots and other herders) and San peoples (desert foragers like the !Kung San) speak languages in the Khoisan language family, the so-called "click languages." Khoisan speakers employ implosive consonants marked diacritically by exclamation points etc., best illustrated in the ethnographic film *The Hunters* or the popular film *The Gods Must be Crazy*. The Capoids differ genetically from other sub-Saharan Africans more than any other group (Cavalli-Sforza *et al.*, 1994: 175), and are genetically most similar to Ethiopians and Middle Eastern (Caucasoid) populations. In 1996, there were 50 000 un-acculturated !Kung San left (Cavalli-Sforza *et al.*, 1994: 174–5).

Phenotypic features

Capoid peoples are now called the !Kung San, but were, at one time, referred to as "Bushmen." According to Coon (1965):

> The Bushmen, who constitute the least-mixed relic population are short, [have] very flat faces and noses and yellowish skin that wrinkles easily in old age. [Capoids] have the world's most tightly coiled hair, spiraled in patches with bare scalp between (peppercorn), moderate beard growth, and little body hair. The head hair is never long. (Coon, 1965: 13)

Cranial features

No dry skull description has been published, but see Lahr (1996: 215). She notes that both African (Negroids/Congoids and Capoids) and Australian populations (Australoids) present long narrow cranial vaults, long palates and low vertex, wide palate breadth, broad nasal apertures, and large teeth (especially molars).

Australoids

General location: Australia and surrounding islands, Tasmania, S. India, Papua New Guinea (Figure 2.1).

Phenotypic features

"Among the Australoids are to be seen the most archaic-looking members of mankind, with beetling brows, sloping foreheads, concave temples, deep-set eyes, fleshy noses, projecting jaws and large teeth. Their hair form ranges from tightly curled or 'Negroid,' to straight, but among the Australian aborigines and most Australoids of India it is usually wavy. Their beard and body hair is distributed as in Caucasoids" (Coon, 1965: 12). Their skin color ranges from a "... sooty near-black, mat [sic] in tone" (Coon, 1965: 12). "Their eyes are brown; hair is usually black, except for 'Tawny' blondes in the Australian interior. Body proportions are similar to [those of] Caucasoids, but with thinner arms and legs." In fact, "owing to their general appearance, the Australoids have been considered by a number of anthropologists as being archaic survivors of the stock from which Caucasoids also evolved" (Coon, 1965: 12).

Craniofacial features

"Australians and Africans share in having a coronally and sagittally prognathic face" (Lahr, 1996: 215). Australoids/(native Australians) appear to be most divergent from other world populations, based on both metric and nonmetric traits, and have the largest within-group variances for the 93 craniofacial dimensions Lahr employed in her study (Lahr, 1996: 216). Note that she did not employ racial terminology but did refer to Coon's "races" as eco-geographic "populations" (Australian, African, and east Asian). Australian populations (Australoids) present long narrow cranial vaults, long palates and low vertex, wide palate breadth, broad nasal apertures, and large teeth (especially molars) (Lahr, 1996: 215).

Negritos ('dwarfed Australoids')

General location: Philippines, the Malay peninsula, Lesser Sunda Islands of Indonesia, the Andaman Islands, and parts of India (Figure 2.1).

Phenotypic features

Hair, eyes, and skin color/tone are similar to that of full-sized Australoids – black to brown skin, curly black hair and broad noses, with endomorphic or steatopygous body proportions, especially among the Andamanese.

2.5   RACE ABANDONED? THE NEW PHYSICAL ANTHROPOLOGY

Race and racism

"Racial science" was initially used by some eighteenth-century scholars (e.g. Morton) to show the intellectual and cultural inferiority of pheno-typically different groups of modern humans and to make the "other" people less than human by placing them in their own separate taxonomic unit or category. Today, race has been recognized as a socio-cultural phenomenon that is more cultural or behavioral than biological (Kottak, 2000: 77–82).

In the USA and other Western countries, *race* is often used as a synonymous descriptor for people of different socioeconomic levels or ethnicities (Kottak, 2000: 71). Geneticists have found that only about 11% of genetic variation in all humans is due to differences between races (Relethford and Harpending, 1995). The remaining 89% of genetic variation is found *within* racial categories. There is no single genetic trait or phenotypic feature that consistently distinguishes human "races" from one another. Features such as skin color vary clinally (Lewontin, 1972; Livingston, 1962), that is, they change gradually across the landscape without clear boundaries (Figure 2.2). This clinal patterning of genetic and "racial" phenotypic variation caused F. B. Livingston and others to declare that "there are no races, only clines."

Genetics and the downfall of race

Is there a gene for race? The answer is "no." Most of the "classic" phenotypic traits described or depicted in the preceding section (craniofacial shape, tooth morphology, eye color, hair color/type, and skin color[24]) are not unique to any one "race." Some do co-vary strongly. Skin color alone is a complex quantitative trait, reflective of at least three to seven major melanin genes, controlling perhaps as many as 50 other separate genetic *loci* (as seen in studies of coat color of mammals (e.g. Cavalli-Sforza *et al.*, 1994). Even more numerous are the genes controlling craniofacial growth, which produce any of the observed differences between and within groups. Boyd (1950) and Livingston (1962) and Lewontin (1972) showed that simple genetic markers are useless for race determination, creating the claims regarding the nonexistence of race that open this chapter.

(a)

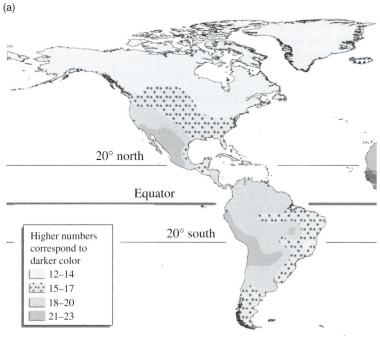

(b)

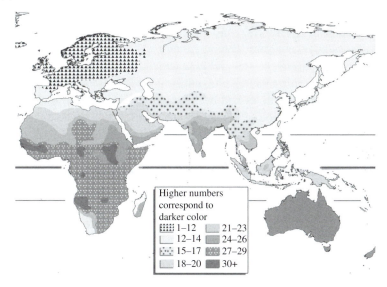

Figure 2.2 Skin color distribution *c*. AD 1500, based on estimations from Biasutti (1959). Reproduction based on compilation by Dennis O'Neil (http://anthro.palomar.edu/adapt/adapt_4.htm).

Genetics of racial features

Most Americans and Europeans feel that races are clear-cut and discrete biological entities (*sensu* Coon, 1965) based on their experiences with racial phenotypes. However, this is actually not the case. This statement seems counter-intuitive, as we can stroll down a busy street in any major city across the globe and find clear and recognizable phenotypic differences between ourselves and others walking past us. Yet, we must remember that our observations of phenotypic variation are strongly influenced by classifications or stereotypes, which are a product of our enculturation.

The idea that the racial differences we perceive are real and significant is based on unscientific observations. Such intuitive assessments can be wrong, and seeing is not always believing. Until the age of Galileo, most people were certain that the Sun revolved around the Earth instead of vice versa, based on their simple empirical observations of the position of the sun in the sky during the course of a day, month, or year. This was just as obvious as the concept of a flat Earth, which apparently still has its adherents. In terms of race, and most other categories based on biology, we typically only see the average phenotype. We do not see the distribution of the variability (in statistical terms, the *variance)* surrounding the mean of a phenotypic feature, because the distributions of trait variation in each "race" significantly overlap with one another, and individuals can only be placed into one racial category at a time (Figures 2.3 and 2.4).

For example, Powell and Rose (1999) found that the Kennewick skeleton had only a 0.001% probability of belonging to the "European" (or Caucasoid) group, as had been suggested from ad hoc analyses of craniofacial morphological features (Chatters, 2000), based on a large number of craniofacial dimensions collected on the original skull. Kennewick was similarly excluded from the Native American samples (Powell and Rose, 1999), based on probability assessments. These results are considered more completely in Chapters 10 and 11.

Quantitative traits

Most phenotypic features used by Coon (1962, 1965) and others to describe "races" are a function of a large number of underlying genes (Lees and Relethford, 1982; Relethford and Lees, 1982), gene–gene interactions between them, and environmental factors. These features (such as skin color, skull length, and nose size and shape) are called

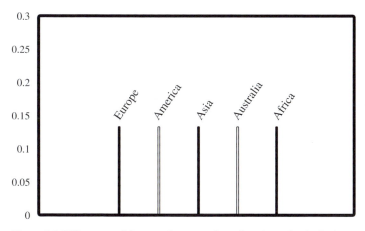

Figure 2.3 Different racial groups' mean values for a hypothetical phenotypic feature. Note that the groups are clearly separated when only the mean value of the trait is examined.

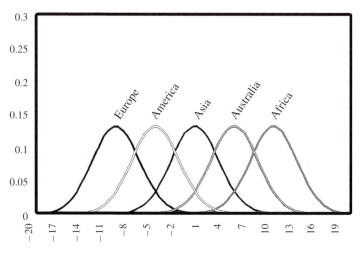

Figure 2.4 Variances for the hypothetical "data" presented in Figure 2.3 with equal but centered variances surrounding each mean. Note that the separation of the groups becomes more difficult, owing to overlapping within-group variances.

quantitative traits, because they do not occur in discrete categories but are expressed along a continuum and must be recorded in the form of measurements. Instead of being expressed in discrete categories by eye (light, medium, or dark etc.), skin color, for example, should be expressed in terms of light reflectance values, because darker skin reflects less light. Skin reflectance values depend on the relative wavelength of light used to assess them and so a skin reflectometer should be used to record these data (Crawford, 1998: 214–5). Figure 2.1 presents Coon's version of Biasutti's pre-1940 skin color map. Figure 2.2 is a map based on Biasutti's compilation of published average skin reflectance values.

Typically, biologists and anthropologists cite maps like Biasutti's as evidence for natural selection being the causative mechanism explaining the geographic distribution of phenotypic features such as skin color. For example, Wilhelm Gloger (1833) noted that animals with darker skin and coats were found near the Equator, where the Earth receives the most intense sunlight owing to the Earth's axial tilt.

Human skin color is also darkest near the Equator, with the exception of those living in shady Amazonian jungles in South America (Figure 2.2). Darker skin provides greater protection from cellular damage and from skin melanomas in areas of intense solar radiation. This is known as Gloger's rule.

Harding and colleagues (2000) showed that darker skin in Africa was under strong selection because of solar radiation levels, while the lighter skins of Europeans and Asians were caused by a relaxation of selective pressures in areas such as northern Europe and northern Asia, which receive less solar radiation. Darker skins also protect individuals from hypervitaminosis D_3, a condition that can lead to developmental defects in the fetus, as they prevent the breakdown of folic acid (vitamin B_{12}), which is needed to prevent fetal neural tube defects. Once human populations ventured north from Africa, the selective pressures for protective dark skin were relaxed and the MCR1 gene was free to undergo change through genetic drift (Harding *et al.*, 2000).

The natural selection causes for skin color differences are, on their own, inadequate for explaining eco-geographic variation in human skin color. Some other types of selection may also have played a role in creating present-day patterns of skin color; Diamond (1994) and Cavalli-Sforza *et al.* (1994: 267) have suggested a theory for skin color distribution, based on human evolutionary ecology. These authors suggest that skin, eye, and hair color may be under strong sexual selection, much like feather color in male birds or mane size in male lions. Halladay (2001), in an interview with two University of California, Los Angeles evolutionary biologists, Jared Diamond and Charles E. Taylor, quoted in *USA Today*:

> "... there is an overwhelming importance to skin, eye and hair color that is obvious to all of us – [in] sexual selection," Diamond says. "Before

reaching a condition of intimacy permitting us to assess the beauty of a prospective sex partner's hidden physical attractions, we first have to pass muster for skin, eyes and hair … "

Charles E. Taylor, UCLA evolutionary biologist, thinks so too;

"Diamond argues for sexual selection because nothing else seems to fit," Taylor says. "This is a cop-out, of course, but it makes sense to me."

Halladay (2001)

Diamond's sexual selection model (a "like-marries-like" view of phenotypes) is used to explain the concentration of certain skin and eye color within an eco-geographic region, because skin color (Figure 2.2) appears to be graded clinally across the landscape and does not display well-defined borders, despite Coon's map to the contrary (Figure 2.1). Another version of the sexual selection model that might explain the clinal distribution of human skin colors may be gene flow in the form of isolation-by-distance (see Chapter 3), or the "odd male model," noted in some lower organisms, in which phenotypic unique-ness in males is favored by females. Experiments have demonstrated that when male fruit flies with red or white eyes are introduced into a population where all the other flies have the opposite eye color, the "odd" males produce more offspring than is predicted from random mating (see Hartl and Clark, 1989). Genetically admixed individuals appear also to have physiological and reproductive advantages ("hybrid vigor") over homozygotes. The "odd male" appears to have a reproduc-tive advantage owing to sexual selection of "odd" males as mates by females (an "opposites attract" version of sexual selection). Any or all of these models of sexual selection may explain the geographic cline in human skin color.

Some facial phenotypic traits, such as nasal size, shape, and volume appear to be adaptations to climatic conditions, such as high or low temperature and high or low humidity (Franciscus, 1995). Natural or sexual selection potentially affects some traits, while other traits may reflect patterns of gene flow or physiological adaptation.

Other phenotypic features, besides skin, hair, and eye color, may result from sexual selection as beauty markers. For example, certain dental features occur at higher frequency among some groups. Lateral incisor insetting in Native Americans in the American southwest is considered to be more attractive than other dental features in some Puebloan cultures,[25] which may help to increase the high frequency of the trait among native populations in the region.

Of course, attractiveness is defined and mediated by culture; the phenotypic trait shown by Chaucer's "gap-toothed" Wife of Bath in

The Canterbury Tales was believed by medieval English men (including, apparently, Chaucer himself) to indicate a bawdy, lewd, and sexually lascivious personality. In most high income–high status families in the USA and elsewhere today, these dental phenotypes would be "corrected" via orthodontics.[26]

Craniofacial variation

Skull size and shape are a reflection of the underlying genes that an individual inherits, as well as the environment in which they live[27] (from mother's womb to climate and diet). Franciscus (1995) and Franciscus and Long (1992) have investigated worldwide variation in nasal shape and have linked this feature to air temperature and humidity. People with flat, broad noses are typically found in warm, humid environments. This nasal shape results in a large interior surface area that enhances evaporation and cooling in high-humidity tropical environments where we find many east and central African, southern Asian, and Negrito groups. Tall, narrow noses are found in cold climates with low humidity. This nasal configuration enhances the warming of cold air as it is inhaled, and can reduce heat and moisture loss in dry cold climates. This configuration is most common in modern northern Europeans and Pleistocene Neanderthals.

Body proportions (Bergmann's and Allen's rules)

Perhaps the most familiar examples of environmental adaptation come from Bergmann's and Allen's rules. Bergmann's rule states that the smaller of two bodies of similar shape has a higher surface area per unit of weight; therefore, mammals, including humans, in hot climates tend to have long, linear body types to increase surface area relative to mass (ectomorphy), helping to dissipate heat more effectively. Those in cold climates have compact bodies (endomorphy) with lower surface area relative to mass, in order to retain body heat. Allen's rule states that appendage (protruding body parts – tail, ears, arms, legs, fingers, toes) length in vertebrates is related to climate, so that longer appendages are found in warmer climates, to aid in heat loss, as they have a lower volume per surface area. Conversely, shorter appendages, with relatively higher volume relative to surface area, are found in cold climates, to help to conserve body heat.

Body proportions are also affected by altitude, with very large chest circumferences or "barrel-chested" populations commonly found in high-altitude populations, as for example in Altiplano Peruvian peoples (Quechua). This developmental adaptation is thought to increase inhalation volume in regions of low air pressure. Siblings of Altiplano individuals who are born in low-altitude coastal regions lack morphology; Tanner (1990: 144–5) shows how this trait is modified by environment.

Biological adaptation and race

Biological variation in humans is not only due to genetic causes but can have environmental components that reflect differences due to the effects of environment during growth and development. As living conditions generally improve over time, health and growth rates also change, depending on the environment, a phenomenon known as *secular trend*. For example, in the period from 1900 to 1940 the average height for 7- to 12-year-olds in the USA increased at a rate of less than 1 cm per decade, but from 1950 to 1970 the increase was 5 cm per decade (Tanner, 1990: 159). The latter period saw tremendous improvements in American diets, living conditions, medical treatment, and economy, all of which helped to improve the growth of individuals. Of course, only those phenotypic features that are easily perturbed from the genetic potential will be affected by the environment and will display such temporal or secular trends. Other traits, such as the arrangement of teeth in the mouth, cannot be altered from their full genetic potential by environmental factors. Such traits are said to be highly canalized. Despite genetically caused malpositioning or mis-eruption, in general mammals have cutting and tearing teeth (incisors, canines, and/or premolars) erupting towards the front of the mouth and grinding teeth in the rear of the mouth, not the reverse. Although tooth position is highly canalized, enamel development and formation are not. Thus, temporary cessation of enamel production at times of environmental insult or stress can result in the formation of enamel hypoplastic defects (horizontal bands in tooth enamel caused by physiological insult)[28] created when ameloblasts temporarily cease functioning normally under stress.

Functional morphological differences between human populations can also explain inter-group differences over time and space. For example, a change in diet can result in changes in the musculature needed for mastication, which results in changes in craniofacial form, as documented in Nubian populations by Carlson and Van Gerven (1977).

The role of race in modern anthropology

Most anthropologists disavow the validity of biological race as a concept for analyzing human diversity.[29] Both the American Association of Physical Anthropologists (AAPA) and the American Anthropological Association (AAA) have statements to the effect that "race" is no longer a useful construct in which to frame discussions regarding modern human biological variation:

> "Race" thus evolved as a worldview, a body of prejudgments that distorts our ideas about human differences and group behavior. Racial beliefs constitute myths about the diversity in the human species and about the abilities and behavior of people homogenized into "racial" categories. The myths fused behavior and physical features together in the public mind, impeding our comprehension of both biological variations and cultural behavior, implying that both are genetically determined. Racial myths bear no relationship to the reality of human capabilities or behavior. Scientists today find that reliance on such folk beliefs about human differences in research has led to misconceptions ... Given what we know about the capacity of normal humans to achieve and function within any culture, we conclude that present-day inequalities between so-called "racial" groups are not consequences of their biological inheritance but products of historical and contemporary social, economic, educational, and political circumstances.
>   American Anthropological Association, 2000, "Statement on 'Race' "

Some anthropologists who reject the validity of a race as an analytical construct in science (Goodman and Armelagos, 1989; Powell and Rose, 1999; Steele and Powell, 1992) use more sophisticated versions of the measurements of early craniometrists like Blumenbach, Morton, and Hooton in their assessment of worldwide skeletal variation (Relethford and Harpending, 1995). However, in using craniometric methods at all, they have been accused of being "politically incorrect" or of having racist motives themselves.[30]

Race and forensic anthropology

> If there is no such thing as "Race" why are forensic anthropologists so good at seeing it? N. J. Sauer (1992)

If we ignore skin color and the genetic data, is it not the case that people within each eco-geographic group share certain craniofacial features due to common biology, similar diet, and common development? The answer is, of course, "yes." However, this does not constitute the use of race as an essentialist notion, as it is clearly not supported empirically. Some anthropologists have to use racial termin- ology in applied anthropological work in order to communicate findings to those who use racial terminology in a social context (e.g. military and law enforcement agencies). The mere act of classify- ing organisms, including humans, does not require racial typologies. I have, myself, used racial terminology in forensic contexts. But, like most of my colleagues, I recognize that our ability to classify different groups of humans (i.e. *races*) is based on non-essentialist concepts of biological variance and covariance in phenotypic traits. What stand out as "clear" phenotypic markers of *race* are merely the mean values of some traits within a very wide range of values in trait distributions that significantly overlap with those of other such groups (Figure 2.1). So, in essence, *race* today exists as a sociocultural label that most people on this planet use to characterize "the other" (see Kottak, 2000: 77–82).

In my opinion, classifications (racial or otherwise) used in foren- sic anthropology must be accompanied by probability statements about the likelihood of correctly assigning a person's remains to a particular category, whether a local population, an eco-geographic population, or a *race*. Despite Sauer's (1992) claim that forensic scien- tists are good at racial classification, this ability is a function of an investigator's experience with the variation in the population in ques- tion, and with eco-geographic variation of certain morphological traits or features. The mis-classification rates for osteologists and forensic anthropologists can be quite high, not only for racial categories but even an individual's sex (D. G. Steele, personal communication, 1991).

Finally, anthropologists know, as did Franz Boas and his col- leagues, that evolutionary *processes* are more likely to be responsible for the *patterns* of human variation we all observe (as opposed to historical– descriptive guessing). This concept is at the heart of this volume.

The application of microevolutionary theory to patterns of past and present human variation involves the use of complex mathemat- ical models (presented in Chapter 3). This methodological approach to human variation is just beginning to be accepted by the majority of the scholarly community, as we dump the essentialist notion that race is a real biological phenomenon with any degree of scientific validity. The understanding of the processes that create the pattern of variation we observe has finally become the focus of research, rather than just the Platonic (Essentialist) descriptions of forms and types.

Box 1 Skin color

Human skin and hair color is the result of the pigment melanin, a secretory product of melanocytes found in the epidermal layer of skin. In individuals with less melanin, blood vessels in the dermis flowing near the epidermis and skin surface can give the skin a "ruddy" hue. Melanin comes in two forms: *phenomelanin*, which is yellow to red in color (typically found in high concentrations among Coon's Caucasoid and Mongoloid groups); and *Eumelanin,* which is dark brown to black and found among Coon's Congoids, Negritos, and Australoids. The secretion of eumelanin can be stimulated by exposure to ultraviolet radiation. The amount of fatty subcutaneous tissue, and the concentration of another pigment, carotene, which provides a reddish or orange color, affect the hue of skin. The yellow-golden skin tone of many Asian populations is not due to excess production of carotene but is due to a slight increase in the density of skin tissues near the epidermis. The pinkish color of many pale-skinned peoples is due to yet another pigment, hemoglobin, which is carried in the blood cells near the skin's surface (the epidermis). Studies of rodents have shown that there are several genes regulating the type of melanin produced. For example, hair/skin (or in mice, coat color) are under the control of a gene called ASIP, located on the q arm of chromosome 20 in humans. Eumelanin production has been mapped to a gene known as MC1R on the q arm of human chromosome 16 (Harding *et al.*, 2000; Oetting, 2002).

NOTES

1 Organisms, including human beings, were placed into species and species grouped into genera (the species name includes the generic portion). For example, chimpanzees (genus *Pan*) include the common chimpanzee, *Pan troglodytes* and the bonobo, *Pan pygmaeus.*

2 Used in the assessment of living and fossil primates and in studies of hominid/hominin paleontology.

3 Classification of Native Americans as part of the human species became possible for Linnaeus because of Pope Paul III's 1537 *Sublimus Deus* bull that the native peoples in the Americas were actually human, so that missionaries might convert them to Catholicism and fulfill their "desire exceedingly to receive it" (Hanke, 1937: 71–2 in Huddleston, 1967: 15).

4 I strongly disagree with this view of Wolpoff and Caspari (1997: 407). Race is a purely biological term and does not (and should not) include cultural or behavioral traits that are learned through enculturation and are not

biologically based. There is also a big difference between race and ethnicity, the latter being a socially based nonbiological term.

5 The *eide* concept is found most clearly illustrated in Plato's analogy of "the cave" found in "The Phaedo"(Benjamin translation 1911).

6 Many consider Blumenbach to be the father of physical anthropology. Brace (1982) notes that Hrdlička considered France's Paul Broca to be the father of physical anthropology.

7 This is because the female skull from the Caucasus mountain region of Georgia was round when viewed from above, and in the essentialist view the circle was a near-perfect form. Blumenbach also stated that it was the most beautiful skull in the university's collection.

8 This was in no way a Darwinian viewpoint.

9 It was also from the hypothesized landing place of Noah's Ark, where Noah's sons created the different races of humanity. Because peoples of the Caucasus were nearest to the Ark's reputed landing place on Mt. Ararat, White people must be closest to God's prototype skull form (of Adam and Eve, through Noah); other races had degenerated from the White prototype, because of differences in climate, etc.

10 Others consider Paul Broca of France to be both the Father of modern craniometric analysis and the Father of modern physical anthropology (see Brace, 1982).

11 Of course, the mustard seeds filling the White crania were compacted more than those in the Native American skulls in order to ensure that White brains appeared to be larger than those of Native Americans (discussed at length in Goulds' 1982 *The Mismeasure of Man).*

12 Caucasians should not be confused with Caucasoids; the latter term includes slightly dark-skinned peoples such as the non-Dravidians of India. Caucasians are very pale-skinned eastern Europeans from the Caucasus mountain region of the republic of Georgia, between the Black and Baltic Seas.

13 Morton's African "Black" skulls were apparently obtained from deceased west African peoples captured and sold into slavery.

14 Polygenists (not to be confused with polygynists) felt that all human races come from a variety of sources and, unlike the monogenists, did not all derive from Adam and Eve, via Noah, as described in Genesis. Polygenists felt that some races were not even divine reflections of the creator, as were the Caucasoid Europeans and Anglo-Americans, who were thought to have had a divine birthright to reign over other races through such despicable institutions as slavery.

15 The practice of phrenology is a system, now rejected, by which an analysis of personality and character can allegedly be made by studying the shape and protuberances of the skull and head. Despite Dewar's (1999: 429) claims, it is not the same as a craniometric analysis.

16 The term is in reference to the Sunda Shelf that once connected mainland southeast Asia to Australia via the Indonesian archipelago (see Chapter 4 for a full description of this land mass) (Turner, 1985b). Northeast Asian Sinodonts are separated from Sundadonts by exhibiting higher frequencies of eight key dental morphological traits (Turner, 1985b).

17 The supposed dental homogeneity proposed for all living and deceased *Amerindians* (*sensu* Greenberg *et al.*, 1986) has been used to suggest that all native peoples in north and south America are a single descendant group derived from a dentally homogeneous founding group of Sinodont Paleoindians (Greenberg *et al.*, 1986).

18 Pecos is a skeletal series that was repatriated to a coalition of tribes and reburied near the original Pecos Pueblo cemetery locale.

19 The long–narrow head/skull type (thought to be characteristic of Caucasoids and African Blacks), was called *Dolichocephalic* (or dolichocranic in the case of skulls), while Mongoloids, including most Native American groups were classified as *Mesocephalic* (Mesocranic), indicating an equality in the length and breadth of the head. Roundness (globularity) was described in the cranial index term *Brachycephalic* (brachycranic), used to characterize some extreme northern or southern Native American populations and those with accidental or intentional reshaping of the head through cradle boarding or head binding.

20 Auxology is the assessment of body proportions and other features in the living, while craniometry is measurement of the crania of the dead.

21 Also referred to as *Negroids* or *American Blacks* (in the USA during the 1960s and 1970s to present); see papers in Gill and Rhine (1990).

22 Here, Coon is referring to individuals with a type of hereditary dwarfism (achondroplasia) using a pseudo-medical term familiar to the general public of his day.

23 Many of the European Upper Paleolithic "Venus figurines" (such as the Venus of Willendorf) appear to represent females with the same hair type and somatotype as living Khoi and San peoples today, suggesting that they may be a remnant late Pleistocene population that was relatively unchanged during the Holocene, and that they occupied marginal areas (deserts) not used by sub-Saharan farmers and herders and were linguistically separated from other African populations by custom, biology, and language.

24 For example, darker skin appears to co-vary with hair color. Light-skinned peoples therefore tend to have lighter-colored hair, but some Native peoples in Australia have genes that produce "tawny" (a dark blonde color) hair, despite having, on average, some of the darkest skin outside of Africa.

25 The late Dr. Al Ortiz, personal communication to the author.

26 Among American and other media-saturated western societies, certain somatypes (body shapes) are considered to be more attractive than others. The American "ideal female" somatype is not often found naturally in humans, i.e. a very thin female body with large breasts is a physiological contradiction, since female breast size is function of body fat. These physical ideals often drive people to undergo painful surgical body modification (liposuction, breast implants or reductions) to achieve the desired appearance. In the past, anthropologists would refer to such body modifications to attain a cultural ideal as "mutilations." Among the Bambara of west Africa, gross obesity in females, resulting in extreme ectomorphy, is considered to be a desired and most attractive phenotype in terms of both physical beauty and socioeconomic status. See Dettwyler's 1994 *Dancing Skeletons* ethnography for an example.

27 Relethford (1994) has noted that 55% of variation in skull size and shape is due solely to the inheritance of genetic material; the remaining 45% of variation is due to effects of the environment, as well as the interaction of genetic *loci* and/or their respective alleles. See Chapter 3 for more mathematical detail on heritability and environment.

28 Insults or stressors may range from poor nutrition and dietary interruption (the most common causes) to illness during enamel formation. Because enamel production seems to have a steady tempo in each tooth class, the number and size of enamel hypoplastic defects can provide information on the age at which the insult may have occurred. A similar linear defect in long

bones (Harris lines) can be seen in radiographs of adult bones and also represent a temporary cessation of tissue development due to external or internal stress.

29 Except for forensic anthropologists, who deal with the general public, and law enforcement officials, who still usually use racial types to describe the victims and perpetrators of crimes. Most physical or biological anthropologists reject the concept of racial types as real biological entities. We do, however, recognize that people within different eco-geographic areas have features that differ to some degree, on average, from people in other areas. We also acknowledge that essentialism has no place in biological science, any more than a flat Earth concept has a place in astrophysics. Most of us avoid using racial terminology, to prevent the type of misconception promoted by the analysts and media and that were, for example, used to oversell the importance of the Kennewick skeleton to the American public in general.

30 Dewar's (1999: 429–31) incorrect account of how one such presentation by me was received by a few anthropologists at the American Association of Physical Anthropologists meeting in 1998 is an example of this.

3

Evolutionary approaches to human variation

We disagree with the notion that this individual [Kennewick Man] is Caucasian. Scientists say that because the individual's head measurements do not match ours, he is not Native American. We believe humans and animals change over time to adapt to their environment. And our elders have told us that Indian people did not always look the way we look today.

Armand Minthorn, 1996
(Umatilla tribal spokesman)

3.1 INTRODUCTION TO EVOLUTIONARY GENETICS

Racial–typological[1] approaches, discussed in Chapter 2, are attempts to interpret human biological variation without making explicit reference to models of population structure and evolution. The alternative to the racial–typological view of human variation is an evolutionary approach. In this chapter, I discuss the forces of evolution and the underlying mathematical models for mutation, selection, migration, and random genetic drift. Human skeletal and dental diversity has an underlying genetic basis. The genes underlying such diversity can be used to create evolutionary models that can tell us about the origin, demographic history, and microevolution of Native Americans over the past 12 000 or so years. Racial typology and categorization cannot provide this information without numerous simplifying assumptions.

These include the primary assumption that each human population is totally distinctive in morphology and changes only as a result of historical events, such as when a racially different group invades/ colonizes and replaces the original population. This, of course, was the story that the Benton County, Washington Coroner's Office told the press to explain why the Kennewick skeleton looked nothing like the Native American tribes in the area. All of the concepts of racial typology presented in Chapter 2 assume that human races are real and very distinctive. This racial–typological approach relies on a kind of non-scientific, model-free thinking known as inductive reasoning, whereas evolutionary approaches to human morphology rely on model-bound deductive reasoning and hypothesis testing using scientific methods. Inductive reasoning is why many perfectly reasonable and intelligent people want to explain natural phenomena as the result of interference from space aliens, or assert that the Earth is flat and not spherical.

The evolutionary approach provides the theoretical foundation for scientific analysis of the phenotypic features of Late Pleistocene and Holocene populations. When phenotypic variation is interpreted within a population genetics framework, it provides a very different picture of the peopling of the New World to the inductive (model-free or *post hoc*) racial–typological assessments. This chapter contains the theoretical basis for using phenotypic variation in the analysis of genetic structure in living and ancient populations.

Basics of genetics

I provide this basic background for those who are unfamiliar with genetics. Readers familiar with the subject might want to proceed to Section 3.2 of this chapter.

The nucleus of every somatic[2] cell in the human body contains 46 chromosomes (23 homologous pairs per cell, one chromosome of the pair from the mother and the other from the father). Each chromosome is composed of two long threads of sugars (polypeptides) that are biochemically linked together by paired nucleotides (bases),[3] tightly wound in a double-helix shape (Figure 3.1). This structure is better known as deoxyribonucleic acid (DNA). The ordering of nucleotides in DNA contains the instructions on how to assemble particular amino acids to make proteins needed for the growth, development, metabolism, and maintenance of the organism. DNA from the cell's nucleus is referred to as nuclear DNA (nDNA), to differentiate it from the circular DNA (mtDNA) found inside the cell's energy-producing organelles located in the cytoplasm, the mitochondria. Both types of DNA have properties that make each useful for different types of anthropological analyses. For example, mtDNA contains a mere 16 597 paired bases, as opposed to over 100 million nucleotides in just a single strand of nDNA, and up to 30 billion nucleotides in the entire human genome. Of these nDNA nucleotides, only

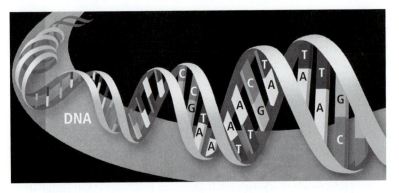

Figure 3.1 Molecular structure of deoxyribonucleic acid (DNA); dark spheres are the peptides; white and gray represent the nucleotides. Graphic modified from the US Department of Energy Human Genome program (http://www.ornl.gov/hgmis). A = adenine; T = thymine; C = cytosine; G = guanine.

Table 3.1 *Possible alleles contributed by parents (top and sides) and possible offspring genotypes (in parentheses) and phenotypes (bold, italic) in the ABO blood system.*

		Mother		
	Possible alleles	A	B	O
Father	A	(AA) = ***A***	(AB) = ***AB***	(AO) = ***A***
	B	(BA) = ***AB***	(BB) = ***B***	(BO) = ***B***
	O	(OA) = ***A***	(OB) = ***B***	(OO) = ***O***

3% to 5% are actually involved in protein synthesis (Crawford, 1998: 139). Shorter segments of nucleotides (genes) code for the production of certain amino acid chains and thus for the shape, structure, and function of different proteins. This property of DNA and protein products permits geneticists to look for the biochemical signature of certain proteins. This method can be used to indicate the presence of a particular version of a genetic *locus* (an *allele*) without tracing the exact sequence of nucleotides.

As an example, the ABO blood group[4] contains A, B, and O alleles, which, in turn, create anti-A and anti-B antigens or no antigens (O) on the surface of red blood cells as a result of the combination of alleles in the *genotype*. From the potential alleles the parents could contribute to offspring (alleles A, B, and O), we get nine possible genotypes but only four possible phenotypes (Table 3.1).

Type A blood has only A antigens, type B blood has only B anti-gens, while type AB blood has both, and type O blood has none. The test for the antigens (in this case the *phenotype* or physical manifestation of the underlying gene and its alleles) indicates the genotype. Other kinds of DNA provide a different view of human genetic variation.

Mitochondrial DNA

Owing to the nature of sexual reproduction, mtDNA is only transmitted by mothers to their offspring,[5] does not undergo recombination, and thus provides better, clearer estimates of the history of female genetic lineages, especially with regard to migration, and the accumulation of mutations. The Y chromosome (a sex chromosome found only in males[6]) provides data on male lineage histories. Both mtDNA, nDNA, and Y-DNA contain restriction sites that allow restriction enzymes to sever the DNA strand at a specific location in the nucleotide sequence.

Different restriction enzymes cut the DNA strand into pieces of a particular length, which can be measured through electrophoresis. These fragments are known as *restriction fragment length polymorphisms* (RFLPs). The discovery of the polymerase chain reaction (PCR) technique, used to make numerous copies of a nucleotide sequence, has enabled molecular geneticists to obtain nucleotide sequence data for mtDNAs, nDNAs, and Y-DNA. The PCR method allows geneticists to examine sequence variation due to mutations or replication errors that can then be used in phylogenetic assessment of genetic sequences. These errors include base-pair deletions or repetitions. For example, the 9 base-pair deletion[7] of mtDNA is frequently seen in persons of Native American and east Asian maternal heritage, as are sets of repeated base pairs in variable numbers (VNTRs and STRs).[8] Replication errors can be distinguished from new bases added to or removed from a sequence as a result of mutation. VNTR and STR variation, as well as nDNA alleles, can be examined using methods from the fields of population and quantitative genetics, which tell us something about the genetic histories and struc-ture of both modern and prehistoric human groups.

3.2   GENETICS OF POPULATIONS

As noted above, allele frequencies can be used to study the population structure in living or prehistoric peoples. Useful studies of the popula-tion structure of living Native Americans have been done using mtDNA (Ballinger *et al.*, 1992; Merriwether *et al.*, 1995) and nDNA (Crawford,

1998). Direct studies of ancient DNA (aDNA) pose a number of potential difficulties, including contamination by modern human or non-human DNAs, the inability to extract DNA from preserved tissues, and recovery of very small amounts of DNA (see O'Rourke *et al.*, 1996; Stone, 1999; Stone and Stoneking, 1996). Given the problems of obtaining DNA sequence data, many researchers have resorted to examining the protein products of particular DNA sequences, such as the human leukocyte antigens (HLAs).

Forces of evolution

Evolutionary biologists have noted that there are four primary forces of evolution that act on populations or subpopulations (Hartl and Clark, 1989). Evolution is narrowly defined as a change in allele frequencies in a population over time. These evolutionary forces include mutation, migration (or gene flow), genetic drift (including founder effect), and natural or sexual selection. If no evolution occurs in a population or subpopulation, the frequency of genotypes is determined by the Hardy–Weinberg equilibrium discussed in Box 3.1.

Box 3.1   Hardy–Weinberg equilibrium

The Hardy–Weinberg equation for expected genotypic frequencies under random mating, where p and q are frequencies of the two alleles at a simple (diallelic) genetic *locus* (A and a alleles, respectively) so that $q = (1 - p)$ and $p = (1 - q)$. Under Hardy–Weinberg equilibrium, which assumes no selection, no mutation, no migration, no genetic drift, and random mating within a population, the expected genotypic frequencies for AA (pp), Aa (pq), and aa (qq) genotypes are given as:

$$p^2 + 2p(1 - p) + (1 - p)^2 = 1 \qquad (3.1)$$

or

$$p^2 + 2pq + q^2 = 1 \qquad (3.2)$$

Mutation

Mutation (μ) is the only way in which new alleles are created. This evolutionary force has been demonstrated to be a rare event, with a probability of occurrence at $\mu < 0.001$ (Falconer, 1989). Mutation and in-migration are the only way that a *deme* (subpopulation) can receive new alleles, thus increasing the genetic variance within and between demes and within the total population.

The probability of fixation[9] of a new mutation is a function of the effective population size (N_e)[10] of the group in question. Mutation, when combined with selection or migration, can be a potent force for the evolution of populations.

Migration

Migration (m), also known as *gene flow*, is when individuals (and their alleles) move from one population to another, either through the physical movement of individuals from one deme to another (Cavalli-Sforza *et al.*, 1994) or by reproduction between members of different demes or populations. Migration can be one-way, balanced, or multi-directional. *Gene flow*, a term that some authors use to indicate a special type of one-way migration (Cavalli-Sforza *et al.*, 1994), can be modeled in a variety of ways. It can occur across space and time (Konigsberg, 1987), and can also take the form of a colonization (i.e. a massive one-way migration, or population relocation), *sensu* Greenberg *et al.* (1986). Long-distance migration (m_∞) occurs when alleles arrive from an external population source at great distance. Such events have a low probability of occurrence,[11] and mutation rates (μ) are only slightly lower than long-distance migration rates (m_μ) (Hartl and Clark, 1989). This fact alone refutes the "lost and wandering Viking" hypothesis proposed to explain the presence of the phenotypically unusual Kennewick Man among the prehistoric peoples of the American northwest. The Lost Viking hypothesis depends heavily on the concept of long-distance migration. Of course, such an event has a phenomenally low probability of occurrence, on a par with being killed by a falling meteorite while driving home from work or school – not impossible, but highly unlikely.

Migration can be structured spatially, as in Wright's (1951, 1978) *island model* (Box 3.2), it can be affected by kinship, as in the case of *kin-structured migration* (Fix, 1999), or structured by space and time (Konigsberg, 1988), as in the case of colonization, when groups enter an unoccupied territory as a "group relocation" (see Cavalli-Sforza *et al.*, 1994).

Box 3.2 Wright's island model

The island model proposed by Sewell Wright in 1951 is the basis for many models. It is used to show the importance of small deme size, i.e. genetic drift, in the evolution of populations and geographic structuring of genes. In the island model, the balance between migration (m) and genetic drift is computed as:

$$f = \frac{1}{4}N_e m + 1 \tag{3.3}$$

Here, f is the inbreeding coefficient within demes. When m is small, then f is large and there is considerable inbreeding within demes, which leads to genetic homogeneity (i.e. homozygosity). This implies that all Paleoindian bands must have had some degree of gene flow to balance the homogenizing effects of inbreeding due to the limited mate choices typical of small hunter-gatherer bands (see Wiessner, 1977).

The value of f is an equivalent to Wright's (1978) F_{IS}, which is a measure of homozygosity of subpopulations due to inbreeding.

The basic model of migration is the *island model*, in which the between-group distance is constant over time because there are no spatial effects (i.e. the demes are arranged in linear fashion and distances between them play no role in the model) and because the migration rate and effective sizes are equal for all subpopulations. Thus, the between-group distance is simply $2F_{st}$ (Konigsberg, 1990) (see Box 3.2).

The island model assumes a somewhat linear arrangement of subpopulations and, as such, is less realistic or appropriate for examining the population structure of humans, because we know that group proximity helps to determine the likelihood of migration/gene flow. For example, up to the 1950s in the United States, most people married and mated with those socially appropriate persons within the same town or village or from nearby towns or villages, or within the same city neighborhood or nearby neighborhoods. Most Americans did not take a boat to China, Zanzibar, or other remote locales to obtain mates. In most cases, reproduction was (and still is) merely an event of convenience and accessibility. The spatial component of genetic drift and gene flow in humans is better described by *isolation by distance* models (Malécot, 1959), which account for the distribution of subpopulations across the landscape. In the unidimensional *stepping-stone* model (Kimura and Weiss, 1964), subpopulations are arranged on a surface so that a subpopulation will exchange alleles with adjacent groups at a rate of m_1, with new alleles added owing to long-range gene flow (or mutation) at a rate of m_∞.

Isolation by distance (IBD) is another popular model for examining migration, and was proposed both by Malécot (1959) and by Wright (1943) (Fix, 1999: 54–5). In an IBD model, genetic distance between demes is a function of the probability that migrants reach other demes at great distances. In the IBD model, inter-demic genetic distance is small when populations are not drifting apart because of large effective sizes; the distance is also smaller when demes are geographically closer, increasing the likelihood of migration between groups. The "isolation by distance" model makes genetic distance a function of geography and deme size, because the larger the group, the greater the number of individuals that participate in migration, and the farther away a recipient population, the less likely it is that any long-term gene flow will take place.

Additional models

Additional models include the *stepping-stone model* of migration, in which alleles hop from one deme to another like a person hopping from one stepping stone to another as they cross a stream. Provided that $m_\infty \ll m_1$, then the correlation of gene-frequency correlation between populations s spatial units apart is defined as:

$$r_s = \exp\left(-s\sqrt{\frac{2\,m_\infty}{m_1}}\right) \tag{3.4}$$

where s is the distance between demes and m_1 is the average migration rate[12] for demes. The value r is a spatial correlation of allele frequencies between demes that exchange migrants.

Although this model is typically applied to populations in linear habitats, Konigsberg (1987) pointed out that a circular stepping-stone model eliminates the problem of "edge effects" associated with uni-dimensional and two-dimensional models, and is similar to some anthropologically documented patterns of mate exchange (Konigsberg, 1987: 39–41). However, this model (Boxes 3.3a and 3.3b) is limited because it accounts for spatial, but not temporal, variation among subpopulations.

Box 3.3a   Time–space migration models

Konigsberg (1990) presented an elegant extension of the stepping-stone model that incorporates both spatial and temporal distance among subpopulations. His derivation was based on the concept of random walks, so that in each generation, an allele can either remain in its original subpopulations with probability $\beta = (1 - m)(1 - m)$, or can move to an adjacent subpopulation with probability $\alpha = m_1/2(1 - m)$. Over time, an allele will move i steps away from its point of origin and j steps back. After t generations of random walks, the probability that an allele is s steps away from its subpopulation of origin is given (Konigsberg, 1990) as:

$$P_t(S) = \sum_{ijk} \frac{t}{ijk} \alpha^{(i+j)} \beta^k \tag{3.5}$$

where $s = i - j$ and $k = t - i - j$.

Konigsberg (1990: 54) then substituted this value into Eq. (3.3) to produce the temporal–spatial gene frequency correlation of subpopulations separated by a spatial distance of s and t generations:

$$r_{ts} = P_t(\phi) r_s + 2 \sum_{k=1}^{t} P_t(k) r_{|s-k|} \tag{3.6}$$

In this equation, the right-hand side represents gene-frequency correlations obtained from Eq. (3.3), and the factor 2 represents symmetric gene flow between adjacent subpopulations (Konigsberg, 1990: 54). The temporal–spatial distances of populations separated by s units of distance and t generations can be obtained by replacing the migration term in Eq. (3.7) (below) with the temporal–spatial gene-frequency correlation from Eq. (3.5), so that

$$d^2{}_{ts} = 2 F_{st}(1 - r_{ts}) \tag{3.7}$$

Here, F_{st} is derived from the ordinary unidimensional stepping-stone model.

Box 3.3b   Wright's F-statistics

F_{is} measures the fixation of alleles due to inbreeding in subpopulation (demes or local populations) relative to diversity in the entire (total) population, or the correlation between uniting gametes relative to the gametes of a deme averaged over all demes subpopulations. This F-statistic measures the effects of nonrandom mating in the form of inbreeding. In diallelic loci, this can be computed as:

$$F_{is} = (H_t/2\bar{p}\bar{q}) - (\bar{p}^2/\bar{p}\bar{q})/1 - (H_t/2\bar{p}\bar{q}) \tag{3.8}$$

H_t is the observed proportion of heterozygotes in the total population, where $\bar{p}$ is the mean frequency of allele p. The latter equation is the correlation between randomly selected alleles relative to the entire population, where V_p is the variance of the p allele in the total population (Crawford, 1998: 151, Eq. 5).

F_{st} is perhaps the best known of Wright's three F-statistics. It is a measure of between-deme variation relative to genetic variation in the total population, which is also the correlation between randomly selected alleles and the entire population. It is equivalent to Harpending and Jenkins' (1973) R_{st} from an R-metric analysis (see below). F_{st} increases over time (t) as $t/2N_e$ in diploid organisms such as humans when t is small relative to the effective size of the population (N_e) (Cavalli-Sforza et al., 1994: Eqs. 5 and 6). For diallelic loci for demes 1 and 2 it is:

$$F_{st} = \frac{(p_1 - q_1)^2}{2(\bar{p} - p_1 q_1)^2} \quad \text{or} \quad F_{st} = \frac{V_p}{\bar{p}\,\bar{q}} \tag{3.9}$$

The last of Wright's F-statistics is F_{it}, which is the sum of the other F-statistics and a measure of inbreeding in the total population (including all demes). It represents the combined effects of nonrandom mating (inbreeding):

$$F_{it} = F_{st} + F_{is}(1 - F_{st}) \tag{3.10}$$

The interpretation of the stepping-stone model of isolation by temporal and spatial distance is somewhat counter-intuitive (Konigsberg, 1990). The within-group distances (i.e. spatial lag $= 0$) increase with time because new alleles are introduced to the population through gene flow. For groups fixed in time but spatially separated, genetic distance increases with spatial distance, as populations that are far apart are less likely to share alleles from gene flow. These expectations are the same as those of the island model. However, in the case of populations at some fixed (non-zero) spatial distance, genetic distances *decrease* through time as a result of the cumulative effects of gene flow. This model predicts that the genetic distances among any set of populations separated in both time and space from the phenotypic distance (i.e. minimum genetic distance) will be positively correlated with geographic distance and negatively correlated with temporal distance (Konigsberg, 1990: 57).

Genetic drift

Genetic drift is a random loss of alleles in a deme due to demographic history of demes (that have small effective size); the probability of allelic loss, like the probability of mutation, is a function of effective population size. Genetic drift leads to a loss of alleles and therefore to a reduction in genetic variability over time. Perhaps the best-known form of genetic drift is founder effect, when a new population includes a founder with a mutation (a rare variant at a genetic *locus*). Cavalli-Sforza and coworkers (1994) note, however, that many authors discuss the founder effect as though it were a different phenomenon to that of genetic drift. Genetic drift typically occurs when the deme has a very small effective size and virtually no in-migration to any populations or demes; the loss of alleles due to random events (drift) is often balanced by the addition of new alleles through mutation or migration.

As mentioned above, the loss of variation due to genetic drift is more likely in small populations.[13] The loss of alleles through drift is concurrent with the addition of alleles between demes through migration, which increases intra-demic variation at a rate of m (Wright, 1951), and decreases inter-demic genetic distances over time, as demes share more genetic material and ultimately become more genetically identical. Wright's (1951) model assumes that the demes are slightly isolated (with low or no migration among them), like a set of islands in the ocean (thus the term "*island model*").

Selection

As Darwin (1859) noted, natural selection can be a primary cause for change through time. We now know that selection can only act on the phenotype, not the genotype, but these are inexorably linked. There are several types of selection, including natural selection, sexual selection (Darwin, 1871), and frequency-dependent selection. Assuming that each genotype produces a different phenotype, each genotype has an associated fitness (w_{ij}) that is a function of the survivorship and fecundity of the genotypes relative to one another, where the fitnesses sum to one. If one homozygous genotype has greater fitness than the other genotypes (i.e. $w_{ii} > w_{ij} \gg w_{jj}$), this condition results in directional selection, which may result in one allele becoming lost and the other fixed in future generations. *Balancing selection* occurs when the heterozygote has greater fitness than any other genotype (i.e. $w_{ii} < w_{ij} > w_{jj}$), and ensures that all genotypes are produced in the next generation; there is, therefore, no loss of allelic variation in this type of selection, unlike directional selection.

Skin color was cited in Chapter 2 as an example of a human phenotypic trait affected by sexual selection, which occurs when like phenotypes tend to select one another for reproduction. Experimental

Figure 3.2 Principal component map for the HLA*A allele frequency in the Americas, modified from Cavalli-Sforza *et al.* (1994).

data from fruit flies, however, indicate that females tend to select males with unusual phenotypes ("odd males") relative to other males in a population. The one well-documented example of natural sexual selection in humans involves the human leukocyte antigen (HLA) complex.[14] The human leukocyte antigen *A (HLA*A) and *B *loci* display a geographic pattern across the Americas and elsewhere, and are described as having a *clinal* distribution (Figure 3.2) that may represent an environmentally correlated type of natural selection referred to as clinal selection (Fix, 1999: 171–2; Sokal *et al.*, 1991).

Measures of population structure

This section is provided to give readers a better understanding of how genotypic and phenotypic variation within and between populations of ancient and modern peoples can be assessed in terms of mutation, drift, migration, and selection. The term "population structure" refers to the degree to which the variation in genotypes and phenotypes in populations (or demes) reflects the effects of the evolutionary forces acting upon them. Such an understanding is crucial in order to see how the pattern of biological variation across space and time, interpreted by racial typology, produces one result while the evolutionary perspective provides a very different interpretation. The following are key concepts in population genetic analyses, along with Hardy–Weinberg equilibrium (Box 3.1), Wright's island model (Box 3.2), and Konigsberg's time–space stepping-stone migration model (Boxes 3.3a, 3.3b).

Genetic measures of variation

In order to assess genetic variation (or the lack thereof) in populations or demes, geneticist Sewell Wright (1951) partitioned genetic variation within or between populations or subpopulations (demes) into three separate components as statistics known as F_{is}, F_{st}, and F_{it}. Here, F or f stand for a *fixation index* (Box 3.3b). For the interested reader, the three F-statistics are given in Boxes 3.3a and 3.3b.

Box 3.4   Additive models

Phenotypic variation is actually a reflection of underlying genetic variation.

The phenotypic variance, σ_p^2 (or V_p^2), of a quantitative trait can be divided into its genetic and environmental components,

$$\sigma_P^2 = \sigma_G^2 + \sigma_E^2 \tag{3.11}$$

where the phenotypic variance is always greater than or equal to the genetic variance (Falconer, 1989: 125). The multivariate extension of this model would be:

$$P = G + E \tag{3.12}$$

where P, G, and E are the phenotypic, genetic, and environmental variance–covariance matrices, respectively.

One way of representing the genetic component of phenotypic variation is through the concept of heritability. The narrow-sense heritability (h^2) of a trait refers to the ratio of additive genetic variance σ_A^2, the variation due to differences in alleles inherited from both parents, to total (phenotypic) variance σ_P^2. Narrow-sense heritability is defined as

$$h^2 = \frac{\sigma_A^2}{\sigma_P^2} \tag{3.13}$$

Because F_{st} is sensitive to its underlying assumptions of infinite subdivisions (Wright's infinite island model), Nei (1973, 1977) proposed a replacement for F_{st} that he called G_{st}, which corrects for the infinite subdivision assumption; this is a measure of the subpopulation or demic variation relative to the total population variance.

The loss of genetic variation through drift or inbreeding is offset by the increase in variation through alleles gained by migration and, sometimes, mutation. Thus, Wright's F-statistics are critical in order to assess whether observed variation is a result of drift or migration. In the Kennewick Man case, this alternative hypothesis was not presented in the first analysis of the skeleton (Chatters et al., 1999), although it was by the US government scientists (Powell and Neves, 1999).

3.3 POLYGENIC MODELS

All phenotypic features, from adult stature to tooth size, nose shape and skin color, are determined by the individual's underlying alleles at one or more genetic *loci*. For many phenotypic features, there are many alleles and dozens or even hundreds of *loci*. Alleles at each *locus* can affect one another, and interact with environmental factors internal or external to the individual. Such phenotypic traits are called quantitative genetic traits because they are generally examined using complex statistical methods. The term *polygenic* refers to the trait as a product of many genes and environmental factors (Box 3.4).

Deviations

In addition to allelic substitutions at a *locus* (additive variance), the total genetic variance (σ_G^2) is the sum of additive variance (σ_A^2), dominance (σ_D^2), and epistatic (gene–gene interaction) effects (σ_I^2), or *deviations*. These deviations can create an amazing amount of complexity in the phenotype expressed in the following, obtained from Eq. (3.13): $\sigma_G^2 = \sigma_A^2 + \sigma_D^2 + \sigma_I^2$.

Numerous studies (Konigsberg and Blangero, 1993; Relethford and Blangero, 1990; Relethford and Harpending, 1994; Sciulli and Mahaney, 1991) have demonstrated that estimates of genetic variation derived from phenotypic variation in humans are relatively insensitive to the value of h^2 used, provided that it is not too low (<0.20).

Environmental variance

In addition to the additive genetic component of phenotypic variance, environmental variation (σ_E^2) must also be considered, as correlation between genotype and environment (and the interaction of these variables) can greatly alter the phenotypic variance (Falconer, 1989: 125). Environmental variance is defined as all variation of a non-genetic origin that reduces the precision of genetic studies (Falconer, 1989). Using the terminology of Falconer (1989), environmental variance can be further broken down into several components,

$$\sigma_E^2 = \sigma_{E_T}^2 + \sigma_{E_I}^2 \qquad (3.14)$$

where $\sigma_{E_T}^2$ is the variation due to "tangible" sources, and $\sigma_{E_I}^2$ is the variation due to "intangible" sources. The type of research and organism under study affect which sources of environmental variance are defined as "tangible" or "intangible."

In the case of phenotypic variation in past human populations, many effects are intangible. For example, most processes affecting the size and shape of teeth act during tooth development, and intangible sources of environmental variation would include maternal genotype, diet, and health, general odontogenetic timing, patterns of tooth or bone mineralization and eruption, the diet of the individual, and genetic abnormalities. External sources of variation, such as climate and ecological conditions, have less impact on dental variation than these because teeth do not respond to environmental stress through size–shape changes at the cellular level.[15] Such variables must, however, still be considered as potential sources of intangible environmental variation (Falconer, 1989).

Tangible sources of variation include external factors acting on the phenotype that are easily controlled in experiments or in research designs (Falconer, 1989: 138). In studies of prehistoric phenotypic variation, it is possible to control for a number of these factors. Sexual dimorphism affecting trait size and shape accounts for a very significant proportion of phenotypic variation. Kieser (1990) provides an excellent review of the considerable body of work on the subject of sexual dimorphism in phenotypic traits, particularly tooth size, which may reflect sex linkage (Alvesalo and Varrela, 1991), differences between sexes in the timing of tooth and bone mineralization and maturation (Moorrees et al., 1963), maternal effects, and the interaction of genetic and environmental factors.

Another important source of tangible environmental variance is observability. Many ancient human remains are represented only by fragmentary crania or worn or damaged teeth and there are any number of causes for environmental variation. For crania, cultural practices, such as cremation of the deceased, clearly affect the bones of the skull and ultimately the researcher's ability to take accurate measurements of how the skull looked in life. Many cultures intentionally modify the skull's shape by head binding, along with unintentional cultural alteration such as strapping a baby's head to a board to support it in a pack carried on an adult's back (cradle boarding), and these alterations also create environmental effects that alter a researcher's ability to observe certain features or dimensions of the skull.

Observability in teeth is often a function of the age and diet of the individual, as well as nondietary factors such as tooth grinding during life (bruxism) or use of the teeth as tools, as this affects dental phenotypic variation by altering the original size and shape of a tooth. Interstitial (between-tooth) and extreme occlusal wear (loss of the tooth crown or just the enamel surface) affect tooth dimensions (Kieser, 1990: 11; Kieser et al., 1985), and even moderate dental attrition can obliterate many dental morphological features (Turner, 1989). Oral hygiene affects dental phenotypic variation through pathological loss or damage to the tooth. Accumulation of dental calculus can affect the size and shape of teeth. Finally, errors in recording traits or measurements between or within observers make a significant contribution to the tangible environmental component of dental and cranial phenotypic variation.

In models where heritability values are set to unity, the environmental variance is zero, since $\sigma_G^2 = \sigma_P^2$. Although this simplifies computations, a more realistic model would include some measure of the environmental variance, as in Eqs. (3.13) and (3.14) above. The goal for researchers is to eliminate as many of the tangible sources of environmental variation as possible, so that any remaining environmental variance can be presumed to be randomly distributed among subpopulations, and can be interpreted as "noise" in subsequent analyses (Buikstra et al., 1990: 6). This allows quantitative traits with low average heritabilities (i.e. those with a significant proportion of environmental variance) to be employed in the analysis of population structure (Konigsberg, 1990; Lees and Relethford, 1982; Williams-Blangero and Blangero, 1989).

3.4   QUANTITATIVE GENETICS OF PHENOTYPIC SIZE AND SHAPE

Craniometric traits

Craniofacial size and shape are a function of several genes that affect both endochondral (within cartilage) and intramembranous (within membranes) ossification that affect the tempo and mode of growth and development, along with environmental factors, during fetal and neonatal, and childhood and adolescent stages (Wilkie and Morriss-Kay, 2001). For example, several craniofacial disorders are associated with mutations in a variety of genes, implying that these genes help to regulate proper growth and development of the skull (Wilkie *et al.*, 2000; Wilkie and Morriss-Kay, 2001).

Genetic/phenotypic distances

An examination of Eq. (3.4) demonstrates that σ_P^2 is always greater than or equal to σ_G^2. From this, the relationship of phenotypic to genetic distance (Williams-Blangero and Blangero, 1989) is that a distance based on phenotypic traits is *always* the *minimum genetic distance*.

Cranial nonmetric traits

Cheverud and Buikstra (1981) conducted a quantitative genetic analysis of cranial nonmetric features in Rhesus macaques (*Macaca mulatta*) from the Cayo Santiago facility in Honduras. Most cranial nonmetric traits are thought to be polygenic and operating under a quantitative model of expression (Konigsberg, 1987). Hauser and De Stefano (1989) present a compendium of craniofacial nonmetric traits, along with information about their possible mode of inheritance (see also Konigsberg, 1987).

Genetics of phenotypic size and shape

One of the properties of teeth and bones that makes them useful in reconstructing population history and microevolutionary patterns is that the size and shape of these phenotypes is, to some extent, under genetic control. Narrow-sense heritability values (Box 3.5) for tooth crown size range from $h^2 = 0.54$ to 0.95, while broad-sense heritability and transmissibility values for dental nonmetric traits are slightly lower (Harris and Bailit, 1980; Nichol, 1989). Human craniofacial dimensions have been estimated to have an average narrow-sense heritability of $h^2 = 0.55$ (Ousley, 1985; Relethford, 1994). The narrow-sense heritability is the proportion of variance directly due to additive changes in alleles inherited from each parent. Broad-sense heritability is the proportion of variance attributed to all genetic effects, including additive and dominance effects.

Genotype and phenotype

Phenotypic traits, including craniofacial and dental morphometrics, have been shown to be correlated with various measures of genetic variation in human and non-human populations. Cheverud (1988) examined the relationship between genetic and phenotypic correlation matrices using data from 41 published studies. He found a significant positive correlation between genetic and phenotypic correlation matrices in 31 studies, with an average matrix correlation coefficient of 0.57. Genetic correlations slightly exceeded phenotypic correlations in most cases. Together, these data indicate that phenotypic variation is a fair indicator of underlying genetic variation (Relethford and Harpending, 1994). According to Cheverud (1988: 965): "... phenotypic correlations may be substituted for genetic ones when genetic correlations are unavailable or not precisely estimated." This relationship of genotype to phenotype makes it possible to employ phenotypic data from the first Americans in microevolutionary models and analyses (Powell and Neves, 1999).

Box 3.5   Heritability

Broad-sense heritability (H^2) is the ratio of total genetic variance (σ_G^2), including all deviations, to the total variance so that:

$$H^2 = \frac{\sigma_G^2}{\sigma_P^2} \tag{3.18}$$

All of the equations above present an additive polygenic model, with no deviation due to dominance, gene–gene interactions (epistasis), or gene–environment interaction, so that the total genetic variance (σ_G^2) is equal to the additive genetic variance. This simplified model is often assumed for analyses of metric phenotypic traits, but many skeletal and dental morphological traits appear to fit a polygenic threshold model rather than a strictly Mendelian model (Konigsberg, 1990; Nichol, 1989).

> The narrow-sense heritability (h^2) is, in reality, untenable for phenotypic traits, since it is the ratio of additive variance to the total phenotypic variance:
>
> $$h^2 = \frac{\sigma_A^2}{\sigma_P^2} \qquad\qquad (3.19)$$
>
> where the additive variance σ_A^2 is due to the additive effect of alleles in which each allele contributes a certain value to the observed trait.

Scott, Sofaer, and their colleagues (Scott, 1973; Scott and Dahlberg, 1982; Scott et al., 1988; Sofaer et al., 1972) investigated the relationship between phenotypic distances and biological distances derived from other features, including tooth crown morphology. They found strong congruence between these data sets, suggesting that dental metric and nonmetric traits produce similar pictures of phenetic relatedness.

Population structure and phenotypic variance

Before discussing data collection methods and analysis techniques (Chapter 6), it will be helpful to discuss how phenotypic variation can be used in the study of past population structure and microevolution. Much of the ground-breaking theoretical work on the use of human phenotypic variation in population and quantitative genetics comes from Blangero and coworkers (Blangero, 1990; Blangero and Konigsberg, 1991), Konigsberg and coworkers (Konigsberg, 1987, 1990; Konigsberg and Blangero, 1993), Lande (1976, 1988), Lees and Relethford (1982), Lynch (1990), Relethford and coworkers (Relethford, 1994; Relethford and Blangero, 1990; Relethford and Harpending, 1994; Relethford and Lees, 1982), Turelli (1988), and Williams-Blangero (Williams-Blangero and Blangero, 1989, 1992).

The greatest problem in studies of quantitative traits is that the proportion of the phenotypic variation due to the additive effects of genes is unknown. This value is required for most methods in which population structure is to be examined, and can be readily obtained through traditional quantitative genetic analysis of familial relationships. These methods, however, require large sample sizes that are rarely available in anthropological studies of living populations, let alone prehistoric groups. Relethford and Blangero (1990) provided a number of methods for estimating the genetic variance from phenotypic data. These methods do not rely on pedigree data, but do make a number of assumptions regarding the additive and equal effects of all *loci*.[16]

If the exact heritabilities are unavailable, then G_i can be estimated using a "reasonable single estimate of the average heritability" (Relethford and Blangero, 1990: 14), h^2, so that $G_i = h^2 P_i$. Again, this assumes that heritability values for all subdivisions are equal. Another approach is to substitute various estimates for the average heritability (Relethford and Blangero, 1990). Perhaps the easiest approach, but the most unrealistic in terms of genetics, is to assume that all phenotypic variation is due to additive genetic variation, so that $G_i = P_i$, and $h^2 = 1$ (Relethford and Blangero, 1990: 14–15). In any case, numerous studies (Konigsberg and Blangero, 1993; Relethford and Blangero, 1990; Relethford and Harpending, 1994; Sciulli and Mahaney, 1991) have demonstrated that estimates of genetic variation derived from phenotypic variation in humans are relatively insensitive to the value of h^2 used, provided that it is not too low (<0.20).

Phenotypic distances as genetic distances

As noted above, the difficulty in deriving the genetic variance from phenotypic variance is that several parameters must be estimated or assumed to be zero. For example, heritability values must be known or estimated, and environmental variance must be controlled or removed. One way of avoiding this problem is to use phenotypic distances as estimates of genetic relatedness among subpopulations, provided that phenotypic variation is, at least in part, a reflection of genetic variation between and within groups. In order to interpret phenotypic distances within a population genetics framework, they must be related to the actual genetic distances between subpopulations in some consistent way.

3.5   THE STRUCTURE OF PAST POPULATIONS

One of the problems associated with hypotheses regarding the peopling of the New World is that they are often not based on explicit population genetics theory and are, in essence, "model free" (Relethford and Lees, 1982). In this section, I present the expectations of phenotypic variation and distance in prehistoric populations under various population genetics models. Konigsberg (1987, 1990) discussed the difficulties associated with this type of analysis:

> There are several reasons for the difficulties in analyzing variation within or between prehistoric populations, for example, (1) only phenotypic, not genetic, distances can be studied; (2) in the archeological record populations or subpopulations are often ill-defined and/or misrepresented; (3) important effects on genetic differentiation, such as mutation rate, effective population size, migration rate, and selection intensity, cannot be directly measured; and (4) temporal and spatial separation and geographic isolation may affect the pattern of between-group biological distances. (Konigsberg, 1990: 50)

In order to examine phenotypic variation in prehistoric populations, it will be necessary to make a number of assumptions. This approach, however, is much better than the *post hoc* interpretation of variation used in many studies of the peopling of the New World, since it explicitly states the assumptions used, and attempts to interpret biological variation within the context of established genetic theories.

Conclusion: problems and solutions

As noted above, the primary concern in the study of the biology of ancient Americans is that studies using prehistoric human skeletal samples are limited to the analysis of phenotypic distances (or ancient DNA). The utility of phenotypic distances and phenotypic variance in the analysis of living and past population structure is now well established in the literature of biology and anthropology (Blangero, 1990; Konigsberg, 1987, 1990; Konigsberg and Blangero, 1993; Lande, 1976, 1988; Lynch, 1990; Powell and Neves, 1999; Relethford, 1991; Relethford and Blangero, 1990; Relethford and Harpending, 1994; Relethford and Lees, 1982; Sciulli, 1990b; Sciulli and Mahaney, 1991; Sciulli *et al.*, 1988; Turelli, 1988; Williams-Blangero and Blangero, 1989).

The second problem, that populations are poorly defined and poorly represented in the archaeological record, is more difficult to address.

- In the case of Kennewick and other isolated skeletal discoveries, we must *assume that the individuals represented have phenotypic values near the mean of the population or deme from which they came.* The variation between individuals from the same place and time can be used to estimate the within-region or the within-group variance. Such an estimation can be a useful proxy for within-group variation among all Paleoindians. Of course, this is a fantastically large assumption to make, but it has support in resampling-based statistical analyses, so that all recovered Paleoindian skeletons might be considered to be random samples of one or two from a set of Late Pleistocene populations or demes. Cadien *et al.* (1974) noted that archaeological samples do not fit the definition of a biological population because more than one generation can be interred in a burial locale. These authors suggested that skeletal samples at a single site (a cemetery) should be considered as skeletal or evolutionary "lineages" that reflect the action of microevolutionary forces on a sequence of related individuals over time, rather than on biologically discrete groups of individuals.

- The time depth of skeletal samples makes analysis of past population structure more difficult, but this is not an insurmountable problem. One approach is to use methods that take into account the diachronic nature of skeletal samples (Konigsberg, 1987, 1990). For example, Konigsberg (1987: 29) was able to demonstrate that the genetic variance (measured with Wright's F_{st}) estimated for several combined generations (i.e. the skeletal lineage) is equivalent to the arithmetic average of the genetic variance of each discrete generation. Although a certain amount of phenotypic variation within a skeletal sample is due to the fact that "interred individuals were not contemporaneous ... it does not necessarily follow that between-site analyses are strongly affected by within-site variation" (Konigsberg, 1987: 195), especially when between-group variation is much greater than the variation within groups. Cadien *et al.* (1974: 197) noted that "comparisons made between lineages ... use the same unit and in that sense they are valid if tested as a statistical population."

- While several factors have a definite impact on the structure of past and present human populations, the effects of some are minimal. Mutation, which inflates the phenotypic and genetic variances by introducing new alleles into a population, is assumed to have a negligible effect on cranial and dental phenotypic variation among Late Pleistocene and Early Holocene populations. Brace *et al.* (1991) felt that the accumulation of mutations due to the "probable mutation effect" (Brace, 1964) was responsible for the dramatic reduction in hominid tooth size after the Pleistocene. However, this model has been challenged on theoretical grounds (Calcagno and Gibson, 1988), and alternative models that do not require mutation have been offered to explain patterns of human phenotypic change (Calcagno and Gibson, 1991). Mutation rates are generally quite low in most organisms, ranging between 10^{-5} and 10^{-6} per generation, per *locus* (Falconer, 1989: 26), and mutation appears to have an effect on quantitative trait variation only at macroevolutionary time scales (Hartl and Clark, 1989: 498–9; Turelli, 1988). Given these facts, and the conflicting data on the mechanism of phenotypic change, mutation is assumed to be negligible in this analysis.

- Migration, like mutation, (especially long-range migration (m_∞), introduces new alleles into a population from some outside population. In the case of Late Pleistocene–Early Holocene populations, long-range migration is presumed to be very low ($m_\infty = 0.001$ to 0.0001). This is assumed primarily for mathematical simplicity, as long-range migration is equivalent to mutation in many population genetics models (Hartl and Clark, 1989: 317). Furthermore, ethnographic data indicate that the territorial range of many hunter-gatherers is quite large, perhaps of the order of 150 to 500 km (Custer, 1990: 15–17). Late Pleistocene and Early Holocene hunter-gatherer bands appear to have practiced *seasonal aggregation*[17] for the purpose of resource use, alliance formation, and mate exchange (Anderson and Hanson, 1989). This could have linked distant groups through marriage and exchange networks (Anderson and Hanson, 1989; Hantman, 1990). In this scenario, migration/gene flow would appear to be "long range" in a geographic sense, but would be equivalent to short-range gene flow between several adjacent demes with extremely large neighborhood sizes.

- Because my studies focus on phenotypic shape rather than on size, the traits examined are assumed to be selectively neutral (see Blangero, 1988: 298). Turner (1985a,b, 1986b) presumes that shape is a selectively neutral trait, and therefore phenotypic changes in tooth shape take place in a clock-like fashion. Kieser (1990: 50–62) has reviewed the literature on phenotypic trends and the possibility that directional or stabilizing selection may act on cranial and dental phenotypes. Other authors (Anderson and Wendorf, 1968; Calcagno and Gibson, 1988, 1991; Sciulli and Mahaney, 1991) have offered evidence of selection in craniodental size. All of these researchers, however, focused on temporal trends in size rather than shape. Perzigian (1984) noted that geographically disparate human populations with similar cultural adaptations, diets, and environments could be clustered by size, a finding that suggests that selection may affect phenotypic size, resulting in an evolutionary convergence in biologically unrelated populations. However, when he examined shape (measured with Penrose's shape coefficient), he found that populations fell into phylogenetically meaningful clusters.

A statistical test for trend in phenotypic data can be used to eliminate selection from subsequent population structure analyses (Konigsberg, 1987). The results of such tests for Late Pleistocene and Early Holocene skeletal samples are presented in Chapter 10, and support the assumption of neutrality for nonmetric traits and phenotypic shape.

- The final assumption employed here regards the heritability of phenotypic nonmetric and metric traits. Because this study involves prehistoric populations, the heritabilities of the dental traits are unknown, but are assumed to be moderate for Native American populations. As discussed above, I assume that environmental variance is randomly distributed in both space and time among skeletal lineages. Under these conditions, environmental variation between groups amounts to "noise" in the data set. Buikstra et al. (1990: 6) noted that "although heritabilities may be low, it is still possible to reach valid conclusions regarding past population structure."

The final and perhaps most important difficulty concerns the effective size of prehistoric populations. Relethford and Harpending (1994) performed an extensive analysis of human cranial data to demonstrate that both the replacement and multiregional models of modern human origins can be supported by these data, depending on whether or not effective population size and number of migrants per generation are taken into account. In this study, effective population sizes (N_e) are assumed to be the same for all Late Pleistocene–Early Holocene groups. Support for this assumption comes from the fact that most of the excavated sites appear to represent peoples with similar lifestyles, diets, and environments that acted to keep their population growth low. Given the assumptions discussed above, it should be possible to test observations regarding the level of variation and phenotypic (minimum genetic) distances among Late Pleistocene and Early Holocene populations against various theoretical models of population structure. Because the focus is on skeletal samples of differing age drawn from a relatively broad geographic region, models must take into account the effects of temporal and spatial distance on biological distance. By using phenotypic distances as minimum genetic distances, it should be possible to examine processes of gene flow and genetic drift in a temporal context (Konigsberg, 1990).

Relethford and Harpending presented an excellent visual analogy of population structure for populations fixed in time but distributed in space:

> Picture a set of populations being represented by particles undergoing random motion but tethered to each other. The size of the particles reflects population size, where the smaller the size, the greater the random motion (drift). The strength of the tether lines reflects migration; the stronger the tether, the more populations are attracted to one another. The overall relationships between populations are determined by the interaction of drift moving particles apart balanced by migration moving them together. In population genetics terms, two populations could be different because they are both small and hence have both drifted strongly, or because they are not tethered by much migration. (Relethford and Harpending, 1994: 259)

As can be seen in this analogy, genetic drift and gene flow (migration) are extremely important in affecting biological distances between groups. The following discussion presents a summary of the theoretical work of several researchers, including Chakraborty and Nei (1982), Konigsberg (1987, 1990), Relethford (1991), and Relethford and Blangero (1990). Rather than reproduce their work, I shall present a brief summary of various population genetics models and the equations required for generating expected phenotypic distances. Readers should refer to the original sources for equation proofs and derivations.

Genetic drift

Relethford (1991) developed a model for examining the potential biological distances between two populations when drift is the sole microevolutionary force affecting them. The model assumes that genetic drift is the *only* factor affecting population structure, and that all populations are completely isolated from one another over time (i.e. there is no spatial component/migration). The effective size of the i subpopulations, N_i, is assumed to be constant over time (Crow and Kimura, 1970), since population growth would dampen the effects of random drift (Hartl and Clark, 1989). All populations are considered to have the same time depth since founding. Chakraborty (1990) provides theoretical support for this.

Phenotypically, this means that founders and their descendants should be quite phenotypically different from one another over large spans of time, due to genetic drift (under the assumptions stated above). In my opinion, this is a much more plausible explanation for the craniofacial divergence of some ancient American skulls from the morphology of modern Native Americans (for example, Kennewick Man and Luzia).

Gene flow

While genetic drift is an important component of population structure, especially among band-level societies, "remarkably little migration is required to prevent substantial genetic divergence among subpopulations resulting from random genetic drift" (Hartl and Clark, 1989: 310). According to the temporospatial model of gene flow and drift discussed above, in demes fixed in time but spatially separated, genetic distance increases with spatial distance, as populations that are far apart are less likely to share alleles from gene flow. These expectations are the same as those of the island model. However, in the case of populations at some fixed (non-zero) spatial distance, genetic distances *decrease* through time as a result of the cumulative effects of gene flow. This model predicts that the genetic distances among any set of populations separated in both time and space (the phenotypic distance, i.e. minimum genetic distance) will be positively correlated with geographic distance and negatively correlated with temporal distance (Konigsberg, 1990: 57). This prediction is one that can be tested using phenotypic data from Late Pleistocene–Early Holocene skeletal and dental remains in the Old and New World.

In my opinion, the evolutionary approach to understanding the peopling of the Americas and origin of Native Americans is a much more informative approach than untestable and unscientific racial-typological models that assume the fixity of phenotypes during the last 12 000 years of human history (Chatters, 2000; Gladwin, 1947; Greenberg *et al.*, 1986; Hrdlička, 1923; Neumann, 1952; Steele and Powell, 1993). Surely humans experienced some degree of genetic and morphological change, in the wake of the last ice age and advent of global warming? In the next chapter, I shall examine sources of genetic and phenotypic variation relative to our understanding of the roles that "race" and evolution have played in our understanding of the peopling of the Americas and Native American origins.

NOTES

1 The racial–typological approach (discussed in Chapter 2) is a simple categoriz-ation of human populations based on similarity of their physical features (the phenotype) or differences between groups without considering within-group variation or the effects of genes, environments, or human behavior.

2 Somatic cells are those composing all tissues except for the sex cells (spermatozoa [sperm] and ovum [egg]).

3 Bases include adenine (A), guanine (G), thymine (T), and cytosine (C), which are paired across polypeptides as $A:T$ and $G:C$ owing to their biochemical shape; these are the only possible pairings of bases.

4 The ABO genetic locus is located on the q arm of chromosome 9 at [9q 34.1–34.2] (see Cavalli-Sforza *et al.*, 1994, for the locations and operation of other important genetic loci).

5 The mitochondrion is an organelle found in the cytoplasm of the female's egg, but only in the base of the tail of sperm – a part of the sperm that does not penetrate the egg's cell wall during fertilization, and which, therefore, does not contribute to the genetic make-up of the embryo. Sperm require a great degree of energy to provide the high motility needed to reach, then fertilize, the egg.

6 Males have a sex genotype of XY; females are XX. Chromosomal anomalies of XYY (Supermale syndrome) and XO (Turner's syndrome) do occur, although rarely.

7 A 9 base-pair deletion, the COII/tRNA L^{ys} intergenic region (Region V).

8 Also known as variable number of tandem repeats (VNTRs) or short tandem repeats (STRs).

9 When the mutation becomes a permanent change in a DNA sequence.

10 The effective population size is assumed to be constant over time, because if it were not, this would indicate the action of other evolutionary forces, such as drift, selection, and migration.

11 For example, the introduction of Australian genes to Icelandic populations during the third century BCE.

12 Assuming that forward and back migration rates are the same.

13 The $4N_e$ term in Eq. (3.3) $[f = 1/4(N_e) + 1]$.

14 For which there are ten nDNA *loci*, with over 38 alleles, 21 of which are alleles for either HLA-A or HLA-B (Fix, 1999: 171–3).

15 One exception is the addition of secondary dentin in cases of extreme dental attrition, but this does not affect the size and shape of the crown.

16 This work (Relethford and Blangero, 1990) extends the Harpending and Ward (1982) R-matrix method for quantitative phenotypic traits.

17 This term refers to a grouping of hunter-gatherer groups (bands) that came together annually during a particular season to exploit a seasonally available resource.

4

Recent population variation in the Americas

4.1 NORTH AMERICA

Genetic markers

Nuclear DNA

Nuclear DNA genotypes are detected primarily through protein electrophoresis or by detection of antigens, such as human leukocyte antigens (HLAs) (see Cavalli-Sforza *et al.*, 1994: 7–10) or immunoglobulins (Crawford, 1998: 93–5).[1] Traditional nDNA serum protein markers include the ABO, MNS, P, Rh, Duffy, Kidd, Lewis, and Diego blood group systems (Figure 4.1), along with the highly variable HLA system, which includes a plethora of informative genetic loci and alleles (Crawford, 1998: 93–4).

North American genotypes include a high incidence of ABO*A2 (Crawford, 1998) among groups classified as Amerind language speakers by Greenberg *et al.* (1986). This finding was supported by the results obtained by Salzano and Callegari-Jacques (1988: 154–5), who noted a high frequency of ABO*O and the O alleles in most Native Americans (Figure 4.1).

MNS blood groups

In the MNS blood system,[2] the genetic locus for MNS is located on chromosome 4 (Figure 4.1). Arctic North Americans have high frequencies of the M allele, with a frequency in some, such as the Naskapi Indians, as high as 90%, but Crawford (1998: 103) notes that the frequency of M is low in native Siberian populations.

Nuclear DNA founder effect and New World mutations

One apparent mutation found only in native North America is the group-specific component GC*ESK found only among Arctic Inuit

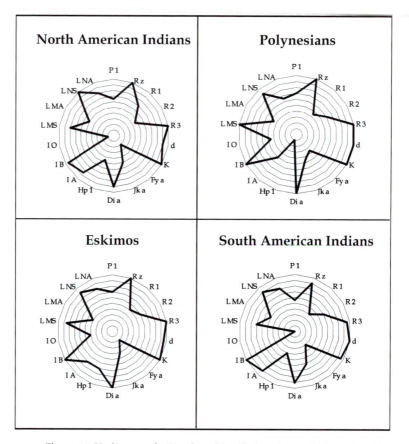

Figure 4.1 Variograms for North and South Americans, Eskimos (Inuit) and Polynesians for allele frequencies for eight major blood systems (Diego, Kell, Duffy, Rh, MNS, ABO, P, and haptoglobin). The center of the chart is 100% (allele fixation), while the outer ring represents 0% (complete loss of the allele). Modified from Salzano and Callegari-Jacques (1988: 17). Abbreviations: P1 = the P allele; K = Kell; Fya = Duffy; R1–Rz = Rh; d, Dia = Diego; Hp1 = haptoglobin 1; IA, IB, IO = ABO; LMS, LMA, LNS, LNA = MNS alleles; Jka = Kidd.

(Eskimo) people. Another mutation is represented by the serum albumin "Mexico" variant. Some of the heavy chain immunoglobulins (IgGs), located on the long arm of chromosome 14, such as gamma-globulins GM and KM, also appear to have a New World origin. Williams *et al.* (1985) felt that the distribution of GM alleles (allotypes) was consistent with Greenberg *et al.*'s (1986) tripartite model of the peopling of the Americas, in which three founder populations (Amerindians,

Na-Dene, and Aleut-Eskimo language speakers) are thought to have been ancestral to all native peoples in the Americas. Crawford (1998) and Schanfield *et al.* (1990) disagree with this tripartite division and typological interpretation because most of the GM system alleles (haplotypes) are found in a single Native American population, or are found in a geographically limited area, suggesting an origin in, and gene flow from, a single population bearing the GM alleles. The GM*A G allele reaches its highest frequency in Algonkian-speaking peoples, in particular among the Northern Cree people (Crawford, 1998: 130; Schanfield *et al.*, 1990).

The kappa blood system

Kappa (KM) is another immunoglobulin[3] system that provides detail about Native American origins, especially regarding the separation of North and South American native populations. North American tribes have only one (KM*1) of three known alleles of the Kappa (formerly Inv), or KM system. Among native North and South American populations, the KM* (1 and 1, 2) alleles reach their highest frequency (59.7%) in the Dogrib, an Athapaskan tribe of northern North America (Crawford, 1998: 126–9).

Human leukocyte antigens

Synthetic gene maps that present principal components analyses of nDNA variation in geographic form provide a simultaneous view of allelic variation in many polymorphic genetic loci (Cavalli-Sforza *et al.*, 1994: 25–8, 39–49). These authors note that I_gG allotypes have considerable variation in North America, with many blood proteins. North American native peoples are characterized by high frequencies of HLA*W28, HLA*W9, and HLA*W5, as well as by the absence of HLA*A1, HLA*A3, and HLA*A10.

To date, there are more papers detailing blood group systems and HLAs of New World peoples than there are papers on New World molecular genetics. As a result, few of the nDNA data sets provide enough detail to test the most complicated of the archaeologically derived models of Native American origins and New World colonization. Torroni *et al.* (1994a,b) have provided enhanced and rather detailed data from mtDNA haplotype (mutation) phylogenies, leading Schurr and Wallace (1999: 43) to write that:

First, the ancestral Amerindian populations brought at least haplogroup A, C, and D mtDNAs during the initial colonization(s) of the New World. Since each haplogroup appeared to have derived from a single haplotype, we proposed that the ancestral Native Americans originated from a limited number of founders, perhaps through a bottleneck effect. We further suggested that the ancestors of the Na-Dene Indians migrated from Asia independently and considerably more recently than the progenitors of the Paleoindians, since the extent of diversity of haplogroup A in the Na-Dene Indians was half of that in Amerindians. Similarly, because of its low diversity relative to the other mtDNA lineages, as well as its non-uniform distribution in Asia and the Americas, we suggested that haplogroup B might represent a second migration, independent of that which contributed the A, C, and, D mtDNAs to the genetic stock of Paleoindians. We concluded that the extent of Paleoindian mtDNA diversity was compatible with a pre-Clovis entry model of the peopling of the New World. (Schurr and Wallace, 1999: 43)

Mitochondrial DNA

Sources on mitochondrial variation in North America include Horai *et al.* (1993), Karafet *et al.* (1999), Merriwether (2002), Neves and Pucciarelli (1991), Schanfield (1992), Schurr *et al.* (1999), Schurr and Wallace (1999), Starikovskaya *et al.* (1998), Wallace and Torroni (1992), and others. These authors interpret their data in a historical framework, using their results to generate models of the peopling of the Americas. Some of their models propose that there were two or more waves of migration from east Asia, with many focusing on at least four New World colonization events (Horai *et al.*, 1993; Neves and Pucciarelli, 1991; Schanfield, 1992; Schurr *et al.*, 1999; Starikovskaya *et al.*, 1998; Wallace and Torroni, 1992). Horai and coworkers (1993) noted that mtDNA haplotype[4] variation within the "Amerind" group of Greenberg *et al.* (1986) represents at least four separate founding lineages.

Other researchers dealing with mtDNA have proposed multiple founding maternal lineages in the Americas (Schurr *et al.*, 1999; Starikovskaya *et al.*, 1998; Wallace and Torroni, 1992). These authors indicate that more than one colonization event, a large colonizing population, or an extended colonization process resulted in significant haplotype diversity in the Americas. Schurr *et al.* (1999) proposed that nearly all (97%) Native American mtDNA variation could be divided into four haplogroups, designated A, B, C, and D (Figure 4.2). These four haplogroups represent founding female lineages in the New World

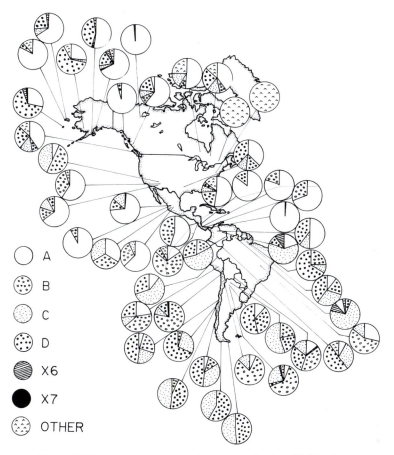

Figure 4.2 Frequency variograms for seven mitochondrial haplogroups
in the Americas, including A, B, C, D, X6, X7, and Other (Brown's X).
Modified from Merriwether (2002) with permission of the publisher.

(Schurr and Wallace, 1999). Haplogroup A is "defined by a *Hae III* site
gain at np 663" (Schurr and Wallace, 1999: 43) and has its highest
frequency among Arctic populations of Alaska and Canada, coastal
Athabaskans, and among Mexican and Central American groups. It
nears a frequency of 99% in northern Canadian and southern Alaskan
coastal groups (Merriwether, 2002: 298). The B haplogroup is characterized by a *COII/tRNA^{Lys}* intergenic (Region V) 9 base-pair deletion, and is
seen throughout North America with the highest frequencies (10%–50%)
among native peoples of the American Southwest (Puebloans) and in
Central America (Hondurans and Guatemalans). Haplogroups C and D

both exhibit the *DdeI* site gain at nt10394, plus an *Alu I* site gain at np 10397. These haplogroups are commonly seen among Native Americans of South America (see Section 4.2 below).

In addition to the four founding haplogroups (A, B, C, D), other founding haplogroups have been described. Brown *et al.* (1998) have discovered an X haplogroup[5] that may or may not represent an ancient Eurasian lineage that came to the New World through the first colonists. Brown *et al.*'s (1998) X group occurs at 100% frequency among tribes of New York and southeast Canada (Penobscot, Pequot, Seneca), who have had the longest contact with English or French colonists and have a documented history of intermarriage (gene flow) with Europeans.[6] Brown's X haplogroup is *separate* from the X6 and X7 haplotypes, which are derived from C and D. The X6 and X7 haplogroups are common among Asians and are found at low frequency in a few North American native tribes of Alaska, but are extremely common among Amazonian and southern cone[7] populations of South America (Figure 4.2). These haplogroups are most likely to be the result of higher European admixture after European conquest, when Europeans invaded the northeast coast of North America (Merriwether and Ferrell, 1996). The X6 and X7 lineages were described by Easton *et al.* (1996) and appear to represent founding New World lineages, as do A, B, C, and D. There are approximately 5–10 haplotypes found within these seven haplogroups (A, B, C, D, X6, X7, and Brown's X) that are shared by all Native Americans and by some Siberian Asian populations (Merriwether, 2002). Just to confuse the issue a bit more, some molecular geneticists refer to Brown's X, as haplogroup N (Fox, 1996; Stone, 1999; Stone and Stoneking, 1998). The N haplogroup in the Norris farms sample were those remains that could not be classified as belonging to haplogroups A–D. Brown *et al.*'s (1998) haplogroup X is considered to be a reflection of European/western Asian (Brown *et al.*, 1998) female gene flow into Native American populations.

Within the category of "other" mtDNAs among native North Americans is the L haplogroup with an African haplotype (AF71), as well as the AM132 of the Seminole tribe of Florida, and the H haplogroup, which contains only a single haplotype (AM028 type) (see Schurr and Wallace, 1999: figure 2). The African type (AF71) is often used to root phylogenetic trees based on mtDNA RFLP variation (Schurr and Wallace, 1999: 48–9). Other haplotypes are less important for assessing mtDNA variation in living native peoples in the Americas, but become critical in studies of aDNA. The X haplogroup proposed by

Bailliet *et al.* (1994) has been renamed the E haplogroup (Stone, 1999: 29), to avoid confusion with Brown's X. Haplotypes X6 and X7 are found in east Asia and the Americas. All of these DNA groups provide a better picture of who the First Americans were and where they originated.

> [The] presence of a small number of founding mtDNAs in Native American populations [including South Americans] which inhabit a broad geographic expanse continues to suggest that the Americas were populated by a *relatively limited number of founders*. (Schurr and Wallace, 1999: 50; italics mine)

One caveat about these mtDNA data was discussed by Merriwether (2002), who notes that the small number of Native American and Asiatic individuals from whom blood and tissue samples were drawn (for mtDNA analyses) may not be a representative sample of all haplogroups present in each region. He also notes that there may be a significant reduction in mtDNA variation among Native Americans due to their demographic history, including female lineage extinction in the wake of European contact and poor sample representation of all American haplogroups:

> [W]e have sampled mtDNA from only a tiny fraction of the individual languages found in the Americas, although at least a third of the higher order groupings of languages have been sampled. So missing data, as always, could change the picture dramatically … (Merriwether, 2002: 299)

Ancient DNA studies in North America

When aDNA results were first presented in scientific publications (Stone and Stoneking, 1996), they were heralded as the best way to understand phylogenetic relationships of ancient flora, fauna, and people, and were touted as making traditional phylogenetic analyses from phenotypic data obsolete. Ancient DNA data were thought to provide a final unarguable conclusion to the debate over Kennewick Man's tribal affiliation (or lack thereof). Unfortunately, as in most situations, including Kennewick Man's, it is difficult, if not impossible, to obtain accurate ancient mitochondrial data. This is due to the nature of the methods, as well as the samples themselves. There are several difficulties in analyzing aDNA, including:

1. Poor preservation, such as when the decay of soft or hard tissues leaves sugar by-products that inhibit DNA replication during PCR amplification. Any preserved DNA is typically in small

fragments due to diagenetic processes that destroy the sugar backbone of the DNA molecule, creating unusably small 2- to 4-bp sequences (Stone, 1999). One solution to the preservation problem is to obtain tissue samples from the dentin and pulp chambers of teeth. These areas are sealed environments that aid in DNA preservation and help to prevent contamination.

2. Possible contamination of archaeological samples by modern mtDNAs. This can occur through improper handling by those submitting samples.[8] The solution here is the use of masks and gloves by any field or laboratory personnel coming into contact with the bone or tooth sample.

However, despite these potential problems associated with recovering good aDNA samples, Stone (1996) was able to examine ancient mtDNA data for the prehistoric individuals ($n = 108$) buried at the Norris Farm site, dated to 600 yr BP, and Hauswirth and colleagues (1994) were able to retrieve aDNA from the well-preserved brains of bodies buried in a bog cemetery (the site of Windover, Florida) dating to the Middle to Early Archaic (5000–8600 yr BP).

Hauswirth et al. (1991) probed one preserved brain sample for nDNA markers and found the presence of sequences for class I HLAs;[9] they were able to amplify a single microglobulin sequence (β_2). This individual and 13 other Windover burials all possessed the A19 allele, a variant found among many modern Native American populations. The Windover samples contained 11 burials with Dan4 alleles ($n = 11/13$; 86%), and three (23%) with the B37 allele. Merriwether (2002: 301) cites a personal communication from Hauswirth, who retyped 40 individuals from the Windover site. Merriwether reports that 20 of the Windover remains presented RFLPs for the X6 haplotype, and the remaining 20 were X7 haplotypes, which would mean that all 40 Windover brains examined by Hauswirth were in the M mtDNA haplogroup, following the groupings presented by Schurr and Wallace (1999: table 1). Like the HLA result, the Archaic data suggest a biological linkage to living native peoples of North America.

Paleoindian aDNA

Three independent laboratories tested the 9600 yr BP Kennewick skeleton, but none could obtain preserved DNA. A Late Paleoindian (Cody-Plano Complex, 8000 yr BP) skeleton from Hourglass Cave, Colorado, produced considerable ancient DNA classified as "other."

This individual was found (Stone and Stoneking, 1996) to have the 9 base-pair deletion that characterizes the B haplogroup. This result refutes the claim made by Cann (1994), that the B haplogroup entered North America as a very recent colonization of North America from Polynesia. It does, however, provide support for those of us who find phenotypic connections between the First Americans and peoples of southern Asia (Sundadonts) such as the Ainu, and Jomon of Japan (see Haydenblit, 1996; Lahr, 1995, 1996; Powell, 1995, 1998; Powell and Neves, 1999; Neves *et al.*, 1996a, 1999a) contra the positions of Turner (1990) and Brace *et al.* (2002).

The oldest mtDNA in North America was recovered from the post-cranial bones (femora) of the Arlington Springs skeleton found on Santa Rosa Island (Orr, 1962), and radiocarbon dated from 10 000–13 000 yr BP cal ^{14}C in the laboratories of Dr. David Glen Smith at the University of California, Davis.[10] This mtDNA sample also produced the 9 base-pair deletion typical of haplogroup B.

aDNA was recovered from the 7000 yr BP preserved brain of one of the Paleoindian individuals recovered from the Little Salt Spring (LSS) site, located in west central Florida. This site consists of a very large vertical shaft cave (and adjacent peat bog) that became flooded during sea level changes in the Early to Middle Holocene. A sample of an ancient brain was tested for the B and C haplogroups, but neither sequence appeared to be present in the sample (Pääbo *et al.*, 1988).

Ancient DNA has also been obtained from mummies in the American southwest and Late Holocene skeletal samples in the Midwest. Several individuals produced the 9 base-pair deletion of haplogroup B, while the C and D haplogroups were detected in others (O'Rourke *et al.*, 1996). The Norris Farm study (Stone and Stoneking, 1998) produced all four of Wallace and Torroni's (1992) founding lineages, (A, B, C, D), as well as Brown's haplogroup X.

The results of all of the aDNA studies indicate that the earlier Paleoindian samples either: (1) do not fit into the range of mitochondrial variation seen today within Native American populations, or (2) are poorly preserved and/or contaminated.

Y-chromosome data

Male Y-chromosome data suggest a colonization/range expansion from Asia that brought haplotype 1F to both Australasia and the New World, followed by a range expansion in Siberia that brought haplotype 1C to the New World (Karafet *et al.*, 1999). However, Karafet *et al.* note that extensive gene flow within Asia or in Beringia, and subsequently in the New World, may have significantly complicated the interpretation of phylogenetic patterns in these data.

4.2 SOUTH AMERICA

Genetic markers

Nuclear DNA

HLA haplotypes present and common among native peoples of South America include HLA*B5, HLA*A2, HLA*AW28, and HLA*BW5. Of the ABO blood system, the O allele is most frequent in South America vs. North America, as noted in Section 4.1 of this chapter.

Mitochondrial DNA

Mitochondrial diversity appears to be greatest among native peoples of South America. All of the four basic haplogroups are found among the native peoples of South America, except in the Yagan of the southern-most tip of Tierra del Fuego, who lack all but the C and D haplogroups. For most tribes south of the isthmus of Panama, the C and D haplogroups are found in highest frequency, and are commonly found in Pacific coast and southern cone populations of Argentina and Chile.

The pattern of haplogroup separation between North America, where A and B haplogroups are most common, and South America is rather striking (Figure 4.2). Among southern cone tribes, C and D are practically the only haplogroups present, especially in Fuegans (C = 55%; D = 45% in the Yaghan; see Figure 4.2). The A and B haplogroups are mostly found in higher frequency among tribes in Bolivia, Venezuela, and other northern areas of the continent (Figure 4.2). The X6 and X7 groups are mostly found in tribes in the Amazon and Orinoco basins. Greater haplogroup diversity is found among inland tribes in Brazil and Argentina. Brown's X haplogroup is present at about 10% frequency among altiplano Peruvians. This pattern of mtDNA diversity may reflect the relative isolation of the Amazon River tribes from those of the South American natives – as has been noted by anthropologists working with them (Salzano and Callegari-Jacques, 1988). The B haplogroup pattern may reflect the retention of an ancient Eurasian mtDNA (Brace *et al.*, 2002), or merely genetic drift since the first occupation of the Americas.

Ancient DNA in South America

Chilean mummies sequenced by Horai *et al.* (1993) and Rogan and Salvo (1990) all lacked the 9 base-pair deletion (haplogroup B) (Stone, 1999: 31), and neither the *Hinc II* site loss nor the 9 base-pair deletion were found in mummies from Colombia (Monsalve *et al.*, 1994). Riberio-Dos-Santos *et al.* (1996) were able to extract and amplify mtDNA from a sample of 26 individuals dating to 500–4000 yr BP from sites in the Amazon basin of Brazil. Eighteen of these individuals had unique sequences in hyper-variable region I (HVI), which may be a result of genetic drift (isolation and founder effect), mutation, or sampling biases. Fox (1996) was able to produce sequences for historical populations in Tierra del Fuego, including the Yamana, Kaweskar, and the Selknam. These populations had wide-ranging frequencies of the C haplogroup, which varied from 15.8% to 90.9%. As noted in previous sections of this chapter, the C and D haplogroups are practically the only mtDNA types/groups seen in the far southern cone of South America, which may reflect both the geographic isolation of these peoples as well as their social isolation as hunter-foragers. The D haplogroup is present in high frequency in these populations, with frequencies ranging from a mere 9.1% to 84%. Stone (1999: 32) reports that the N haplogroup (referred to here as Brown's X) is virtually absent in these populations (except for 7% in the Selknam), again reflecting their isolation.

Because ancient preserved tissues (mostly from mummies) can be tested for the presence of certain antigens without DNA sequencing, nuclear loci controlling those phenotypes, such as HLA system antigens, can be detected in well-preserved soft tissues of some pre-Ceramic (older than 3000 yr BP) individuals. Salzano and Callegari-Jacques (1988: table 1.6) summarize data from an HLA study by Hossani and Allison (1976) on temporally and geographically grouped South American mummies; groupings include pre-Columbian (older than 500 yr BP) and Colonial (500 to 200 yr BP) periods, with the former category subdivided into Ceramic (4000–500 yr BP) and pre-Ceramic ("Archaic"; 9000–5500 yr BP) periods, and the Colonial Period divided into Peruvian and Chilean individuals.

Among the pre-Ceramic sample ($n = 8$), a wide variety of antigens for two loci, HLA*A and HLA*B, were detected. (The most common antigen in this tiny sample was HLA*A2, followed by *B5, then by *B13, *B17, *AW19, and, finally, HLA*AW28.) Salzano and Callegari-Jacques (1988) also note the possible inaccuracy of the HLA antigen frequencies due to non-representative samples and denaturation of proteins in the tissue sample from hot dry environments.

Salzano and Callegari-Jacques also summarize frequencies for several blood systems in pre-Ceramic populations (Salzano and Callegari-Jacques 1988: table 1.5). They note that for the ABO system, type AB is most common, with a rare variant of AB, "*cis*-AB," found in a sample of pre-Columbian Ceramic period remains in altiplano Peru.

An examination of Figure 4.1 shows that, of the nine genetic systems depicted in variograms, North and South American natives are most similar to one another in the patterning of their frequencies for blood systems and HLA types shown. Arctic North American natives (Inuits) are differentiated, as are Siberians, whereas for the Kell, Diego, and Duffy systems, the North and South American samples are most like Polynesians (Figure 4.1; Salzano and Callegari-Jacques, 1988: 154). There appears to be a significant difference in haplogroup frequencies and diversity between the continents (Figure 4.2). The mtDNA mutation rates and diversity have been used to suggest a common ancestor for Old World Asian and New World mitochondrial haplotypes dating to the earlier part of the Late Pleistocene (~25 000 yr BP) (Torroni *et al.*, 1992, 1994a,b). While this is potentially problematic (see discussion by Merriwether, 2002: 299), it does provide a lower limit for the timing of human migration to the Americas, provided that the mtDNA mutation rates used in the estimates are accurate.

North America

Nuclear DNA

Nuclear DNA variation in the Americas appears to indicate long-term effects of evolutionary forces, primarily genetic drift, in the wake of a migration of native peoples from North America to South America. Torroni *et al.* (1992).

Mitochondrial DNA

Multiple migration/founder models of the peopling of the Americas have been presented by Greenberg *et al.* (1986), Horai *et al.* (1993), Karafet *et al.* (1999), Neves and Pucciarelli (1991), Schanfield (1992), Schurr *et al.* (1999), Starikovskaya *et al.* (1998), Wallace and Torroni (1992), and others. These models propose two or more waves of Late Pleistocene migration from Asia, with many focusing on at least four

New World founding events. Horai *et al.* (1993) noted that mtDNA variation within the Greenberg *et al.* (1986) model's "Amerind" group represents at least four separate founding lineages. Likewise, other researchers dealing with mtDNA have noted multiple founding lineages in the Americas.

Researchers dealing with geographic patterning in Y-chromosome (Karafet *et al.*, 1999) and mtDNA (Templeton, 1998a,b) variation have employed a novel phylogenetic method (Templeton *et al.*, 1995) for detecting range expansions and restricted gene flow among Native American populations. The mtDNA data (Templeton, 1998a) indicate either more than one colonization event, a large colonizing population, or an extended colonization process that resulted in significant haplotype diversity in the Americas.

Wallace and Torroni (1992) viewed patterns of mtDNA variation as reflecting four founding lineages in the Americas (the A, B, C, and D haplogroups), while Ballinger *et al.* (1992) observed that the 9 base-pair deletion present in the Americas also occurs in Australasian groups, suggesting some support for the Neves *et al.* (1996a,b) version of the four-wave model. Merriwether and colleagues (1995) have proposed that at least four haplogroups represent four founding mtDNA lineages in the Americas. Again, critics have pointed out that the problems noted for the tripartite model apply to migrations of four or more groups (Weiss, 1994).

Y-chromosome data

The Y-chromosome data suggest that a colonization/range expansion out of Asia brought haplotype 1F to both Australasia and the New World, followed by a range expansion in Siberia that brought haplotype 1C to the New World (Karafet *et al.*, 1999). However, these authors note that extensive gene flow within Asia, or Beringia, and subsequently in the New World, may have significantly complicated the interpretation of phylogenetic patterns in these data.

Phenotypic data

Neves and Pucciarelli (1991) used craniometric data to present a "four-wave" model of colonization that simply added an additional migration event to the three proposed in the tripartite model of Greenberg *et al.* (1986) (represented by Amerind, Na-Dene, and Aleut-Eskimo populations). The four-wave model was based on the distinctive "non-Mongoloid" morphology of the earliest crania in South America, which, according to these authors, differs too greatly from Late Holocene northern Asian populations in the New World to be explained by an ancestral–descendant relationship between them (Neves *et al.*, 1996a,b). These populations were described in racial terminology as "Mongoloid" which was used to denote Late Holocene populations of northeast Asia and the Americas, who share certain phenotypic features such as facial flatness, epicanthic folds, and shovel-shaped incisors (Hanihara, 1968; Hrdlička, 1920; Lahr, 1996; Turner, 1989, 1990) that distinguish them from southeast and southwest Asians.

Neves and Pucciarelli (1991) and Munford *et al.* (1995) postulated that the earliest colonists of the New World were derived from a population of anatomically modern *Homo sapiens sapiens* in east Asia that eventually migrated north to Siberia/Beringia and south to the Sunda Shelf,[11] leaving descendants in Australia and the Americas (as Paleoindians). Sutter (1997a) and Haydenblit (1996) have presented dental data to support this view, while Powell's (1995) analysis of North American dental data has been interpreted as supporting a "non-Mongoloid" presence in the Americas (see Lahr, 1997). In actuality, Powell (1995) found less dental similarity between Middle Archaic (5000–8000 yr BP) populations from eastern North America and modern "Sinodont" Asians and Native Americans, and greater similarity of Archaic samples and southeast Asian "Sundadonts" (*sensu* Turner, 1985a).

4.3 SUMMARY

The modern and ancient blood markers and molecular DNAs indicate some degree of diversity (see Cavalli-Sforza *et al.*, 1994), perhaps representing a degree of isolation of populations within the New World. This suggests the possibility that deme (subpopulation) sizes were small and therefore susceptible to genetic drift during the majority of the Holocene. The nDNA patterns, especially the HLA types, seem to separate the native peoples of North and South America, which may indicate a degree of separation of genes and low levels of gene flow for the few loci on which we have data.

The mtDNAs are perhaps the most informative for reconstructing the peopling of the New World. It appears that the B haplogroup (with its 9 base-pair deletion) is found at its highest frequency in North America, with lower frequencies in South America, but is at higher frequency in northern South and Central America (Figure 4.2), perhaps due to southward gene flow to Mesoamerica, and then to South America.

Although Crawford concluded that the only external source for Native Americans (both North and South) was from Siberia, Salzano and Callegari-Jacques (1988) presented data in Figure 4.2, suggesting that allele frequencies for the major blood systems (summarized from a variety of studies) were similar for sub-Arctic North Americans and Arctic Inuit (Eskimo) groups. There was also a strong similarity between North and South American groups in terms of Rh, ABO, and MNS patterns (Figure 4.2). Contra Crawford (1998), there is no similarity in blood system patterns of variation between Native Americans and Siberians (Figure 4.1), but there is some degree of similarity for Native Americans and their Polynesian contemporaries (Figure 4.1). There is shared variation between native peoples in the Americas and Siberia for HLA frequencies (a single locus with many alleles).

Molecular DNA results indicate a minimum of four autochthonous founding female lineages, and perhaps five (A, B, C, and D, and possibly Brown's X) originating from Asian types (Merriwether, 2002; Schurr and Wallace, 1999: 43). Ancient DNAs, although difficult to obtain (Stone, 1999) from some ancient skeletons sampled in the Americas (e.g. Kennewick), appear to exhibit the mutations defining the X and A haplogroups (Stone, 1999: 33).

Turner (1985a) found at least three possible dental groups in the Americas, using dental morphological data that corresponded to Greenberg et al.'s (1986) three major language groups in the Americas: Amerindians, Na-Dene, and Aleut-Eskimo, which he felt represented three founding lineages from northeast Asia. The majority of genetic data seen today in the Americas are consistent with one or more migration/colonization events, during which Asian (or western Pacific) peoples entered North America and traveled southward, which were followed by considerable differentiation through microevolutionary forces during the 12 500 years of occupation of the two American continents.

NOTES

1 In this section, I have found Crawford's (1998) review of North American nDNA studies, and Merriwether (2002) and Schurr and Wallace's (1999) reviews of mtDNA helpful. Stone's (1999) thorough presentation of aDNA research was also invaluable.
2 I, like Crawford (1998), opted to use the older, pre-ISGN nomenclature because most readers are more familiar with alleles M, N, S, and s.

3 With three alleles *1, *2, and *1, 2, nucleotides coding for immunoglobulins in the KM system are found on the short arm of chromosome 2.

4 Haplotypes are certain variations in mtDNA sequences; different haplotypes can be included in a larger category called the haplogroup, all of which are useful for phylogenetic studies of mtDNA within and among human populations.

5 Hereafter referred to as "Brown's X," following Merriwether (2002).

6 For example: the John Smith–Pocahontas union.

7 The *southern cone* of South America includes Uruguay, Paraguay, and portions of Argentina, Chile, and the regions of Tierra del Fuego and Patagonia.

8 Such as handling bones or teeth without gloves, or coughing or sneezing on specimens.

9 Heavy-chain gene families β_1 and β_2.

10 $10\,080 \pm 810$ to $10\,960 \pm 80$ uncal ^{14}C.

11 Sundaland refers to a Pleistocene land mass connecting what are now the separated islands/land masses of Indonesia, Malaysia, Australia, New Guinea, and New Zealand. Like the Sibero–Alaskan Bering shelf, Sundaland was submerged during the rise in sea levels brought about by glacial and ice sheet melting during the terminal Pleistocene.

PART II   The Pleistocene peopling of the Americas

5

The Pleistocene and ice-age environments

5.1 WHEN AND WHAT IS THE PLEISTOCENE?

The Pleistocene geological epoch began 1.8 million years ago (mya) and is the geological period directly following the Pliocene (1.8–5.2 mya), the epoch in which all hominids and hominins evolved. For most of the Pleistocene, ice sheets and glaciers covered the Earth's major land masses. Within this epoch are several "stadials," or cooling events, when glaciers and ice sheets expanded their ranges.

The cold stadials are separated long warming periods, or inter-glacials. In the most recent interstadial, today's Holocene Epoch, there were stadial-like cooling periods – short, abrupt returns to ice-age conditions, the most significant and recent being the Older (13 840–13 590 yr BP) and Younger Dryas (12 680–11 560 yr BP). During these cooling periods, average global temperatures decreased rapidly by 2–5 °C (Straus, 1996). The end of the Pleistocene, or "terminal Pleistocene," was the time of a huge global warming event (the Holocene) that thus far has lasted for the past 12 000 years. All through the Pleistocene, huge sheets of ice covered Europe and Asia.[1] Two large ice sheets also covered the majority of North America: these were called the *Laurentide* and *Cordilleran*[2] sheets. The *Laurentide* sheet was centered over present-day Hudson Bay in Canada, while the *Cordilleran* was a west coast ice sheet extending down from the western mountains of Alaska and Canada (British Columbia and Saskatchewan) to the present-day Sierra Nevadas in northern California, and Nevada to the Pacific shore. One important feature to note is that during the Last Glacial Maximum (LGM), at about 18 000 yr BP, the Cordilleran coast-line contained a number of "coastal refugia" (unglaciated pockets that held abundant plant, avian, and marine animal life[3]). The two North American ice sheets periodically coalesced, but even during full glacial

Table 5.1 *Epochs of the Quaternary Era.*

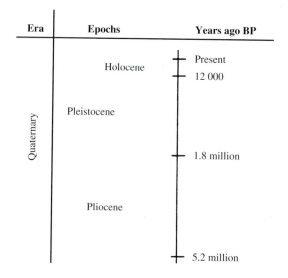

Era	Epochs	Years ago BP
	Holocene	Present / 12 000
Quaternary	Pleistocene	
		1.8 million
	Pliocene	
		5.2 million

conditions were separated by an "ice-free corridor" one to several kilometers wide. In the terminal Pleistocene, this corridor was open wide
enough to allow the north-to-south passage of Asian megafauna, such
as the woolly mammoth, musk oxen, giant elk, giant beavers, giant
ground sloth, and other large, now-extinct mammals that were well
adapted to ice-age conditions.

5.2　WHAT CREATES AN ICE SHEET?

In 1920, while studying the mathematical properties of wave forms and
phase shifts, Serbian mathematician Mulutin Milankovich (1879–1958)
created a prediction model for past and future glacial advances (stadials)
and retreats (interstadials), based on the convergence and divergence of
three important astrophysical cycles:

1.　the eccentricity of the Earth's orbit;
2.　its axis obliquity (wobble); and
3.　seasonal precession (i.e. precession of the equinoxes).

Eccentricity cycle (every 100 000 years)

Since the development of post-Copernican astronomy, we have known
that the planets do not orbit round the Sun in a circular path but have

elliptical paths of varying sizes and eccentricities, due to the gravitational pull of other bodies in our Solar System. The Sun is also not centered within these orbital ellipses. This affects the amount of sunlight or insolation (incident solar radiation) that the Earth receives. At the Earth's furthest point away from the Sun (aphelion), it receives less solar radiation, while the reverse occurs when the Earth is close to the Sun (perihelion) (see Figure 5.1a).

Every 100 000 or so years, the Earth's orbit shifts from a very elongated ellipse at great distance from the Sun at aphelion to a more circular orbit at perihelion (see Figure 5.1a). The Earth's greater distance from the Sun causes a reduction in insolation, which ultimately results in cooling, while the more circular orbit at perihelion increases insolation, and creates warming.

Obliquity cycle (41 000 years)

The Earth wobbles on its axis every 41 000 years, much like a top that is winding down. This obliquity cycle occurs when the Earth's axis moves from its current "normal" 23.5° slightly off-vertical orientation, to one in the range 21.8° to 24.4° (Figure 5.1b). The net effect of obliquity is that it causes the northern and southern hemispheres to tilt. It is also the cause of a "wandering" north pole, which has, in previous times, been far from its position today, and as far south as the 45th parallel. The changes in orientation of the pole affects the severity of the seasons – greater "tilt" means more severe seasonal conditions: very hot summers and bitterly cold winters. Less "tilt" produces mild winters with cooler summers.

Seasonal precession (19 000 and 23 000 years)

The "tilt" of the earth relative to its plane of travel around the Sun causes the seasons we experience today. Today, when the northern hemisphere is orientated toward the Sun at perihelion, insolation increases and the north experiences summer. In past millennia, this sunward tilt occurred at aphelion, when the Earth was farthest from the Sun, which means that past summers were cooler and milder than today (Figure 5.1c). Conversely, as the northern hemisphere tilts away from the Sun, the north experiences winter, but it is summer in the southern hemisphere.[4] The equinox precession occurs when the northern hemisphere is tilted toward the Sun at aphelion, when it is farthest from the Sun, thus reducing summer insolation (Figure 5.1c), and is

(a) Eccentricity cycle (100 ky)

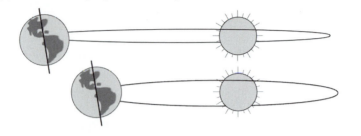

(b) Obliquity cycle (41 ky)

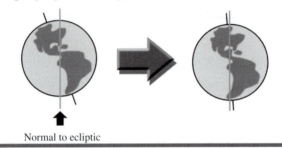

Normal to ecliptic

(c) Precession of the equinoxes (19 and 23 ky)

Northern hemisphere tilted away from the sun at aphelion

Northern hemisphere tilted toward the sun at aphelion

Figure 5.1 Diagrams of the Milankovich cycle. (a) The eccentricity cycle, every 100 000 years; (b) the earth's orbital obliquity cycle, every 41 000 years; (c) the equinox precession every 19–23 million years. Reproduced with permission from S. Rutherford (http://deschutes.gso.uri.edu/~rutherford/milankovich.html).

tilted away from the Sun at perihelion, when it is closest to the Sun. When orbital obliquity and seasonal precession cycles are in phase (i.e. are synchronous), the result is a change in insolation (Figure 5.2), such that summers are mild and cool and winters are cold and wet, as normal. This allows more snow to accumulate on glaciers during the

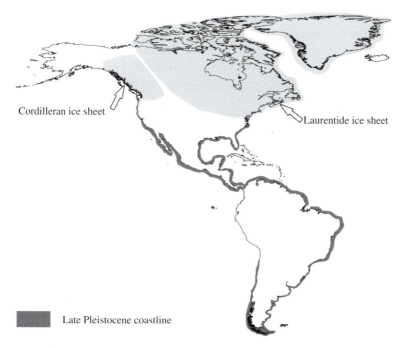

Cordilleran ice sheet

Laurentide ice sheet

Late Pleistocene coastline

Figure 5.2 Late Pleistocene coastline and position of the Cordilleran and Laurentide ice sheets (generalized).

winter, while the mild summers[5] mean that the accumulated snows do not melt and thus persist year-round. The result during the Pleistocene is that the northern hemisphere glaciers accumulated ice at a rate of meters of thickness per year rather than at a rate of several centimeters (Meltzer, 1993b: 26).

Milankovich cycles therefore resulted in thick and expansive ice sheets in North America. The Cordilleran, Laurentide, and Greenland sheets covered a total of 18.06 million km^2 of land mass and were 2 to 3 km (1.2 to 1.9 miles) thick. In the late Pleistocene of South America, which had "normal" winters and summers, only the Andean valley glaciers coalesced into a large, montaine ice mass. However, the major Pleistocene ice accumulation in the southern hemisphere is still with us in Antarctica. The Antarctic ice sheet is a mere 1.28 million km^2 smaller today than at its Pleistocene maximum; but it is now melting at an abnormally fast rate, perhaps due to "global warming" induced by carbon dioxide and pollutants accumulating in the atmosphere since the industrial revolution, which increase insolation and trap heat.[6]

During the Pleistocene in North America, there were four sequences of major[7] stadials (glaciation events), followed by an equal number of interstadials or warming periods. The first of these was the Nebraskan stadial, followed by the Kansan, Illinoian, and, finally, the Wisconsin stadial. The Wisconsin glaciation was followed by the Holocene interstadial, and what we consider to be today's "normal" weather. The Wisconsin glaciation is important to our discussion of the First Americans and Native American origins. Owing just to a decrease in summer insolation, the Wisconsin stadial had an enormous influence on later Pleistocene geography and environments, which led to dramatic climate changes that allowed the passage of the First Americans from the Old World to the New. The change that had the greatest impact on contemporary humans, however, was the post-glacial Holocene warming, which led to population stability and the development of towns and cities and to the development of horticulture and agriculture as a primary form of subsistence. These impacts are discussed at length in Chapters 10 and 11.

Insolation patterns

As the various parts of the Milankovich cycle come in or out of phase, we get peaks and troughs of solar radiation measured in watts of radiation per square meter (m^2) of Earth surface. These insolation values have ranged between a maximum of $550\,W\,m^{-2}$ at about 1 mya, to a minimum of $425\,W\,m^{-2}$ at 210 000 years ago. As previously stated, low insolation leads to cooling of the globe (an ice age), while high insolation is a global warming event. Over the last 1 million years, there have been at least 17 distinct low points representing 17 glacial periods of the Pleistocene. The most recent low insolation point represents the "Little Ice Age" of the sixteenth century. Seasonal changes resulting from the three Milankovich cycles affected seasonal temperatures throughout the Pleistocene, so that between 6000 and 12 000 yr BP, and with a maximum at 9000 yr BP, solar radiation was greatest in the northern hemisphere, and summer insolation was 8% greater than today (COHMAP Community climate model, Kutzbach and Webb, 1993). This means that summers were drier and warmer than present conditions. This served to increase the seasonality of the northern hemisphere, with continental interiors warmer in summer than at present.

Ice sheets and weather patterns

To further complicate the issue, the overall global response to insolation differs between land and sea. Land has less heat capacity than water, and radiates more solar heat than water, which means that the 5 °C land surface temperature increase in the northern hemisphere in the Late Pleistocene was matched by only a 1 °C increase in water surface temperatures in the North Pacific and North Atlantic. The differences in land–sea surface temperatures led to a vertical expansion of air columns over land, so air flow was primarily from land to oceans when the land was relatively warmer than the sea (June, July, and August) and the reverse occurred when the land was cooler than the oceans (December, January, and February). Increases in summer ocean temperature resulted in a pattern of greater evaporation of lighter fresh water from the ocean's surface, leaving mineral salts behind, and thus increasing sea salinity.[8]

An inflow of air from ocean to land also occurred during the northern hemisphere winters, which were 5 °C colder during the late Pleistocene (16 000–12 000 yr BP) than they are today. The result was a shift in monsoonal patterns, so that the Pleistocene winters were rainy on land and relatively drier over the oceans. This helped to move the evaporated ocean water in the atmosphere to the cold winter land, resulting in snow and ice formation in the northern hemisphere. After hundreds of years of such patterns, huge glacial sheets began to form and grow over much of North America, Siberia, and northern Europe.

5.3   LATE PLEISTOCENE NORTH AMERICA

The environments of Paleoindian occupation in the southern High Plains of the United States (including portions of Texas, Oklahoma and New Mexico) are based on Holliday's (1997) analyses of the valley fill fluvial stratigraphy from upland eolian deposits, along with stable carbon isotope data. During the Clovis occupation (~11 200–10 900 yr BP), the valleys contained perennial streams. However, this was followed by the Folsom-age (10 900–10 200 yr BP) environments, characterized by a shift from relatively wetter to relatively drier conditions with periodic drought, and therefore with an abrupt change from lakes, ponds, and marshes to the accumulation of sheet sands on uplands, starting the earliest phase of the construction of regional dune fields. Stable carbon isotopes from the southern plains indicate that warming characterized the Clovis–Folsom transition, referred to by some archaeologists as the "Clovis drought." During the rest of the Paleoindian period, the environment was relatively cool but fluctuated between wetter and drier conditions, with an overall trend toward drying that resulted in further enlargement of the dune fields and culminated in the warm, dry Altithermal (or Hypsithermal) period, beginning at ~8000 yr BP. Of all the archaeological periods discussed here, the Clovis period was probably the wettest in terms of runoff and spring discharge. In the southern plains, the Folsom period was drier and was the earliest episode of regional wind erosion (Holliday, 1995, 1997). The Younger Dryas warming might also have been a source of problems for Clovis-age and early Folsom-age people. There is evidence for a drought during Folsom times, which may have affected the behavior of Folsom-age peoples at the Gault site in Texas. These peoples placed "offerings" (stone projectile points, slabs engraved with depictions of Clovis-age mammoths) within or near a now-dry spring. A post-Clovis/late-Folsom drought may also explain the pattern of human burials dating from between 8000 yr BP and 10 200 yr BP which took place in or near water features (springs, sinks, marshes, and pluvial lakes).

Geography

We know that at 14 000–12 000 yr BP the Laurentide ice sheet had reached its fullest southward extent. Between 18 000 and 14 000 yr BP, sea levels were lowered by at least 200 m (650 ft), exposing a significant portion of the current coastal shelf (Figure 5.2). In the Midwest region, several lobes on the southern front of the Laurentide ice sheet had scoured out large, deep basins that later filled with glacial melt water to become today's Great Lakes (Figure 5.2).

Younger Dryas (13 000–8000 yr BP)

Arguably, the most important paleoclimatic events, besides the ice sheet expansions, were the Older and Younger Dryas global cooling events (Straus, 1996). At the Pleistocene–Holocene boundary during the Younger Dryas, some regions became drier because of reduced precipitation in winter, spring, and summer. In many northern lati-tude areas, the boreal and temperate forests expanded, while in a few equatorial regions, tropical (formerly continuous) lowland forests became fragmented rainforests and dry savannas. The Younger Dryas expanded and accelerated the process of ecosystem fragmentation and led to a degree of isolation of various species in refugia and to the formation of new species or subspecies of flora and fauna within them (Endler, 1986). Humans were also required to alter their foraging and hunting strategies, and show a worldwide shift from inland occu-pations and subsistence to littoral (seaside) living once sea levels stabilized (Erlandson, 1996: 172). Some have argued (Bar-Yosef, 1996; Powell, 1995; Powell *et al.*, 1999) that in human populations in some areas, the Younger Dryas gave rise to sedentism, towns and villages, along with all that goes with a sedentary behavioral adaptation. The Natufian cultures of the Middle East and northern Africa, predynastic villages in Egypt, and sedentary Archaic foragers in Florida (Windover), Louisiana (Spiro), and other areas in the Americas seem to be synchronous with the end of the Younger Dryas of 11 000 to 10 000 or 9000 yr BP.

5.4   THE PLEISTOCENE ENVIRONMENT

Ecosystems

Based on geological and palynological studies of sediments in the eastern half of North America (Goodyear, 1999; Webb, 1981), we know that 14 000 years ago the areas adjacent to the ice sheets were tundra environments occupied by Pleistocene versions of caribou, elk, and woolly mammoth, while the region just south of the tundra was boreal forest, also occupied by mammoth, elk, and caribou, as well as by walrus in the riverine areas (Webb, 1981). This band of boreal forest (mixed jack pine and spruce) extended from the Atlantic to the Mississippi, with broad spruce forest across the central and southern plains from about 35° to 45° north latitude. South of the boreal forests were temperate forests (oak, hickory, and southern pine), typical of modern ecosystems in the deep south. These temperate forests followed the Gulf of Mexico shores south to what today are Texas and Mississippi. The riverine basins and Gulf shores contained cypress and gum trees typical of today's Louisiana and southern Alabama. Because so much of the Earth's water was land-locked as ice, the Pleistocene shoreline extended several kilometers further out than today, to what is the modern edge of the continental shelf, especially in the southern Atlantic coast of North America and the Gulf of Mexico. Below about latitude 30° north, ecosystems shifted to subtropical flora intermixed with temperate oak–spruce–hickory forests occupied by deer, mastodon, ground sloth, and giant tortoise (Goodyear, 1999; Webb, 1981).

The Rocky Mountains, foothills, and inter-montaine regions were covered by alpine or peri-alpine plant communities that included sedges and grasses favored by mammoth, bison, pronghorn, mountain sheep, deer, and smaller fauna (rodents, reptiles), especially during terminal Pleistocene conditions (Frison, 1990). At the onset of

Holocene warming, dramatic changes in vegetative zones were accompanied by human populations producing an increasing diversity of projectile point types (previously dominated by Clovis, Folsom, and Goshen) and possible shifts in subsistence strategies (Frison, 1990).

The Pacific coast from Anchorage, Alaska, south to San Francisco Bay, California, were "highly productive marine ecosystems" between 13 000 and 8000 yr BP (Erlandson and Moss, 1996: 279), although rising sea levels in the Early Holocene led to rapid adjustments in flora and fauna communities. In Alaska, glacial retreat at 13 000–14 000 yr BP led to shifts from tundra to grassland and scattered patches of scrub grasses (sage, sedge) and pine forests (Erlandson and Moss, 1996: 280). The southern Pacific coastal areas contained some large fauna, such as mastodon and ground sloth, whose abundant remains were recovered at Rancho La Brea in present-day Los Angeles, California. Prior to 14 000 yr BP, much of the coast was a dangerous and relatively unpredictable place for human occupation, owing to sudden storms and heavy seas that were not hospitable to land animals, plants, or humans. The Cordilleran ice sheet, along with several montaine glaciers, extended up to the ocean in some locations, but there is good evidence that small refugia areas were available for human occupation up and down the Pacific coastline (Fladmark, 1978, 2002). These refugia were, of course, accessible only from the ocean – a critical component in archaeological models for coastal migration to the Americas (Dixon, 1999; Fladmark, 1978, 2002).

5.5 LATE PLEISTOCENE SOUTH AMERICA

Geography

For the most part, glaciation in South America was limited to the expansion of enormous montaine glaciers in the Andes, down-slope toward the Pacific. Very little of the southern hemisphere was covered with sheet ice, with the obvious exception of Antarctica and portions of Tierra del Fuego.

Ecosystems

As in North America, the Pleistocene epoch brought about considerable cooling, with associated changes in flora and fauna, although the temperature and the paleoclimate in South America appear to have oscillated rapidly between a very cold dry climate to warm and wet conditions (Borrero, 1996: 339). As in North America, there appear to be significant regional differences in Pleistocene conditions. "Magellenic Tundra" ecosystems, similar to tundra in Arctic North America, appeared near glacial areas in Tierra del Fuego. Borrero suggested that the unpredictable changes in climate and therefore in ecosystem dynamics led to the extinction of some plant and animal species, including a few human populations, presumably leading to the development of founder effect in remaining human and other animal populations (Borrero, 1996: 349–50).

NOTES

1 The Laurentide has been estimated to be at least 1.5–2 km thick in places.
2 Pronounced "Core-dee-err-ann."
3 Including marine mammals such as seals and avifauna like seabirds and their eggs – all possible resources for human exploitation.
4 The southern hemisphere seems to have been less affected by Milankovich cycles, as demonstrated by the lack of large glacial masses and the presence of temperate species in what are now tropical regions during the Pleistocene epoch.
5 Contrary to the popular concept of the ice age, winters were not unusually cold below 65° north latitude. Cooler summers are the key to the formation of huge, thick ice sheets.
6 Aerosol propellants, along with natural processes, have "eaten" a hole in the Earth's protective ozone layer, especially over Antarctica. Carbon dioxide serves to hold heat in the atmosphere under a protective "blanket," preventing insolation from being siphoned back into space.
7 Within each major stadial, there are smaller expansions totaling 17 or so over the past 1.8 million years (see Figure 5.2).
8 Salinity affects surface and deep ocean currents, as the more heavily salinated water sinks to the ocean floor after summer surface evaporation. This has had its most obvious impact in the recent-day changes in global weather patterns (such as a shift in the Gulf Stream).

6

Ancient cultures and migration to the Americas

6.1 PLEISTOCENE CULTURES IN THE AMERICAS

Back in the old days, say about three years ago, we had a pretty compelling scenario for the peopling of the Americas. We believed the first Americans came out of northeast Asia during the latest Pleistocene, crossing the Bering land bridge into Alaska during a period of lowered sea level. For a time the massive North American ice sheets blocked their way south, but after the Laurentide and Cordilleran glaciers melted, back say 12 000 years ago, a group or groups of these hunters sped south through the newly opened "Ice-Free" Corridor between them (Wright, 1991). Once they reached the unglaciated lower 48 states, they radiated out across the length and breadth of North America with what appears to be archaeologically breathtaking speed (e.g. Haynes, 1964, 1992). (Meltzer (2001: 27))

Clovis first?

Anthropologists David Meltzer (2001) and Nina Jablonski (2002) have noted that our view of the peopling of the Americas is moving away from the traditional "Clovis-first" view described in the above quotation. Significant changes in our understanding of Paleoindian archaeology have occurred in the past few decades, with old ideas challenged by new theories and data. We now know that humans have occupied the New World for at least the past 11 000 to 12 000 yr BP[1] (Meltzer, 2001). As Meltzer (1993b, 2001) and others (Dixon, 1999; Powell and Neves, 1998, 1999; Wright, 1991) have remarked, the colonization of the New World seems to be an unbelievable feat of hunter-foragers traveling thousands of miles south from Beringia in "blitzkrieg" waves of advance, with their descendants arriving in Tierra del Fuego, South America, in a mere 500 to 600 years. This feat would be difficult, if not impossible, to accomplish without fantastically high population growth to buffer extinction due to demographic collapse.[2] Population growth would be needed to avoid random events (genetic drift) and violations of incest taboos.[3] The traditional Clovis-first model of New World colonization therefore appears to be less than realistic, given these evolutionary factors.

The Clovis complex

The oldest indisputable archaeological/cultural complex in North America is the Clovis complex, which dates from the terminal Pleistocene (11 500 yr BP to 10 900 yr BP)[4] (Collins, 1999; Haynes, 1964), a range most recently trimmed to 11 200 to 10 900 yr BP (Haynes, 1992), although some anthropologists argue that 11 500-year-old Clovis lithic technology has its origins in the 14 000-year-old Solutrean cultures of western Europe (Stanford and Bradley, 2002), contra the traditional view of Clovis. Clovis tools are characterized by large (up to 11 cm long, 3–4 cm wide) bifacially flaked spear points with a central flute or "channel flake" and concave bases enclosed by small, thin ears (Figure 6.1a). The fluting flake is a thinning flake driven from the base toward the tip. Thus far, no hafted Clovis or Folsom points have shown up in the archaeological record of North America.

One explanation for the channel flake is that because it is so difficult to produce, it became a status marker, indicating the skill of

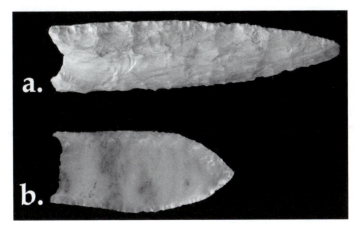

Figure 6.1 (a) Clovis point. Surface find from 35 miles south of Albuquerque, NM. Courtesy of Maxwell Museum of Anthropology, 68.94.5. (b) Folsom point. Rio Rancho Folsom site. Located 20 km north west of Albuquerque, NM. Courtesy of Maxwell Museum of Anthropology, 69.20.374.

the flintknapper, much as it is among modern flintknappers; an alternative explanation is the functional hypothesis that the fluting flake makes the point easier to haft onto a wooden, bone, or ivory foreshaft (Bonnichsen, 1978). Support for this view comes from a pair of incised bone rods with angled tips (parts of a foreshaft) that fit neatly into most Clovis point fluting channels, which were discovered with the Clovis-age child burials from the Anzick site in Montana (for further discussion, see Chapter 7).

Clovis points are also defined by a characteristic basally fluted spear point with delicate parallel flaking (Figure 6.1a). Other Clovis tools include bone shaft wrenches, the aforementioned bone fore-shafts, as well as unifacial blades, gravers, and shavers (for use on wood, bone, or ivory) and prismatic blade cores.

Late Clovis cultural materials have been discovered very close to water sources such as seasonal playa lakes and marshes, near semi-permanent springs (the Gault, Warm Mineral Spring, and Little Salt Spring sites are examples), or on the margins of Pleistocene riverbeds, such as the Ancilla River in Florida. The discovery of Clovis tools in or around ancient water sources hints at the possible importance of freshwater ecosystems in the diet of Clovis humans, an idea supported by Holliday's discovery of numerous freshwater turtles in association with a Clovis occupation stratum at the Aubrey site in north central Texas. Tree-ring and other paleobotanical data suggest that at this time there was a "Clovis drought" and that the tools were likely to have been an animistic[5] offering to the spirits or forces controlling these scarce and valued water sources.

Other evidence that provides support for the "offering theory" includes a set of chert blanks (unchipped "preforms" used to manufacture finished points) covered by incised limestone slabs discovered along the edge of a terminal Pleistocene (10 000 yr BP) spring at the Gault Site, Texas, which also contained 30 limestone rocks[6] with incised geometric designs atop a different set of unfluted Clovis points. These items may indicate that offerings were made to those spirit beings who controlled water in the spring, which was dry in Clovis times; this is a good indication that water was a scarce commodity that affected Clovis-age peoples in North America.

Folsom culture

Between 10 900 and 10 600 yr BP, we see a new cultural complex called Folsom, which was briefly discussed in Chapter 1. Folsom, like Clovis, is defined by a characteristic basally fluted spear point with delicate parallel flaking[7] (Figure 6.1b) that is nearly as ubiquitous in North America as are Clovis points and other artifacts of the Clovis complex (Faught and Anderson, 1996; Meltzer, 2001).

Folsom points in the plains and southwest are part of a great number of contemporary and regionally specific point types such as Barnes, Bullbrook, Chessrow, Cumberland, Great Basin Stemmed, Midland, Peace River Fluted, and Simpson (Meltzer, 2001). There is an increase in the number of point types and their morphological diversity in the Eastern Woodlands of North America after 10 500 yr BP (Cleland, 1976). Artifact variability after the terminal Pleistocene (~10 600 yr BP) may be a material cultural marker, possibly linked to tribalization among prehistoric populations (Powell, 1995), or may simply be related to the function of projectile weapons (darts vs. Clovis and Folsom spears). The explosion of point types after Folsom appears to give rise to a series of region-specific, Archaic projectile point types in North America by 9000 yr BP (Anderson and Sassaman, 1996; Meltzer, 2001; Morell, 1998; Powell, 1995).

Is there a pre-Clovis?

Most archaeologists in North America would answer the above question with a resounding "No!" However, an increasing body of new and convincing evidence does point toward the likelihood of human entry into the Americas prior to Clovis. This evidence has been produced at the Monte Verde site in southern Chile (Dillehay, 1989), as well as at Meadowcroft Rockshelter, Pennsylvania (Adovasio et al., 1990); at Cactus Hill (44SX202), Virginia (Hall, 1996; McAvoy and McAvoy, 1997); and at Pedra Pintada, Brazil (Roosevelt et al., 1996).

Actual human remains from Clovis and Folsom sites are quite rare (recall Hrdlička's requirement for Holmes and Putnam to prove their hypothesis of an "American Paleolithic," by finding securely dated human remains or artifacts in indisputable Pleistocene geoarchaeological contexts). In fact, only one Clovis site has produced human remains (Anzick, Montana), but there may be others out there. There are only a handful of North American human skeletons (or bits thereof) that have been recovered in indisputable Clovis or Folsom (Paleoindian) contexts, at least in areas where these archaeological complexes are typically recovered. There are a few human remains from South America that are associated with uncontaminated pre-Clovis and Clovis-age radiocarbon dates. Because these sites are poorly known among

North American scholars, I present each in some detail in later sections of this chapter. We do know that humans arrived in North America at the end of the Pleistocene, but anthropologists are now re-examining their views of the route (or routes) taken by these first colonists.

6.2   MIGRATION OF THE FIRST AMERICANS

Introduction

Our species, *Homo sapiens sapiens*, has a tendency to move about the landscape, a behavior we seem to have inherited from our 100 000-year-old ancestors in Africa. As humans in the Americas did not arise *de novo* (as far as we can tell from scientific analysis), they must have come from somewhere else – the question is, where? Scholars have been working to answer that question since the sixteenth century. In 1590, Jose de Acosta, proposed in his volume *Historia natural y moral de las Indias* ("Moral and Natural History of the Indians"), that an unknown land connection from east Asia to the New World allowed settlers to enter North America on foot. Gregorio García (1607) followed suit by including a land bridge theory among the many possibilities he examined for the origin of humans in the Americas (see Chapter 1).

6.3   LAND ROUTES

... there is nothing new under the sun. (Ecclesiastes 1: 9)

The Bering Land Bridge

Acosta (1590) and García (1607) were the first to suggest a land connection between Asia and the Americas. This idea remained unproven until the 1728 North Pacific voyage of Vitus Bering, during which he demonstrated that no such land connection was then in existence. In the late nineteenth century, scholars realized that the islands of the Aleutian chain were only a few nautical miles from the Kamchatka peninsula of Russia. Researchers also discovered that the continental shelves of Alaska and Siberia are contiguous, not very deep, and would have been exposed as a dry land connection during the last glacial maximum (18 000 yr BP). This was a time when much of the Earth's water was locked up in glacial ice sheets, thus exposing the continental shelves for human habitation and pedestrian travel. Direct scientific evidence of a Pleistocene land bridge connecting the New and Old Worlds came in the 1930s (Johnson, 1933):

Direct evidence that proves the existence of the former Land Bridge has been discovered in recent years. The remains of extinct animals have been dredged from the ocean floor [of the Bering Sea] (Dixon, 1983). In addition, ancient river channels that could have only been formed by water flowing across the surface of the land have been documented on the sea floor (McManus *et al.*, 1983). Cores taken from the sediments of the Bering and Chukchi Seas contain deposits such as peat, that could only have formed when the continental shelf was exposed as dry land (Elias *et al.*, 1992; Hopkins, 1967; McManus *et al.*, 1983). (Dixon, 1999: 25)

This evidence has been so solid that very few archaeologists have disputed that a 1000 km (620 mi) wide land connection between Siberia and the New World existed, dating from approximately 18 000 years ago to as recently as 14 000–10 000 yr BP (Dixon, 1999: 27; Hopkins, 1982). The real question is not whether such a land bridge existed, since it clearly did (Hopkins, 1982), but rather, did humans cross it along with the fauna they hunted? Once humans arrived in eastern Beringia, what then? The traditional archaeological view (called the Ice-Free Corridor) is that:

1. After pausing briefly in eastern Beringia, Asian big-game hunters followed herd movements south, to the top of the Laurentide and Cordilleran ice sheets.
2. The Laurentide and Cordilleran were fused and impenetrable during stadials (glacial periods).
3. Fusion was sporadic and the ice sheets were separated during interstadials such as during the most recent (14 000–12 000 yr BP).[8]
4. A hypothetical opening, or "Ice-Free Corridor" or "McKenzie Corridor," was located as follows: the southern-most opening near present-day McKenzie, Alberta, Canada, at 22° latitude and 112° longitude, and the northern opening just east of the present Alaska–Canada border at about 64° latitude and 136° longitude (Figure 6.2).

The Ice-Free Corridor supposedly used by Clovis-age people from Beringia is not without its critics in the academy (Mandryk, 1990, 2002) or the media:

Science writer Dietra Henderson parodies the Clovis-first theory as a "'cartoon version' ... of human migration ... with Big Game Hunters breaking through the ice sheets (KAPOW!) and descending in blitzkrieg fashion (BAM!) into this New World.'" (Henderson, 1998 quoted in Thomas, 2000: 168)

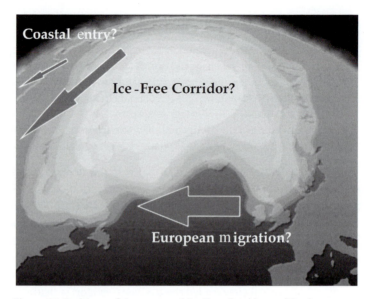

Figure 6.2 Positions of the proposed Ice-Free Corridor and Soultrean migration routes.

Harvard geologist Carole Mandryk has long been a critic of the Ice-Free Corridor route[9] since the days we were both writing our Ph.D. theses. She has always claimed that such a corridor was open to human and animal entry only at 30 000 and 12 000 yr BP. While open, it was a sterile, hostile, forbidding environment for cold-adapted Pleistocene fauna, and more so for human hunters, with howling gale-force winds laden with dust and sand. The winds were channeled by the kilometer-high walls of the Laurentide and Cordilleran sheets, across a relatively bleak landscape which had very little in the way of kindling for cooking fires and only a scattering of small pluvial lakes and ponds from which to obtain potable water. In an article written by Charles Petit of *US News and World Report*, Mandryk states that Clovis-first is a fantasy created by "macho gringo guys [who] just want to believe the first Americans were these big, tough, fur-covered, mammoth-hunting people . . ." (Mandryk quoted in Petit, 1998).

6.4   SEA ROUTES

A Pacific invasion?

After visiting the Alaska territory in 1930, Ales Hrdlička suggested that the diverse native peoples of the North American Arctic and Subarctic

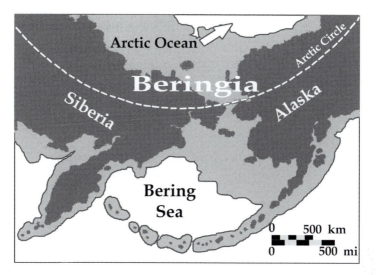

Figure 6.3 Map of Beringia (Bering Land Bridge) at 13 000 yr BP.

arrived in a series of short island hops across the now-flooded Bering Strait. Hrdlička thought that the First Americans originated from the East Cape of Siberia and went via the Diomede and Prince of Wales Islands to the Steward Peninsula or via St. Lawrence Island to the Norton Sound of Alaska (Figure 6.3). He eliminated the possibility of an Aleut migration from the Kamchatka Peninsula (Siberia) via Commander Island, to the Attu and Agattu Islands in the western Aleutian chain, to Umiak Island, then finally to the Alaska Peninsula (Harper and Laughlin, 1982; Hrdlička, 1930), as depicted in Figure 6.3, simply because he found modern Siberian seafaring technology to be inadequate for such a long journey in small vessels (kayaks).

In *Men out of Asia* (1947), Harold Gladwin suggested that long-distance migration by sea was a viable route for the prehistoric human colonization of the Americas. Gladwin felt that no fewer than six trans-oceanic migration events were needed to accomplish the peopling of the Americas. These migrations would have included at least two by Australoid groups represented by Clovis and later Folsom peoples, and separate post-Pleistocene voyages by the ancestors of the Algonquians, Eskimo (Inuit), and Mongoloids.[10] In addition to these migrations, Gladwin hypothesized a fanciful and final Polynesian/Arawak migration, based on archaeological and biological character-istics of Caribbean natives and native Hawaiians.

Fladmark/Dixon's North Pacific refugia coast migration model

Those who have suggested that pedestrians could have moved southward along the Northwest Coast . . . have never visited this region of steep-walled fjords, where the bases of mountains often jut directly out of the sea with no beach. (Bryan, 1969: 339)

According to Canadian archaeologist, Knut R. Fladmark, "statements like this have usually sufficed to dismiss the Northwest Coast as a possible route for migration" (Fladmark, 1978: 119). However, he provided information that made a coastal route seem not only plausible, but also quite likely, including such evidence as small (less than 1 km long) refugia along the icy coastline of Alaska and Canada. These areas could have provided resting areas for large numbers of marine mammals, such as seals and walruses, and also nesting areas for seabirds. The coastal refugia would be nearly perfect microenvironments for coastally adapted humans to exploit during southward migrations by boat.

In the past ten or so years, the coastal migration model has experienced a resurgence in interest, as demonstrated in the works of E. James Dixon (1999), Tim Heaton (2002), Knut Fladmark (1978, 2002), and others. For example, in 1997, Dixon *et al.* discovered a late Pleistocene-age human skeleton in "On Your Knees" Cave, located on Prince of Wales Island in the Bering Sea. Their ethnographic and ethnohistorical research on Umiak skin boats (Figure 6.4) suggested that 20+ people[11] could have been carried in each boat during relocation of hunting and fishing camps along the coasts of Alaska and Canada (see Chapter 7). Similar boats may have provided a means for the First Americans to travel quickly southward along the Pacific coastlines of the New World.

The Solutrean ice-sheet theory

Like so many theories of how humans colonized the Americas, the prescient fifteenth- and sixteenth-century papal scholars of Spain, Acosta and García, anticipated the possibility of early European or Mediterranean peoples having crossed the Atlantic Ocean to people the Americas from the east coast of the New World. García had, of course, ruled this model out based on historical documentation and observed biological difference between Europeans and South American native peoples, with whom he was most familiar.

Figure 6.4 A 1928 photograph of an Umiak skin boat carrying a family along the Alaskan coast during a hunt. Cape of Wales, 1901. Photographer, Suzanne Bernardi. Courtesy of Maxwell Museum of Anthropology Photo Archives.

In 1997, after the discovery of the Kennewick Man and the pronouncement to the press of his supposed "Caucasoid features" (Begley and Muir, 1999; Chatters, 2000), an article by Douglas Preston (1997) published in *The New Yorker* carried a story about a controversial view held by two Paleoindian specialists, Dennis Stanford and Bruce Bradley, regarding a possible colonization of the Americas by Upper Paleolithic Solutrean peoples of western Europe (France, Spain, and Portugal). This view was also presented in articles and interviews in popular media outlets (the *Associated Press*, *Newsweek*, *The New Yorker*), at the for-profit "Clovis and beyond" conference in Santa Fe, New Mexico (1999), and other venues, as well as in a book chapter (Stanford and Bradley, 2002). Straus has elegantly pointed out that Emerson Greenman (1960, 1963) and Art Jelinek (1971) were the first to suggest the idea that American Paleolithic peoples may be directly derived from European Paleolithic cultures, such as the Solutrean culture (20500 to 17000 yr BP) (Straus, 2000: 220). However, the arguments offered to support the Solutrean model have few hard data to back them up, but a great deal of conjecture.

The Iberian invasion model of Stanford and Bradley (2002) goes something like this: at about 21000 to 16500 years ago, a group of

Upper Paleolithic European peoples bearing Solutrean material culture[12] began to move from Iberia up to the British Isles, then west
across the margin of the frozen North Atlantic Ocean either on foot
or by boat, arriving on the coast of Canada's Maritime Provinces, before
moving inland just below the Laurentide ice sheet. Stanford and
Bradley have suggested that the potentially pre-Clovis site of
Meadowcroft Rockshelter is archaeological evidence for the presence
of Solutrean people in eastern North America, despite the fact that the
controversial site contains no humanly modified lithic material that is
unequivocally "Solutrean" in style or manufacture. Once ensconced in
the east, the theory suggests that these colonists made their way west,
and by 12 500 yr BP had reached the area of southern Alberta, Canada,
with a new Solutrean-derived lithic technology later known as Clovis.
From this starting point, the Clovis peoples dispersed to the south,
west, and southeast, terminating their expansion at the Isthmus of
Panama. Stanford was quoted by the *Associated Press* (1998) as stating
that "[I]t is not farfetched to imagine Solutreans sailing to the New
World in skin boats. With a strong current and favorable weather, the
trip might have taken as little as three weeks. By this time in prehistory South Pacific islanders had been sailing open waters for at
least 20 000 years" (Begley and Muir, 1999).

Criticism of Solutrean theory

Stanford and Bradley's (2002) Solutrean model for the peopling of the
Americas received support from a few Americanist scholars (Kenneth
Tankersley, as reported by the *Associated Press*, 1998; Begley and Muir,
1999) and a sound thrashing from archaeologists specializing in the
Paleolithic Solutrean cultures of Europe, mostly in presentations by
Clark, Straus, and Zilhao at national or international meetings (Straus,
2000). The best of these critiques was written by my University of New
Mexico colleague, Dr. Lawrence Guy Straus, whose *American Antiquity*
article (2000) was entitled "Solutrean settlement of North America?
A review of reality."

Why is the Stanford and Bradley Solutrean model unfeasible?

Straus (2000: 220–4) noted the following issues:

1. "The latest Solutrean stone points are more than *5000 radiocarbon
   years older* than Clovis points."

2. "During the LGM [Last Glacial Maximum] (i.e. during the Solutrean), human occupation was limited to a few refugia in southwest and southeast France and (mainly) to the lowland peripheries of the Iberian Peninsula (Vasco-Cantabrian, eastern and southern Mediterranean Spain, and Portugal) ... The very northernmost Solutrean site, Saint-Sulpice-de-Favióres ... is south of Paris. *In sum there were simply no people living in the regions north of Paris ... and there were certainly no people living in southern or any other part of England until ca. 12 500 BP.*"

3. "... the distance from Portugal to Virginia is 5000 km straight across the open mid-North Atlantic Ocean."

4. There are "vast differences between Solutrean and Clovis technologies." As an example, Straus states that Solutrean point *"bases are never fluted"* [italics in the original]. Furthermore, stemmed and shouldered foliate points typical of Solutrean lithic assemblages are not found in Clovis complex sites in the northeast USA.

5. "The fact that red ocher is used in both techno-complexes – as noted by Stanford and Bradley [on the Smithsonian website] – is meaningless, as such pigment is used universally among *Homo sapiens* foragers worldwide."

6. A journey on foot along the margin of the frozen North Sea would have been difficult, if not impossible, as there were no sea mammals, birds, or other fauna accessible from the ice. Hunting was not a possibility, and technologies for fishing (fishhooks, twine) are not known in the Solutrean archaeological record.

7. Finally, there is absolutely no evidence for the use of watercraft in the Solutrean, nor is there archaeological evidence for the manufacture of ropes, cloth, or other items needed to construct a vessel capable of crossing the open North Sea. Straus concludes: "... Clovis is merely one more instance of widespread archaeological convergence or parallelism in prehistory. Rather than requiring the presence of "sophisticated" Paleo-European immigrants to develop Clovis technology, it was the work of Native Americans, undoubtedly of trans-Beringian Asian origin."

The Clovis-first and Solutrean migration models appear to be crumbling under closer inspection. New techniques and theoretical viewpoints have permitted this closer inspection. However, there is now a growing body of evidence to support most of the sea and coastal routes proposed above, with the exception of the North Atlantic Solutrean model (Stanford and Bradley, 2002). First, there are several Paleoindian human remains recovered in areas that would have been exposed during glacial periods, but which are now in the Bering Sea, including the "On Your Knees" Cave skeleton on Prince of Wales Island (Dixon, 1999; Dixon *et al.*, 1997; Heaton, 2002). Other coastal human remains have been recovered on the Channel Islands (Arlington Springs site, Santa Rosa Island) off the California coast. We also know that the ancient peoples of the western Pacific had sufficient knowledge of boats (probably with sails) to be able to cross large stretches of open water (up to 90 km) in the Indonesian Archipelago and travel to Australia and New Zealand. Much of this technology appears to date to about 50 000 years ago (in the case of Australian colonization by humans). Other west Pacific peoples with documented open ocean vessels are the Jomon and their Ainu descendants of northern Japan (Hokkaido Island).

Conclusions

Two main views of how humans migrated to the Americas have been presented over the past 400 or so years of scholarship on the subject. One long-held view is that ancient peoples migrated from northeast Asia during cold (stadial) periods when ocean waters were locked inside ice sheets, and inter-continental land connections (land bridges) were exposed. Asian hunters followed large game across the exposed Bering Land Bridge to reach what is present-day Alaska about 13 000–12 000 yr BP. This view is still the status quo version of Paleoindian migration, despite a growing number of inconsistencies in the archaeological and geological record (Dixon, 1999; Fladmark, 1978; Mandryk, 2002).

An alternative view invokes the long (50 000–500 000-year-long) history of coastal migration along the archipelagos of Australasia, and the east Pacific coast by humans using boats. A growing body of biological (Merriwether, 2002; Powell and Neves, 1999; Powell and Rose, 1999; Schurr, 2002), archaeological (Akazawa, 1999), and linguistic (Nichols, 1990, 1995, 2002) data are making the coastal migration route a bit more plausible. American anthropology appears to be at a crossroads in belief or, as some might say, "a paradigm shift." Regardless of how the first Americans came to the Americas, their camps, burial sites, and skeletal remains are scattered from Alaska to Patagonia.

NOTES

1 All radiocarbon ages presented in this chapter are in uncalibrated form, and not adjusted to a calendrical scale, unless otherwise noted (cal = calibrated to calendrical).
2 A loss of all reproductive-age males or females in a group.
3 Inbreeding in demes can be measured using Wright's (1951) equation for F_{is}, presented in Eq. (3.8).
4 Most recently calibrated to 12 900 to 12 400 yr BP (Fidel, 1996).
5 Animism is the belief (common among some foraging peoples) that spirit beings inhabit and control features of nature, such as springs, ponds, rivers or mountains, or trees. To change nature, the spirit being must be beseeched typically with offerings at the site of the spirit's habitation. This belief system is seen in prehistoric western European belief in wood sprites, fairies, elves, and gnomes. The beseechment occurs by knocking on the trunks of hollow trees where tree sprites live. Of course, western peoples have retained these beliefs as "superstitions" of "knocking on wood" to invoke good luck or to ask for its continuance.
6 Only two other Paleoindian sites in North America have produced such portable art: one incised stone each at the Wilson–Leonard site, central Texas, and the Clovis-type site in eastern New Mexico (both of which have produced human burials, as discussed in Chapter 7).
7 This flaking is sometimes referred to as "overshot" flaking because the pressure used to create the thin, narrow, parallel flakes travels from edge to edge across the blade (see Collins, 1999).
8 These dates are a source of considerable controversy, with some authorities claiming that the Ice-Free Corridor was open only at 30 000 or 12 000 yr BP (Mandryk, 1990, 2002), neither of which would adequately accommodate a Clovis-first entry.
9 The Ice-Free Corridor between the Laurentide and Cordilleran sheets is the essential component of the Clovis-first view of the peopling of the Americas.
10 Here, Gladwin's (1947) meaning is clear: Mongoloid describes the very Asian-looking peoples of the Pacific northwest (the Athabaskans, or Na-Dene peoples) using the terminology of Greenberg et al. (1986).
11 This number is close to the size of a band in a few contemporary hunter-gatherer populations.
12 The Solutrean material culture is typified by distinctive, finely flaked, shouldered, stemmed, and foliate bifacial projectile points as well as by worked bone and ivory rod "tools" (Straus, 2000: 220).

Kennewick Man and his contemporaries

7.1 PALEOINDIAN OR EARLY ARCHAIC?

The bulk of ancient skeletons in the Americas date to the warmer post-glacial period known geologically as the early Holocene (10 000– 8500 yr BP), or culturally as the *Early Archaic period*. People from this period have been thought of as direct descendents of the Clovis (11 500–10 900 yr BP), and later Folsom (10 000–8500 yr BP) colonizers in the Americas (Fagan, 1987; Meltzer, 1993b, 2001). While most skeletal biologists who deal with ancient American skeletons recognize that these remains are not truly Late Pleistocene or "Paleoindian" in age, several of us continue to use the Paleoindian moniker to distinguish early skeletons dating from about 10 900 to 8500 yr BP. The rest of this chapter provides an overview of Paleoindian and Early Archaic skeletons found in the Americas.

7.2 SUMMARY OF ANCIENT SKELETONS IN NORTH AMERICA

Northeastern USA

Trenton site, NJ (1877–1892)

As discussed in Chapters 1 and 2, the Pleistocene gravels of Trenton, New Jersey, produced what appeared to be Paleolithic tools in association with fragmentary human skeletal remains (Abbott, 1876a; Holmes, 1892). However, the Trenton remains have recently been proven to be a modern skeleton incorporated into Pleistocene deposits. Other than this set of remains, there are no other suspected ancient human remains in the northeastern USA, which argues against the Solutrean model of colonization.

Southeastern USA

I have excluded several sites in the southeast USA, especially those from Florida, that were purported to be Late Pleistocene in age, but are now known to be Middle to Late Holocene in age. These localities, therefore, are of little or no consequence for understanding the First Americans and the origin of Native Americans. The remains of historical note, with the dates of the discussion of their antiquity in this area, include Vero Beach, Florida (1917–19) and Melbourne, Florida (1925–7). For more information and citations dealing with these sites, see Meltzer (1991).

Natchez pelvis site, MS

The "Natchez pelvis" was an early twentieth-century discovery initially thought to represent a person from Holmes' American Paleolithic culture. It is mentioned here more for its historical role as the first human bone thought to be evidence of Late Pleistocene human occupation in the Americas. This bone was found in an alluvial deposit that also contained the remains of the Late Pleistocene megafauna (mastodon and mammoth). Initially, the human pelvis was thought, on the basis of the faunal association and of fluorine analyses of the bone, to have considerable antiquity (>12 000 yr BP), but recent accelerated mass spectometry (AMS) ^{14}C dates produced an age of 5580 ± 80 yr BP (AA-4051) (Cotter, 1991), placing it in the Middle Archaic period. The "Natchez pelvis" appears to be the *os coxa* of a Middle Holocene individual of unknown biological affinity.

Little Salt Spring site, FL

The Little Salt Spring site is located in Sarasota County in southwest Florida. W. R. Royal first carried out exploratory work here in the 1950s and various multidisciplinary teams have subsequently excavated here since the 1970s. These excavations are reported in Clausen *et al.* (1975), Goggin (1962), Merbs and Clausen (1981), and other data are summarized by Purdy (1991: 139–58). Work at the site continues under the direction of Dr. John Gifford, at the University of Miami.

The site consists of a flooded sinkhole, approximately 60 m deep, with an adjacent erosional drainage that is now a muck-filled slough. The sinkhole deposits produced preserved wooden artifacts and tools dating to early Clovis times (12 030 yr BP), along with the remains of an adult male who was trapped in the sinkhole during the Late

Pleistocene, when water levels were considerably lower than they are today (Clausen *et al.*, 1975). Clausen discovered a series of wooden stakes, dated to 9500 ± 120 yr BP, driven into the sinkhole wall, leading down to a set of small ledges and small rockshelters about 8 m below the current surface (Clausen *et al.*, 1975). One of the ledges produced wooden tools and the skeleton of the above-noted adult male, along with a large, burned, inverted tortoise shell that had been penetrated by several wooden stakes; the turtle seems to have been cooked on the half-shell by the Little Salt Spring man. The man's personal effects included a nonreturning boomerang[1] made of oak. The hypothesis of Clausen *et al.* (1975) was that the man became trapped while trying to reach scarce spring water[2] about 35 m below the edge of the sinkhole rim, just a few feet below the ledge on which he was discovered. After falling into and being trapped in the sink, the man apparently caught, then killed and cooked a large tortoise. Bone dates on the man's remains produced conventional ^{14}C ages of 10 190 ± 1450 (TX-2595) and 9660 ± 160 yr BP (Beta-26591).

During the Middle Holocene, the spring attracted Archaic populations who occupied the adjacent ridge, and buried their dead in a 600 m^2 area of the muck-filled slough. Dates for the slough cemetery have a median calibrated age of 7157 ± 90 yr BP. The archaeological materials are all under water at present, which, in part, accounts for the remarkable preservation of perishable artifacts and human soft tissues at this site.

Burials at the site were in an extended position, and many appear to have been covered with mats or biers of wax myrtle (*Myrica cerifera*), or even shrouds (Clausen *et al.*, 1975; Purdy, 1991: 154). Other burials appear to have been placed inside small structures or surrounded by posts (Merbs and Clausen, 1981). Artifacts recovered from the cemetery include a variety of projectile points, basketry, wooden tools, and a carved wooden tablet. The Little Salt Spring cemetery and artifact assemblage is nearly identical to that of Sarasota County's Bay West and Republic Groves sites, as well as to several other Middle Archaic period cemeteries in Florida that are now destroyed (Beriault *et al.*, 1981). It also has some affinities with later Glades traditions in the Okeechobee basin of Florida (Clausen *et al.*, 1975).

Skeletal remains representing 35 individuals were recovered from test excavations in the slough and from the spring itself (Goggin, 1962). Given the extent of the cemetery, 1000 individuals may be buried there (Clausen *et al.*, 1975). Anaerobic conditions in the pond and slough have contributed to the preservation of human brain and other soft tissues in some of the recovered burials, which have provided material for mtDNA analysis (Pääbo *et al.*, 1989). The population appears to have been affected by enamel hypoplasia, *cribra orbitalia*, and subperiosteal reactions (Merbs and Clausen, 1981; Powell, 1995).

Warm Mineral Spring site, FL

The Warm Mineral Spring site (WMS) is located near the city of North Port in west central Florida, at the edge of Florida's central ridge, near the Myakka River. During the terminal Pleistocene, WMS would have been considerably further inland than it is in today's higher Holocene sea levels. Warm Mineral Spring is geologically situated much like its neighbor to the east, Little Salt Spring (8SO18), and is composed of a deep karst sinkhole formation (vertical shaft cave) filled by geothermally warmed water, fed in part by small karst fissures originating near the Gulf of Mexico. Warm Mineral Spring is actually a slightly smaller sinkhole (61 m deep and 70 m in diameter at the surface) than Little Salt Spring and has a large (23 m high) "debris cone" at the bottom (Figure 7.1). This debris cone contains detritus that has washed into the sink, large spalls, and ceiling blocks from the collapse of the massive

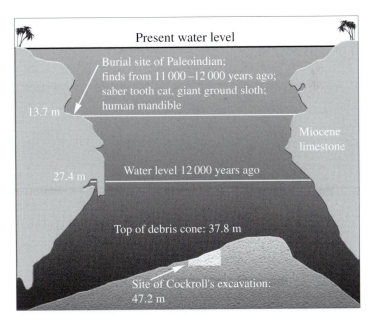

Figure 7.1 Cross-sectional diagram of the Warm Mineral Spring site, Florida. Note the location of the burial cave.

cave roof which created the sinkhole. The debris cone also contains the bones of Pleistocene fauna that appear to have fallen into the spring and drowned. The Terminal Pleistocene water level was about 27.4 m below the present water surface (Figure 7.1). Like Little Salt Spring, the sinkhole rim contains small caves[3] and rockshelters, which were explored by amateur underwater archaeologist Lt. Col. William Royal in the mid to late 1950s. Royal reported that he recovered at least seven complete human skulls and parts of at least 30 other bodies in the "Stalactite" Cave. Royal's notes for this discovery are sketchy at best and apparently were not recorded while at the site. Because of these provenience problems, the site was re-examined by Dr. "Sonny" Cockrell, who discovered a large humanly modified log partly buried in silts in Royal's "Stalactite" Cave. Just below and behind this artifact, Cockrell discovered oak and hickory leaves and other preserved plant material (such as oak and hickory nuts) as well as three human skulls in various degrees of completeness and fragmentary post-cranial skeletal remains of at least two of the skulls.

The most complete skull (the "Brown" skull) was that of a young adult female about 20–25 years of age. This young woman presented excessive alveolar (lower facial) prognathism, a very narrow face, and tall and broad nasal aperture and dolichocranic neurocranium (Figure 7.2), similar in overall form to the young adult female skulls at Pelican Rapids (MN) and La Brea (CA). The two other WMS skulls include the sphlanchnocranium (face) of a robust adult male (30–50 years of age),

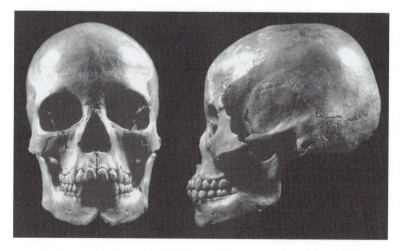

Figure 7.2 Frontal and lateral view of the Warm Mineral Spring "Brown" skull.

dubbed the "Black" skull.[4] The third skull consisted of articulated fragments of the bones along portions of the fused coronal, sagittal, and lambdoid sutures (frontal, both parietals, occipital) that were sun-bleached to a white or ivory color (the "White" skull). These cranial fragments appear to be from an older adult (50+ years of age) female with an associated edentulous (toothless) mandible. In addition to these remains, a fragmentary cranium and pelvis, plus a few vertebral pieces from a young child (0–5 years of age, but more likely to be 2–4 years of age) were recovered. There are 16 radiocarbon ages for the skeletons, logs, and other organic materials (leaves) in the sinkhole, ranging from 8030 ± 120 (UM-111) to $10\,630 \pm 210$ (UM-111). Direct conventional bone dating from a post-cranial fragment that probably belonged to the Black skull individual yielded a ^{14}C age of $10\,260 \pm 190$ (Gak-3998) (Clausen et al., 1975).

The current owners of the spring property have developed it as a spa, and some local citizens suggest that it is the long-sought "Fountain of Youth" of Ponce de Leon. Warm Mineral Spring has been promoted for many years as a tourist attraction for its "warm healing waters," in which one can bathe or swim for a modest fee. The "Stalactite" Cave is only 6 m underwater, so someone with great lung capacity can reach it without benefit of breathing apparatus, albeit not for very long.[5]

Cutler Fossil site, FL

This site is located in southern Dade County, near Miami, Florida, and is the southern-most locality on the eastern American seaboard to yield Late Pleistocene human remains. The Cutler Fossil site (12 000–7000 yr BP) is a dry sinkhole filled with Pleistocene-age faunal remains, including horse, peccary, dire wolf, and jaguar. Upper layers of the fossil deposit contained a "spear tip" and several other nondescript stone tools, a hearth, along with human bone and tooth fragments found in association with fragments of Pleistocene fauna. The human remains represent a minimum of ten different individuals, and do not appear to be in primary context as intentional interments.

Windover site, FL

The Windover site in Florida, although not a Paleoindian site, contains one of the oldest and best preserved Archaic cemeteries on the eastern seaboard, and dates to the Early and Middle Archaic periods, which overlap partly with post-Folsom Paleoindian occupations in the region.

Because of the fabulous preservation at Windover (including preserved matting, twine, and basketry, and brains inside the skulls of individuals interred there), it is certainly worth mentioning here.

This site, actually a shallow pond located on the Atlantic ridge near Cape Canaveral, Florida, was excavated during the 1980s by a team of archaeologists from Florida State University under the direction of Dr. Glen Doran. Results of the multidisciplinary investigations are reported in a variety of publications (Doran, 1992; Doran and Dickel, 1988a,b; Doran et al., 1986; Estes, 1988; Hauswirth et al., 1991).

Human skeletal remains were recovered from the saturated peat deposits at the site in association with woven fabric, cordage, wood and bone artifacts, basketry, stone tools, and a wide variety of preserved plant and animal remains (Doran, 1992; Doran and Dickel, 1988a,b; Tuross et al., 1994). A series of 15 radiocarbon dates from human bone, wooden artifacts, and peat were obtained for the Upper Red Peat deposit, the stratum that contained virtually all of the human remains from the site (Doran and Dickel, 1988b). Calibrated ages ranged from 7777 ± 90 yr BP (Beta-19316) to 8988 ± 100 yr BP (Beta-13909), with a median date of 8095 ± 100 yr BP (Beta-5803). As Doran and Dickel (1988a,b) note, this makes the Windover material the largest human skeletal collection in North America that is indisputably older than 5000 yr BP.

The Windover site appears to have functioned exclusively as a cemetery location. Individuals were interred or submerged within 48 hours of death (Doran et al., 1986), and were often covered with fabric or basketry (Doran, 1992; Doran and Dickel, 1988b). Bodies were held in place in the marsh deposits by means of wooden stakes penetrating the textile wrappings of the burial (Doran, 1992) or by branches placed over the remains (Doran, personal communication).

Use of ponds and bogs as cemeteries has been documented at other Middle Holocene sites in south Florida including Bay West (Beriault et al., 1981), Little Salt Spring (Clausen et al., 1975), and the Republic Groves (Wharton et al., 1981). Wet site burial appears to be a practice that is atypical of other pre-5000 yr BP populations in North America (Doran, 1992). However, it is similar to that of later Holocene Belle Glade populations in the Lake Okeechobee basin of Florida (Clausen et al., 1975; Milanich and Fairbanks, 1980: 60).

Human skeletal remains representing a minimum of 172 individuals were recovered from the site (Hauswirth et al., 1991: 63). Some researchers believe that an additional 100 to 150 individuals are interred in deposits that have not yet been excavated (Hauswirth *et al.*, 1991). Excellent preservation conditions at Windover, brought about by an anaerobic burial environment and neutral water pH, resulted in the recovery of 91 saponified human brains, as well as organic artifacts and stomach contents. Genetic material from these individuals is currently undergoing analysis (Doran, 1992; Hauswirth *et al.*, 1991; Lawlor *et al.*, 1991; Pääbo *et al.*, 1989).

The Windover site is also unusual among Middle Holocene cemeteries in that over half of the recovered individuals (52%) were sub-adults. Adult males and females were represented in nearly equal numbers. Several individuals exhibited pathological conditions. Traumatic injury, including parry fractures of the ulna and radius, puncture wounds to the face and pelvis, and blunt trauma to the head, was common in both males and females (Dickel and Doran, 1989; Dickel *et al.*, 1989), and has been offered as evidence of interpersonal violence between different populations in the Middle Holocene (Purdy, 1991: 216). Other health conditions included high levels of anemic response (41.6% of skeletal sample), enamel hypoplasia, and other indicators of physiological or nutritional stress (Estes, 1988: 132–7; Estes and Dickel, 1989), as well as severe neural tube defects (Dickel and Doran, 1989) and dental anomalies (Powell, 1995). The latter possibly reflects limited mate choices in a group with a small effective population size, leading to unintentional inbreeding over time (Powell and Neves, 1998).

Mid-continent

Pelican Rapids site ("Minnesota Woman")

In 1931, workers widening and grading a highway near Pelican Rapids in western Minnesota, bladed through shallow deposits of silts and glacial loess which were the remnants of the bottom of a small, shallow Pleistocene-age pond or playa lake. Within these silt deposits the workers discovered the grave and skeletal remains of the "Minnesota Man." The workers then contacted Dr. Albert Ernest Jenks, the founder and chair of the Anthropology Department at the University of Minnesota who, along with his assistant Mr. Lloyd Wilford, went to the site to examine the grave and skeleton.

Jenks was a firm believer in the Pleistocene antiquity of humans in the Americas (Holmes' American Paleolithic) and had published an *American Anthropologist* article to that effect. He claimed that the Arvilla gravel pit skeletons from Nebraska were extremely old because of the skeletons' association with a collection of Yuha points (now known to be a Folsom-age [10 200–9500 yr BP] point-type specific to the Upper Midwest region). Smithsonian Institution Director Ales Hrdlička engaged Jenks in a lengthy argument via mail[6] about the antiquity of the "Minnesota Man" skeleton, which to Hrdlička must have been like a modern, Late Holocene (no older than 4000 years old) Native American skeleton. Hrdlička, who became Jenks' harshest critic, was able to prove that Jenks was wrong, not about the antiquity of the skeleton, but about its sex, which turned out to be female rather than male.[7] Hrdlička used this mis-identification as the focus of an article entitled "The Minnesota 'Man'," published in *American Anthropologist*. After this paper was published, the press dubbed the Pelican Rapids skeleton "Minnesota Minnie," now referred to as the "Minnesota Woman" (still a misnomer, as the individual was not fully mature).

Steele and Powell (1992) and Nelson (1998) found the "Minnesota Woman" to be a subadult, about 15–18 years of age at death. More recent investigations have shown that the Pelican Rapids girl is only marginally associated with the Terminal Pleistocene, despite a possible Folsom association and is well dated to the Early Archaic period in the Holocene, with an uncalibrated radiocarbon age of 7840 yr BP (Myster and O'Connell, 1997).

Browns Valley site, MN

On October 9, 1931, William H. Jensen, a farmer in Browns Valley, western Minnesota, discovered stone tools and human bones among the quarry gravels dumped on a road on his farm. He then contacted Jenks and Wilford, who later examined the gravel pit site, which ultimately produced numerous Terminal Pleistocene Yuha and Folsom-like points along with a burial feature containing a male skeleton that cane to be nicknamed "Browns Valley Man." Jenks and Wilford excavated the site in 1933 and 1934. Jenks published his account of the site and skeleton as an article in the journal *Science*, entitled "Ancient Minnesota maker of Yuma and Folsom flints" (Jenks, 1936), and in *Minnesota's Brown Valley Man and Associated Burial Artifacts*, a book in which he compared the skeleton to Pleistocene finds from Europe (Jenks, 1937). This time there was no doubt that the ancient skeleton was a male; it was extremely robust and, according to Jenks, had a mandible and maxilla ("jaws" *sensu* Jenks, 1937) comparable to the "Heidelberg Man" (*Homo erectus*, also known as *Homo heidelbergensis*).[8]

More recent investigations have shown that the Browns Valley skeleton is only marginally associated with the Terminal Pleistocene and is firmly seated in the Early Archaic period. Recent AMS dating of the skeleton yielded ^{14}C ages of 8700 ± 110 yr BP and 8900 ± 80 yr BP (Myster and O'Connell, 1997).

Sauk Valley site, MN

The skeleton found in Sauk Valley, western Minnesota, also associated with periglacial geological deposits, was first described by Jenks and Wilford (1938). Albert Jenks also used the Sauk Valley Skeleton (probably representing an Archaic period fairly robust male) to support the Holmes' "American Paleolithic" culture (see Chapter 1). They saw the Sauk Valley Skeleton's "primitive features" and robust skull as Neanderthal phenotypic traits, instead of what they really were: a very robust male dating to between the Terminal Pleistocene and Early Holocene. The report on the site and skeleton was published as "The Sauk Valley skeleton," oddly enough in the *Bulletin of the Texas Archaeology and Paleontological Society*[9] by Jenks and Wilford in 1938, as Jenks neared retirement from the University of Minnesota.

Northern and central plains

Anzick (Wisall) site, MT

A construction project brought to light skeletal fragments representing two individuals: parietal fragments and an associated clavicle of an 18-month-old child of indeterminate sex, and cranial fragments from an older (7–10-year-old) child, also of indeterminate sex. The younger child was coated with red ocher pigment prior to interment[10] and both were buried in association with over 100 non-human bones and stone artifacts, all suspected to be of Clovis-age. The burials were recovered in deposits at the back of a small rockshelter in the inter-montaine basin separating the Belt and Crazy Mountains on a tributary of the Shields River. During the 1968 discovery, many of the artifacts appeared to be Clovis-age grave goods.[11] Both sets of remains were tested for collagen preservation and both produced ^{14}C ages based on specific amino acids in bone collagen (Stafford, 1990; Taylor, 1994: table 2): the older subadult bones produced ages ranging from $10\,240 \pm 120$ yr BP (AA-2978) on pure aspartic acid from human collagen, to $10\,940 \pm 90$ yr BP (AA-2981) from purified glycine (Roosevelt *et al.*, 2002: 228). A third collagen date from the older of the Anzick juveniles produced an uncalibrated age of $10\,600 \pm 300$ (Taylor, 1991: 102). The average of five radiocarbon dates on the older child was $10\,680$ yr BP (Owsley and Hunt, 2001: 312). Lepper (2001) reported that a research team, comprising D. Owsley, L. Lahren, D. Hunt, and T. Stafford,[12] examined the Anzick remains and concluded that the younger child was of Clovis age, given the ^{14}C ages, and was associated with the huge Clovis tool cache just above it in the shelter deposits. Owsley *et al.* felt that differences in ocher staining between the two skeletons indicated that the children were products of two separate interment events at the site, one during a Clovis occupation (the 18-month-old child) and the other of an Early Archaic occupation (the 5–6-year-old child) dating nearly 2000 years earlier than Clovis (Lepper, 2001). A new AMS date by Stafford places the 18-month-old child at $11\,550 \pm 60$ (CAMS-35912) (Dixon, 1999: 121). If Owsley *et al.* are correct, then the traditional interpretation of the Anzick burials as a "Clovis-age double child burial" is completely incorrect. The Anzick remains have already been subject to NAGPRA claims, but have been available in the past few years to scientists and scholars and have not, as at the time of writing, been repatriated or reburied. The Anzick Clovis tool cache remains the largest such cache yet discovered.

Nebraska and Kansas

Several sets of potentially ancient human remains have been recovered in Nebraska and Kansas in the central Great Plains. Other Nebraska and Kansas skeletons suspected to be ancient include the Wet Gravel site male and female skeletons, and male skeletons from the Lime Creek and Swanson Lake sites, along with two skeletons (one male and one female) from the Plattsmouth Ossuary site. These skeletons were once thought to be ancient based on their possible stratigraphic association with terminal Pleistocene deposits. However, no chronometric ages were obtained for them, and they have now been repatriated and reburied with very little scientific study, except for a few measurements by Jantz and Owsley (2001) and their students (Key, 1983).

Gilder Mound site, NE

On occasion, the skeletons from this site pop up in the literature about the First Americans, and so they are discussed here. Human bones from Gilder Mound, Nebraska, were discovered during the

1906 construction of a root cellar. Later, the skeletal remains were identified as those of an adult male and adult female, of indeterminate biological age. These remains were buried in a glacial moraine and, hence, the name "mound" (not in the late Middle Woodland earthwork sense) was applied, and they were thought to belong to the newly proposed American Paleolithic (Holmes, 1892). Despite their association with Holmes' "paleoliths," which are now recognized as chert blanks from the initial stages of stone tool manufacture, they are now known to be Holocene in age (Meltzer, 1991). Unfortunately, the skeletons were repatriated to local tribes, during the University of Nebraska's NAGPRA debacle, before complete scientific studies could be conducted. They have since been reburied somewhere on sacred tribal lands of the Omaha tribe.

Southern Plains

Midland site, TX

The Midland site (41MD1) (or Scharbauer site) was located in 1953, when the skull of an adult female was discovered in the exposed deposits of the basin of Monahans Draw, just south of Midland, Texas, along the southern escarpment of the Llano Estacado. Wendorf (1953–4) and Sellards (1953–4) conducted later sets of site surveys in the area of the skull discovery. The cranium appears to have eroded from a Pleistocene-age sand dune blow-out and was initially dated by stratigraphic association with a white sand deposit dated to $13\,400 \pm 1200$ yr BP, a date supported by fluorine analysis of a fragment of the cranium. The site also contained overlying gray sand that contained Folsom and Midland (a Folsom regional unfluted point variant) points. The stratigraphic position of the skull prompted Wendorf and his fellow investigators to declare the skull as pre-Folsom, and others later to claim it as a pre-Clovis person. A 1995 verification of Midland Site stratigraphy by Holliday and Meltzer (1996) and Hofman (1992) demonstrated that the "Midland Woman" was probably a Folsom–Midland ($11\,000$–$10\,000$ yr BP) age human burial that was covered by Holocene dune sands. This hypothesis was verified in 1990, when a new ^{14}C date was obtained from the cranium, which yielded an age of $11\,600 \pm 800$ yr BP (Holliday and Meltzer, 1996); this is now consistent with the corrected stratigraphy and associated artifacts.

In this case, the Midland Woman really is female, aged 30–40 years at the time of her death. Her well-worn teeth showed little sign of dental decay, but the wear is consistent with the pattern of wear that has been observed on other Folsom-aged human teeth, including the subadult teeth from the nearby Shifting Sands, Horn Shelter, Wilson–Leonard, Browns Valley, Warm Mineral Spring, Little Salt Spring, and Kennewick remains. Each of these early Americans shows a pattern of wear seen among mixed economy and generalized foragers of the Late Archaic period and later Holocene peoples in the Great Basin and elsewhere (Powell and Steele, 1993), possibly indicating that Terminal Pleistocene peoples ate a wide range of foods, including fruits, vegetables, nuts, and other gathered foods.

The few facial bones present were consistent with those of other First Americans examined by Steele and Powell (1992), with a greater degree of facial flatness than is typical of northeast Asian populations. Midland Woman's teeth (despite their heavy wear) present a pattern of dental morphology that Turner (1983b) described as Sinodont. In my, and a few of my colleagues', assessments, the Midland Woman's teeth express traits like those seen among most of the ancient Americans; a pattern intermediate between the Sinodont[13] extreme and the generalized Sundadont pattern (Neves *et al.*, 1999a; Powell, 1997; Powell and Neves, 1998).

Shifting Sands site, TX

This site, located in the Texas Panhandle, near the Oklahoma border, is a sand dune "blow-out" which produced several Folsom-derived Plainview points, human tooth crowns representing at least one subadult of indeterminate sex and possibly 5–9 years of age based on dental maturity. A few additional, very weathered fragments of human bone that could not be attributed to the subadult individual were also recovered. The teeth of the subadult indicate a strong expression of incisor shoveling and double shoveling, dental traits common among Native Americans of the southwest and southern Plains regions.

Seminole Sink site, TX

The Seminole Sink is a small karst cyst formation located in arid Val Verde County, Texas, just east of the confluence of the Lower Pecos and Rio Grande River drainages, on the north side of Seminole Canyon. The Canyon is well known for its large Paleoindian period mammoth, camel, and horse drive-and-kill site at Bonfire Shelter. Seminole Canyon contains huge Archaic period rockshelters of the Lower Pecos region, known for their spectacular Archaic age pictogram panels rising, in some cases, nearly 12 m (at Panther Cave) above the shelter floors (see Shaffer, 1986; Turpin, 1991).

Seminole Sink, while not a pictogram site, is a long-term burial locale or cemetery used by Native Americans from the Early Archaic to the historic periods. It is actually a very small sinkhole, by Warm Mineral Spring standards. The sink's small surface opening leads 3–8 m down to the ceiling of an elliptical cave. Beneath this opening was found a small talus cone of materials such as surface wash detritus and human skeletal remains (minimum number of individuals, MNI = 22), some as old as the Early Archaic period (10 000–5000 yr BP), that had been dropped into the opening of the sink, along with historic period "metallic trash" (tin cans, pistol shell casings), and prehistoric period human remains. Seminole Sink provided indications including an assumed receptacle (animal skin pouch or woven basket)[14] containing the cremated remains of a 5–6-year-old child.

Rocky Mountains

Hourglass Cave site, CO

In July of 1988, three members of the National Speleological Society (NSS) discovered a small cave, 3000 m up on the eastern face of the Rocky Mountains in west central Colorado. In what appeared to be an untraveled passage of the maze-like cave, they discovered a set of prehistoric skeletal remains that were fairly complete, lying on their right side in a muddy area of mixed clay and drip water in the unusually cold (4–5 °C) and humid cave environment. By 1989 the cavers returned with a multidisciplinary team of cave archaeologists, physical anthropologists, and speleologists. This team recovered the skeleton, which probably pre-dated the modern era. The prehistoric man provided material for dating data from collagen in a rib, and from a split sample from his tibia. These samples produced AMS ages of 8170 ± 100 (Beta-38554) and 7944 ± 84 yr BP (ETH-6765) for rib fragments, and 7714 ± 77 yr BP (AA:11808) for fragments of the tibiae. These radiometric ages are fairly consistent in placing this Man in the Early Archaic period. The skeleton was that of a male, 35–45 years of age at the time of death, with no skeletal manifestations of trauma or disease except for minor spinal degeneration in the cervical area and tibial shafts that were "unusually thick" (Mosch and Watson, 1997: 11). The latter condition may be due to post-mortem accumulation of carbonates in the long bones, resulting from the absorption of lime-stone drip water from the muddy water on the cave floor at the recovery site. The man's cranium was only partial, with most of the calvarial portions preserved, and some of the sphlanchnocranium (face) and basilar portions were missing or damaged, but it did contain 11 maxil-lary teeth.

Numerous faunal remains were found just inside the cave entrance. The cave walls and ceiling contained smudge marks and radiometrically recent charcoal left by later prehistoric peoples, or perhaps by the man, during his exploration of the cave; these marks extend 36 m beyond the location of his body. Because the Hourglass Cave skeleton was so well preserved in the cave environment, aDNA from his skeleton was easily extracted (Stone and Stoneking, 1996). The aDNA results indicated the presence of the 9-bp deletion (Stone and Stoneking, 1996), typical of the B haplogroup (see Chapter 4), which has a high frequency among prehistoric and modern Native Americans. The Hourglass Cave skeleton was an inadvertent discovery of human remains on federal (US Department of Agriculture Forest Service) land, and based on the aDNA data was declared to be from a prehistoric Native American man. The remains were returned to the Southern Ute tribe for repatriation.

Central Texas

Horn Shelter No. 2 site, TX

The Horn Shelter No. 2 site, located in central Texas, just south of Waco, was investigated by avocational archaeologist Al Redder[15] in the 1970s and analyzed by Redder, along with D. G. Steele, D. Young-Holiday, B. Baker, and J. F. Powell in the late 1980s and early 1990s. A Terminal Pleistocene/Early Holocene occupation floor yielded thou-sands of faunal remains representing several species of small fauna, including mice and voles (possibly contained in owl pellets dropped onto the occupation surface; Baker, personal communication) along with many other species, ranging in size up to deer. The occupation also produced fragmentary bison bones, which are appropriate to the shelter's position on the interface between southern plains and the westernmost margin of the Eastern Woodlands. Horn Shelter also yielded a shallow, slab-covered burial feature containing the partially crushed remains of two ocher-covered individuals: an adult male 35–40 years of age at death and an adolescent (possibly male) estimated to be

12–14 years of age at death. The double burial also contained grave offerings of perforated marine shell beads, flintknapping tools (a set of chert blanks and a limestone abrader, the latter probably used to dull the edges of a striking platform, along with what might be a small hammerstone). The adult's head was found resting on a "pillow" made from the carapace of a Pleistocene turtle species that is now extinct (Baker, 1998).

Wilson–Leonard site (41WM235), TX

This site, a large stratified rockshelter in Williamson County, Texas, produced a skeleton with a series of ^{14}C ages ranging from 10 000–9500 yr BP, as well as evidence of late Paleoindian unfluted point types and a wide range of preserved floral and small faunal remains. The site's significance, beside the ancient human remains discovered therein, is that the bioarchaeological data from the burial (Powell, 1993) indicate that users of Plainview Paleoindian projectile points during the terminal Pleistocene were not just large game hunters focusing on Pleistocene fauna, but were much like modern foragers and practiced broad-spectrum foraging as early as 10 000 yr BP (Bousman *et al.*, 2002; Powell and Steele, 1994). The 1983 excavation of the site by archaeologists from the Texas Department of Transportation yielded a shallow grave pit containing the badly compressed, but nearly complete skeleton of a 20–25-year-old female, buried in a tightly flexed position. The skeleton produced ^{14}C ages on organic material in the grave feature and associated with the skeleton of 9490 yr BP (TX-4787). Recent dates for the Wilson–Leonard Woman place her at 11 500 yr BP, making her the oldest human skeleton in North America (Bousman *et al.*, 2002).

Ages for the Leann stratum, from which the burial feature originated, range from 9990–9750 yr BP. Plant remains in this stratum include black walnut shells and juniper wood. Along with remains of two rabbit genera (*Sylvilagus* and *Leptus*), there were charred remains of five rodent species including field mice, cotton rats, squirrels, small carnivores such as raccoons (*Procyon lotor*), and some larger fauna, including fragments of Late Pleistocene bison (cf. *Bison antiquus*) and a possible new subspecies of deer (*Odocoileus* spp.) (Baker, 1998). Several bird species are also present in the stratum, as are a variety of snakes in the genera *Columbridae* and *Viperidae*, fish (*Chondrichthyes*), and turtles (*Kinosternidae* and *Emydidae*) (Bousman *et al.*, 2002).

The burial was accompanied by a Cretaceous-aged fossil shark tooth (perhaps part of a necklace), three pieces of worked hematite,

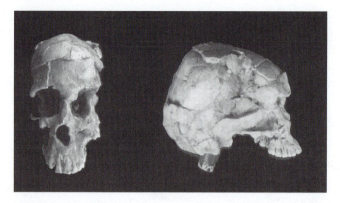

Figure 7.3 The Wilson–Leonard Woman from central Texas. Photographs of the epoxy cast of the skull and facial reproduction, prepared by Betty Pat Gatliff. Photos courtesy of D. Gentry Steele. Modified with permission from Steele and Powell (2002).

and a groundstone chopper made of feldspathic sandstone from a mineral outcrop 15–20 km away from the Wilson–Leonard locality. The body was positioned on its right side, knees bent toward the chest in a tightly flexed position in a shallow grave feature. The cranium was resting on the palmar surfaces of the bones of the right hand. The left arm was flexed with the left hand near the face.

The reconstructed cast of the woman's crushed and distorted skull indicates a woman with extreme alveolar prognathism and a broad nasal aperture (Figure 7.3). This combination of phenotypic features is most often seen among some living peoples of the South Pacific, especially Australomelanesians and Polynesians (Steele and Powell, 1992), and among Native Americans in Tierra del Fuego, Chile (Neves *et al.*, 1999b).

The overall craniofacial appearance of the Wilson–Leonard female compares favorably to the 26 000-year-old Pleistocene Czech Republic skeleton of Predmostí III (Larsen *et al.*, 1991) or the 11 000-year-old Terminal Pleistocene Brazilian skull nicknamed Luzia (Figure 7.4). The possible implications of these similarities for the First Americans will be discussed in Chapters 10 and 11.

Southwestern USA

Whitewater Draw site (Sulphur Springs), AZ

Like so many other "Paleoindian" skeletal finds, the two adult skeletons found here were discovered during the excavation of a backhoe trench

Figure 7.4 Photo of the facial reproduction of Brazil's Luzia ("Lucy").
Photo courtesy Dr. Walter A. Neves.

being used to establish the geomorphological history of Whitewater
Draw as part of Dr. Michael Waters' 1986 geoarchaeological field work
near Sulphur Springs in south central Arizona. Most archaeologists
familiar with the region initially thought that the sites there were likely
to be associated with Paleoindian-age peoples. However, by 1986, Waters
proved the human remains to be more recent in age; in this case the two
adult skeletons produced ^{14}C ages placing them in the Sulphur Springs
stage (10 000–8000 yr BP) of the Early Archaic period in Arizona prehistory. This late date does not negate their scientific importance, as
very few human remains from the Sulphur Springs stage have been
documented (Sayles and Antevs, 1941).

In this case, the bones appear to represent two fairly complete skeletonized adult individuals. The first was initially recovered by Sayles and Antevs (1941) and was a fragmentary adult of unknown sex, with partial cranium (Sulphur Springs I). Waters' Sulphur Springs II feature contained the nearly complete skeleton of a female 20–35 years of age at death, placed in a flexed position, and facing the northwest. The "Whitewater Draw Woman" (Sulphur Springs II) was clearly associated with a burial feature originating from Sulphur Springs-age deposits dating to 8000 to 10 000 yr BP (Waters, 1986: 56).

The overall morphology of the Sulphur Springs crania is meso-cranic to brachycranic (globular or "round-headed") like the cranial shape of Late Holocene populations in the southwest and unlike the appearance of most Paleoindian crania, which tend to be dolichocranic ("long-headed"). Sulphur Springs II possesses very large teeth (Powell, 1997: unpublished report to Waters[16]) whose morphology is consistent with Turner's (1983b) Sinodont pattern. Her teeth were heavily worn, indicating a gritty diet or possible use of the teeth as tools.

Southern California

Many of the skeletons listed in this section were initially dated using new and sometimes experimental methods such as amino acid racem-ization (AAR), which relies on temporally created changes in amino acid structure and shape from the L to the D form. This method of dating was invented by biochemist Jeffry Bada in the early 1970s (Bada and Protch, 1973; Bada et al., 1974) and was applied to faunal bones and teeth (especially in humans). For a detailed description of the technique, see Bada and Protch (1973) or Taylor (1991: 89–91). Because Bada worked in southern California, the AAR method was mostly applied to Californian skeletons thought to be significant for their possible pre-Clovis geological or archaeological contexts. Many of these skeletons also produced anomalous radiocarbon dates, all in excess of 20 000 yr BP,[17] as a result of the unrefined carbon extraction and decontamination methods used in the early days of ^{14}C methods (Taylor, 1991).

Other "early skeletons" in California that were thought to be pre-Clovis or much older and subsequently turned out to be very recent include Mostin, Del Mar, Yuha, and Los Angeles Man (see Lorenzo, 1978; Taylor et al., 1985). These remains are of historical interest only. They are rarely mentioned in the recent literature on the First

Americans and need not be discussed in detail here. Interested readers should consult Taylor *et al.* (1985), Taylor (1992), Lorenzo (1978), Larsen *et al.* (1991: 174–5), and Rogers *et al.* (1992, 1999). As an example of how improvements in radiocarbon dating improve the clarity of our understanding of the First Americans, the Del Mar skeleton (San Diego Museum of Man, SDM #16704) was thought to be 11 800 yr BP from a total carbon fraction ^{14}C date on the partly fossilized skull, but re-dating of just the collagen fraction revealed it to be a mere 4900 yr BP (Taylor *et al.*, 1985) – a Late Archaic forager at best.

Rancho La Brea tar pit (La Brea tar pit), CA

The La Brea tar pit is located in the West Hollywood area of Los Angeles, on the former Rancho La Brea farm property, now owned by the city. The locality is now adjacent to the George C. Page Museum of La Brea Discoveries. The tar pit associated with the site was created by massive underground deposits of petroleum. Throughout the Pleistocene the tar pit was a shallow pond of rain water resting on the surface of the highly surfactant tar bubbling up from the oil deposits deep below. Thirsty Pleistocene megafauna (ground sloth, mammoth, and, at certain times, mastodon) in search of water during the periodic droughts that occurred throughout the Pleistocene (including the so-called "Clovis drought") would have waded into the pond and became ensnared in the subsurface tar deposits. At that point they either died from liquefaction or exhaustion, or were killed and eaten by large Pleistocene predators and scavengers such as saber-tooth cats and dire wolves, many of which also became mired in the tar along with their prey. In early 1919, an unexpected predator species (*Homo sapiens sapiens*) was recovered along with the bones of the megafauna and predators (Berger, 1975; Kroeber, 1962). The human skeleton was that of a female, 20–25 years of age at death, according to Kroeber (1962). A radiocarbon age of 9000 ± 82 yr BP (UCLA-1292B) was obtained from the total amino acids in the bone sample (Berger, 1975; Taylor, 1991: 90, table 3.2).[18] This woman may have been intentionally deposited within the tar pit, although this is still a subject of speculation. Her cranium was extremely dolichocranic with a broad nose set on a narrow face, like that of most other ancient Americans. Her post-cranial skeleton was fairly complete except for some of the small bones of the hands and feet (Powell, unpublished research notes on file, UNM Clark Field Archive, 1994).

Arlington Springs, CA

This skeleton was discovered eroding from a cut bank near the Arlington Springs fossil locality on Santa Rosa Island by the anthropology curator of the Santa Barbara Museum of Natural History, Phil Orr (1962, 1968). He was in search of bones of a species of dwarf mammoth (*Elephas exilis*) that evolved on the island as a result of its isolation from mainland mammoth species (*Elephas mammuthus*). The Arlington Springs Woman appears to represent one of the oldest skeletons from North America, with an initial conventional radiocarbon age of $10\,080 \pm 810$ yr BP (UCLA-1899). One important aspect to note is that Santa Rosa is one of the Channel Islands, several nautical miles off the coast of Los Angeles, California, and could only have been reached by boat in the Late Pleistocene. Re-dating by Orr's curatorial replacement, John Johnson and his colleagues (Johnson, 2001) produced an uncalibrated age of $10\,960 \pm 60$ yr BP (CAMS-16810). The latter date produces a calendrical age close to $13\,000$ yr BP (Johnson, 2001).

Great Basin, NV

The majority of sites in this section are on the far western edge of the Great Basin, on the east side of California's Sierra Nevada mountain range in and around the small seasonal lakes and saltwater marshes. At the time of their discoveries, most of these sites and the skeletons buried in them were thought to be from the Archaic period.

As part of the Nevada State Museum's NAGPRA inventory process, many of the perishable materials and human remains in the museum's collections (including one or two naturally mummified bodies) were dated using the AMS radiocarbon method. The dating of these collections was paid for by state and federal funds to help the Nevada State Museum meet its NAGPRA inventory deadline. Each skeleton in the collection, in addition to being dated, was fully inventoried in order to assess cultural and biological affiliation with the many Native American tribes that have occupied the mountains, deserts, and marsh lakes of the state.[19] One surprise for the Nevada State Museum staff was that several of their previously unassuming "Late Archaic" skeletons and mummies produced ^{14}C ages falling in either the Terminal Pleistocene or earliest Archaic ($10\,600$–9000 yr BP) periods. Once the media heard of these "new discoveries," they became big news, setting the stage for the limelight shone on the discovery of the Kennewick remains.

Fishbone Cave, NV

Fishbone Cave is one of many caves located in the dry Winnemucca Lake area of southwest Pershing County, Nevada. The site was recorded and reported by P. C. Orr (1965), and is in the same general area as the Wizard's Beach (Pyramid Lake) remains. The site contained fragmentary post-cranial human bones of a single prehistoric individual of unknown age or sex in association with cultural remains dating to about the same time as late Clovis or early Folsom in the southern plains (*c.* 11 200–10 900 yr BP) (Orr, 1956, 1962).

Grimes Burial Shelter (26CH01c), NV

Grimes Burial Shelter is located in Churchill County, Nevada, near the Spirit Cave site and was found to contain a human subadult skeleton (AHUR-743) of indeterminate sex. This skeleton is that of an older child/ adolescent, 10 to 12 years of age at death based on the pattern of dental eruption (Powell and Neves, 1998). Like the other Nevada skeletons discussed in this chapter, the Grimes Burial Shelter skeleton was originally thought to date to the Late Holocene or Middle Archaic period, but produced a radiometric age of 9700 ± 80 yr BP. Carbonate in the site deposits that held this young person's mortal remains has produced a radiometric age of 9470 ± 60 yr BP (UCR-3477) (Dixon, 1999: 133; Nelson, 1998: 155).

Spirit Cave, NV

Like the Grimes Cave skeleton, this well-preserved human mummy (AHUR-743) dubbed the "Spirit Cave Man" was considered to be only 1000 to 2000 years old at the time it was discovered and excavated in 1940, along with remains at nearby Grimes Burial Shelter. Total amino acids from Spirit Cave Man's bone collagen revealed an age of 9430 ± 60 yr BP (URC-3260/CAMS-12352). This body is, without a doubt, the best preserved of the First American remains, right down to his hair and the nits in it,[20] leather moccasins, rabbit-skin blanket, and sage-filled burial mats which form a burial bundle (a mortuary form typical of Archaic foragers in the region). In addition to the mummified body, the site produced a contemporaneous cremation representing one or two persons and dated to 9040 yr BP. The Spirit Cave mummy bundle was placed on the man's right side with his legs and arms very tightly flexed. His intestines contained the tiny bones of many minnow-sized fish, which represented his final meal.

The Nevada State Museum (NSM) produced a highly accurate epoxy resin cast of the Spirit Cave Man's skull. CAT-scan data were then used to allow the skull dimensions to be recorded without added error from overlying soft tissues or inadvertent damage to those tissues from craniometric calipers. This established that he was 35 to 40 years of age at death. His teeth showed signs of an unusually abrasive diet for a forager of his age; the dental wear may have led to multiple abscessed teeth and severe periodontal disease. In fact, he was in poor overall health, suffering from a partly healed pre-mortem fracture of the right wrist, a small ("hairline") fracture on the left side of the skull[21] with accompanying damage and blood clots in the associated tissues over the impact site, and arthritic degeneration and osteophytic growth in several vertebrae, indicative of extrusion (herniation) of the inter-vertebral disk.

Cranial and dental dimensions from the Spirit Cave skeleton were recorded by Steele and Powell and Ozolins, and later assessed by Powell and Neves (1999) and Steele and Powell (1999). These research-ers came to the same basic conclusions about the Spirit Cave as Jantz and Owsley (1997), who recorded the material independently. The Spirit Cave Man's dolichocranic (long, narrow) cranium, high nar-row orbits, and low face make it morphometrically similar to skulls of some Sundadont southern Asian groups (*sensu* Steele and Powell, 1992, 1999; described by Brace and Hunt, 1990), especially the Ainu of Japan (Jantz and Owsley, 1997: 82; Powell and Neves, 1999). Several native American tribes in the area made NAGPRA claims based on the antiquity and geographic proximity to their traditional lands. The US Bureau of Land Management, the federal agency responsible for the Spirit Cave Man's remains, made a statement that "There is no bio-logical information available at this time, given the state of current scientific technology, methodology and theoretical framework, which would allow the assignment of Spirt Cave Man to an affiliation with a particular tribe. There is no available biological information which clearly supports cultural continuity with contemporary North American Indians. The biological information does not indicate that there is, 'a relationship of shared group identity which can reasonably be traced historically or prehistorically between members of the present-day Indian tribe … and an identifiable early group,' as required by NAGPRA. No biological findings to date indicate by a 'preponderance of the evidence' that there is 'affiliation' of Spirit Cave Man to an affiliation with a particular tribe" Barker *et al.* (2000: 64). The remains, including Spirit Cave Man, will therefore remain in federal ownership and protection. The importance of the scientific analyses and results carried out on the remains played a key role in the federal agency's decision to keep the Spirit Cave Man's body in receivership.

Wizards Beach (26 WA1605), NV

The Wizards Beach site is associated with Pyramid Lake in Washoe County, just west of dry Winnemucca Lake, Nevada, on the Pyramid Lake Indian Reservation. The skull was discovered in 1978, on a small ancient beach exposed by low water levels in Pyramid Lake. Wizards Beach Man's skull had been only partly buried in beach deposits along the sagittal plane. The left side of the skull is stained a dark brown to black, while the right side is sun-bleached to a dull ivory color. The right side also exhibits surface exfoliation from either solar or water weathering, with numerous small flakes (spalls) of bone having exfoliated from the right side of the frontal bone, right parietal bone, and right temporal bone. The skeleton is that of a man in his mid to late 40s with extremely poor dental health, numerous periapical and gingival abscesses, and extreme periodontal disease. The rather mesocranic brain case of the Wizards Beach skull and his broad, flat cheeks (zygoma), tall projecting nose, and overall robust appearance are a good morphometric match to either east Asian populations or North American natives (Steele and Powell, 1999), a pattern noted by other researchers (Nelson, 1998).

Rocky Mountains and foothills

Gordon Creek, CO

The Gordon Creek Woman, like so many of her ancient compatriots, was initially misidentified as a male (Breternitz *et al.*, 1971: 174), as noted by Anderson (1966). Initially the woman had been coated with red ocher and placed on her left side in a flexed position in a burial pit with her head to the north, along with several artifacts, including a smooth grinding stone, two bifaces, a few flakes, and a hammerstone (Breternitz *et al.*, 1971).

A reanalysis of the body by a group of anthropologists who were not part of the original study team identified her correct sex (see Swedlund and Anderson, 1999), and produced a conventional ^{14}C age from acid-insoluble organic compounds in her bones, which resulted in an age of 9700 ± 250 yr BP (GX-0530). A 1987 reanalysis of the Gordon Creek remains (Swedlund and Anderson, 1999) suggested a new ^{14}C age of 9400 ± 120 yr BP, consistent with the first age assessment by Breternitz and colleagues (1971). The Gordon Creek Woman's craniofacial appearance is like many other skeletons from this period.

Buhl, ID

In 1989, a human skeleton was discovered during operations at a rock quarry near the town of Buhl in southern Idaho. A radiocarbon age obtained from an unknown piece of bone using total acid-insoluble organics (collagen and other organic material not removed during sample processing) was 10 625 ± 95 yr BP (BETA-430055/ETH-7729) (Taylor, 1994: table 2). The remains were those of yet another late teen to early adult, 17 to 21 years of age at death. Her teeth were fairly worn, suggesting a diet high in grit, which might be expected from someone eating lots of cooked meat, fish, and other soft materials pounded into a pemmican or jerky (Green et al., 1998).

The Buhl Woman was accompanied by an unused obsidian biface placed just under the skull, and the eyelet of a bone needle, similar to the one found with the Horn Shelter juvenile. A radiograph (X-ray) of the young woman's femora reveals several Harris lines in the bone indicative of periodical (seasonal?) physiological or nutritional stress since adolescence. According to the researchers who examined the Buhl skeleton, the placement of the obsidian biface is an indication that the body had been intentionally buried (Green et al., 1998).

Green et al.'s (1998) analyses of the woman's craniometric data showed that the Buhl Woman's cranial shape was similar to that of living Native Americans and living east Asians (Japanese, Chinese, Siberians). However, Neves and Blum's (2000) reanalysis of the published cranial measurements determined that the Buhl skeleton's measurements were completely unlike those of native peoples anywhere in the western hemisphere. Neves and Blum performed complex multivariate analyses in their assessment, which indicated that the woman's craniofacial shape was more similar to southeast Asians, Africans, and aboriginal Australians. This result indicated that the earliest Americans were derived from two waves of Pleistocene population expansion, originating in Asia and moving into the New World during the Late Pleistocene, a view which has yet to be independently substantiated by solid archaeological evidence.

Pacific Northwest

Kennewick, WA

Because this skeleton was discussed at length in the Prologue, I shall provide only a brief summary of this First American. As noted in many places in this chapter, Kennewick Man is not the oldest human skeleton in the Americas, but it is important because of its completeness, and also just because each new skeleton helps to fill in our picture of the First Americans.

Kennewick Man's mortal remains had been badly damaged prior to their 1997 recovery on the bank of the Columbia River. The skeleton was that of a middle-aged (40–45-year-old) male with a considerable amount of dental wear and some moderate dental disease, in addition to a possible minor fracture to the left side of the skull and some arthritic degeneration to some joints. The most amazing traumatic lesion was the presence of an Early Archaic stone projectile point embedded in the right iliac blade. According to Powell and Rose (1999):

> There would have been no organ damage, minimal muscle damage, and no major blood vessels would have been severed. Considerable force would have been needed for the point to penetrate the bone so deeply. The stone dart point's tip was facing to Kennewick's ventral (belly) side, suggesting the weapon entered from behind and just barely missed penetrating the right kidney, which would have been a fatal wound. The bony defect containing the projectile point was smooth internally suggesting that this trauma occurred earlier in Kennewick Man's life, and was not a perimortem fatal wound as some suggest (Chatters, 2000). This conclusion was supported by some of our colleagues who participated in the later assessment of taphonomic features in the Kennewick remains.

"Stick Man," WA

Very little is known about the archaeological context of this lone calvarium from an adult male, except that it is supposedly from somewhere in south-central Washington state and currently resides in the collections of a northwest US museum or other institution (Chatters, 2000).[22] The "Stick Man" is so named because the calvarial fragments were glued together and supported using wooden matchsticks. The calvarium has no currently known archaeological provenance except that described by Chatters (2000). The Stick Man calvarium is suspected by some anthropologists to be the proposed 10 300-year-old calvarium from Lyon's

Ferry, Washington. As with so many skeletons suggested to be ancient, Chatter's primary basis for the age given is the long and low (dolicho-cephalic) neurocranium, together with a low frontal bone, a combination of features that is atypical for native peoples in that area of the north-west. The antiquity of "Stick Man" seems to be based on its "non-native" appearance, which is in fact similar to that of the Kennewick skeleton. Such features are not commonly seen in Native Americans of the north-west coast, whose crania *tend* to be brachycranic with high frontal bones.

Prince of Wales Island, AK

Originally, this site, a small cave located on a rocky rise on Prince of Wales Island, Alaska, was dubbed "On Your Knees" Cave, because the investiga-tors had to crawl into the cave's tiny entrance on hands and knees. The cave appeared to be an abandoned bear den because of the large number of Holocene-age faunal remains recovered by the investigators.

The fragmentary skeleton of an older adult male was nearly edentulous. His remains were found in a muck-filled crevice at the base of a small ledge during a site survey by E. J. Dixon, T. Heaton, and coworkers. The purpose of the survey was to find evidence of Clovis-age occupation of the Pacific Northwest coastline to prove that a coastal migration route might have some plausible archaeological evidence (Dixon, 1999). The AMS radiocarbon date from XAD-treated gelatin (collagen) from this man's skeleton produced a ^{14}C age of 9730 ± 60 yr BP (CAMS-29837).

Valley of Mexico

Peñon Woman

The "Peñon Woman III," like Spirit Cave Man, has been sitting in Mexico City's National Museum of Anthropology since her initial recovery near the Mexico City airport in 1959. Since 2001, anthropologist Sylvia Gonzales has been radiocarbon dating suspected ancient human remains in the Museum's collections. She found that this one female skeleton from the Valley of Mexico dated to older than 13 000 yr BP, like all other skeletons of the First Americans. Based on photographs in the press and Dr. Gonzales' descriptions, Peñon Woman III has a long, low brain case with a long, narrow face similar to other skeletons in North America. In her analyses, Gonzales found a morphological similarity of the skull to the Ainu people of Japan and attributes this result to a common ancestry between the First Americans and ancient southern Asians like the Jomon and their Ainu descendants.

Tepexpan, Mexico

"Tepexpan Man," along with several other "Clovis" skeletons in Mexico, has been gunned down by AMS radiocarbon dating. Once thought to be 11 000 yr BP, because of an association with mammoth bones, we now know the human remains at Tepexpan to be those of a Late Archaic person with a ^{14}C age (from total organics in (see AQ77c7) the bones) of less than 2000 yr BP (Owen, 1984; Taylor, 1992). Because it is always listed as being among the oldest human skeletons in Mexico despite being Late Archaic in age, it still holds a place as being historical among early American remains, and I shall briefly describe it here.

The Tepexpan skeleton was found in 1949 by paleontologist Helmut de Terra, who was using a mine detector[23] to search for Pleistocene-age sites along the north shore of Lake Texcoco in the Valley of Mexico. The human skeleton was very near the bones of a mammoth, and was interred in a tightly flexed position. Owen (1984) suggested that the skeleton is intrusive in the Becerra deposits and is not ancient at all; this has subsequently been proven to be absolutely correct (Taylor, 1992: table 25.5).

The Tepexpan skull represents an adult male, probably 35 to 50+ years of age at death, based on suture closure and dental loss patterns. The mandible is robust, with a square chin and 90° (vertical) gonial angle, with strong eversion, and large mastoids. However, like many other First American males, the browridge is not very pronounced, and *unlike* most Paleoindians, regardless of sex, the Tepexpan face is broad, short, and orthognathic (flat faced), with a broad, nonprojecting nose, and the neurocranium is somewhat brachycranic. These features are more typical of modern Native American peoples in the Valley of Mexico. The Tepexpan skeleton's most striking feature is the very poor state of his dentition, with heavily worn lower teeth, periodontal disease, and a nearly edentulous maxilla and distal mandible. The skeleton is housed in the collections of the Instituto Nacional de Antropología y História (INAH, National Institute of Anthropology and History).

Tlapacoya XVIII, Mexico

Lorenzo and Miriambell (1999) reported other ancient human remains in Mexico. In 1968, a fragmentary adult human cranium was located out of archaeological context in the vicinity of the Paleoindian-age site of Tlapacoya XVIII in Mexico (Lorenzo and Miriambell, 1999). This skeleton was described as a robust person (male?) with a dolichocranic neurocranium, and may be associated with deposits dating to 9730 and 9920 ± 250 yr BP (Dixon, 1999: 140). A second, more complete, brachy-cranic cranium was discovered in later excavations of site deposits dating to 9920 ± 250 yr BP (I-6897).

7.3   ANCIENT SKELETONS IN SOUTH AMERICA

Pacific coast

Paijan Woman, Moche Valley, Peru

Peru has a very rich prehistory ranging from complex Archaic shell-fishers of the northern coastal area to the agriculture-based high civilizations of the Altiplano region (Moche, Inka). Although numerous Paleoindian sites have been located in Peru, only two localities, to the best of my knowledge, have produced ancient human remains.

The Paijan culture is the earliest identified cultural complex in Peru. It is contemporaneous with Folsom culture in North America but differs in being characterized by a thin, stemmed and shouldered projectile point (a "Paijan point") and by large numbers of small razor-like unifacial flakes (Ossa, 1978). The Paijan Complex is associated with megafauna kills and dates from about 11 000 to 10 500 yr BP, although dates as old as 12 795 ± 350 yr BP to as young as 8645 ± 370 yr BP (Ossa, 1978: 293) have been derived from charcoal in hearths that contained such points.

Chauchat and Dricot (1979) discovered the skeletal remains of an adult female of indeterminate age in association with the remains of Pleistocene fauna (mastodon) in an open air location along the slopes of the Moche Valley, near the site of la Cumbre. This human skeleton was described as an adult (20–50 years of age) female whose cranium was extremely dolichocephalic and less robust than the Punin skull (Ecuador) and was quite similar to the ancient skulls from the Lagoa Santa sites in Brazil (Chauchat and Dricot, 1979).

Quirhuac, Peru

This Moche Valley site is an enormous rockshelter that has a large Paijan occupation floor. Two burial features were found originating from the Paijan surface of the shelter, very near the drip line (Blocks I3 and H3).

One burial contained the skeletal remains of an adult (20–50 years of age at death) of unspecified sex, along with teeth from a second adult, near the skull of the first (Ossa, 1978: 293). The second burial feature contained the remains of a subadult. The adult skeleton provided a radiocarbon age of 9930 ± 820 yr BP; the subadult's radiocarbon age was 9020 ± 650 yr BP (Ossa, 1978: 293). No other information about these ancient remains is available, including their current curatorial location.

The average of "acceptable" (i.e. uncontaminated) ^{14}C ages ($n = 8$ conventional dates) at the Quirhuac site, including bone collagen from the burials, was 10 650 ± 180 yr BP. This average age is consistent with the ages of other Paijan Complex sites in northern Peru.

Ecuador

Otavalo skeleton, Ecuador

Once in a while, this skeleton is cited in texts or articles dealing with South American pre-Clovis, so I shall include it among the many other "dating mistakes" described in this section. British zoologist David M. Davies (1978: 273) describes the discovery in this way: "While looking on the shelves of a museum belonging to the Technical University in Quito, Ecuador, I noticed a lump of 'conglomerate' out of which was protruding a human rib … " Three other lumps of breccia were located in the museum, each of which produced portions of the same partially fossilized skeletal individual. Davies, after contacting the museum staff about his discovery, then accompanied zoology professor Orcez Villagomez to visit the original site, just north of the city of Quito. Radiocarbon ages from the breccia deposits clinging to the bone produced fantastically old ages (as one might expect) from the sample carbonates, ranging from 29 023 ± 1800 to >36 000 yr BP. However, direct dates on bone collagen placed the Otavalo skeleton in the Early Ceramic period at 2300 yr BP (Taylor, 1992), not even Archaic by today's standards (Davies, 1978; Roosevelt et al., 2002: 181).

Punin, Ecuador

This site, located on the high plateau of Ecuador (Andean highlands), was explored in 1923 by an American Museum of Natural History team. The Punin skull was the Kennewick man of its day, owing to claims by several authorities (the British Museum's Sir Arthur Keith and Harvard's Ernest Hooton among them) that it, like most Lagoa Santa ancient skeletons, such as the recent Luzia skull, had strong similarity to native peoples of Australia owing to its exceptionally pronounced supraorbital robusticity and alveolar prognathism. This similarity came to be accepted in scientific circles as "strong" evidence for the point of origin for Native Americans in South America (Gladwin, 1947). Modern physical anthropologists have rarely heard of the Ecuadorian Punin skeleton.

The Punin skeleton was recovered, like so many South American human remains, in direct association with extinct Pleistocene mega-fauna (horse, glyptodon, and ground sloth, etc.) and was presumed to be at least 10 000 to 12 000 years old – which may be the case, because no radiometric dating of the cranium has ever been conducted. The Punin skull was found in a fossiliferous bed of partially consolidated volcanic ash and rock and belonged to an older adult female (45–50+ years of age).

Amazon Basin, Brazil

Many North American archaeologists seem to assume that because of shallow acid soils leading to poor preservation, and poor accessibility for site surveys, the Amazon Basin and floodplain have produced relatively few Paleoindian sites, let alone skeletal remains of the First Americans. This is not the case. While it is true that no true Clovis sites have been found, nor any Folsom archaeological sites south of the isthmus of Panama, South America has its own unique and diverse stemmed and triangular projectile points dating to pre-10 000 yr BP within Brazil, Chile, and Uruguay. These sites are similar in many ways to post-Folsom (*Archaic*) stemmed point traditions in the USA, but many of these points in South America are associated with radiocarbon dates as old, or older, than Clovis.

Pleistocene human occupation appears to be limited to the limestone escarpment forming the southern margin of the Amazon floodplain. This is not to say that ancient peoples did not occupy closed canopy tropical forests in South America. In fact, there are early triangular and stemmed points recovered from the lower Amazon, Rio Negra, and Rio Cuua, as well as the Rio Sao Francisco. Radiocarbon-dated sites (some containing human remains) at these localities have produced ^{14}C ages ranging from 11 200 to 10 000 yr BP (Roosevelt *et al.*, 2002). However, in nearly all of South America, including portions of the Amazon, we do see "evidence of a near instantaneous radiation of people throughout the hemisphere soon after 12 000 years ago"

(Roosevelt *et al.*, 2002: 202), which surely must have included late Pleistocene tropical areas in South America.

Southeast Brazil and the Southern Cone

Eastern Brazil (cerradão forest)

The Lagoa Santa plateau of the state of Minas Gerais is located in southeast Brazil. The site is in an area currently covered in rocky grassland fields and dry savanna forest (Neves *et al.*, 1999a) and is sprinkled with caves and rockshelters in the ubiquitous limestone outcrops in this region. Most of these shelters and caves served as habitation and mortuary locales during the Terminal Pleistocene through the Late Archaic periods (12 000–3000 yr BP). The sites are filled with several styles of red or black rock art depicting human figures spearing or darting Pleistocene megafauna such as ground sloth or glyptodon (a giant armadillo-like animal) and mastodon, as well as more modern prey.

Santana do Riacho ("Saint Ann of the Creek") I

This site is part of a complex of four Paleoindian and Early Archaic sites along a narrow river valley near Cerro do Cipó in Minas Gerais. The four rockshelters contain a total of 1500 individual rock art panels among them, most depicting daily living scenes (animals, hunting, travel, human copulation, etc.) or abstract geometric designs.

Lagoa Santa sites

Lapa Vermelha

A Paleoindian skeleton was discovered here in 1975, at the site of Lapa Vermelha IV, one of a series of Archaic-period rockshelter sites recorded by the Franco-Brazilian archaeological mission of the early 1970s under the leadership of the late Annette Laming-Emperaire. The mission's work continues under the direction of her student Dr. André Prous. The rockshelter of Lapa Vermelha IV is located in the Lagoa Santa region, in the state of Minas Gerais, central Brazil, and is part of a karst complex of caves, shelters, and underground rivers (Laming-Emperaire *et al.*, 1975). The archaeological excavation of Lapa Vermelha IV started in 1971 but was abruptly interrupted in 1976 with the death of Dr. Laming-Emperaire (Prous, 1986, 1991). For this reason, the published material regarding the site is poor or completely lacking (Laming-Emperaire *et al.*, 1975; Laming-Emperaire, 1979; Prous, 1986). The Lapa Vermelha IV rockshelter was filled by a thick layer of Pleistocene and Holocene deposits extending from the present to as old as 22 410 yr BP. Deposits dating to about 11 000 yr BP contain evidence of human occupation of the site, which includes structured hearths and flaked quartz tools (Dillehay *et al.*, 1992; Prous, 1980, 1986, 1991; Schmitz, 1984, 1987). Bones of a giant sloth (*Glossoterium gigas*) were found in deposits as deep as 11 m, and date to 9580 ± 200 yr BP (Laming-Emperaire, 1979). A single human skeleton was recovered during the 1975 excavation, in a stratum below the sloth bones.

Approximately 2 m below the bones of the giant sloth, unarticulated remains of a human skeleton were found bracketed by two archaeological levels which produced radiocarbon ages on associated charcoal of 11 600 and 12 960 yr BP, respectively. Although Laming-Emperaire (1979) and Prous (1986) described the skeleton as an *in situ* intentional interment, Cunha and Mello e Alvim (1971) questioned its stratigraphic positioning in the shelter's deposits simply because the bones were not found in complete articulation. Direct dating of bone collagen was impossible to obtain owing to poor bone preservation (Stafford, personal communication, 1997). However, an AMS date on total organics after an acid wash preparation of the sample resulted in a *minimum* age of 9330 ± 60 yr BP (Beta-84439), placing the Lapa Vermelha skeleton between approximately 11 000 and 12 000 cal yr BP.

Professor Walter Neves (University of São Paulo) and I conducted an analysis of the Lapa Vermelha Woman (whom Dr. Neves named Luzia ["Lucy"]), in reference to the oldest hominid in Africa. We concluded that all of the bones belonged to a single individual, a female aged between 20 and 25 years at death, confirming a previous independent assessment carried out by Alvim (1977). Her neurocranium is dolichocephalic and she presents extreme alveolar prognathism similar to other female first American skeletons, such as those found at Pelican Rapids, Warm Mineral Spring ("Brown" skull), and Wilson–Leonard.

Luzia's nasal aperture is broad, like Wilson–Leonard Woman, and her facial reproduction (Figure 7.4) is also quite similar to that of the Wilson–Leonard Woman, making both of them appear similar to living subtropical peoples from Africa, Australasia, and Polynesia rather than Native Americans of North or South America. Luzia's craniofacial morphology is similar to the facial configuration of the

Yanomamö, Mikiritare, and other Native American tribes of the tropical Orinoco Basin in the northern Amazon, who also present broad noses, wide faces, and long, low crania (Neel *et al.*, 1974). The multivariate analyses of Luzia's craniofacial morphology confirm the Australian morphology, although Dr. Neves has theoretical reasons to prefer the African comparison (Neves *et al.*, 1998).

Cerca Grande 6 and 7

These two large rockshelters were discovered by Swedish paleontologist Johannes Lund in the late nineteenth century, and excavated by Wesley Hurt (1960) in the late 1950s and early 1960s. The sites are very similar in configuration to others in the Lagoa Santa area, but contain only ten fairly complete skeletons (with complete crania) and many other fragmentary human remains, all in association with the remains of extinct megafauna. Lund removed many of the human remains, which are simply labeled as "Lagoa Santa," to museums in Europe. My colleague Walter Neves (University of São Paulo) has examined all the Lund collection materials, and together we examined the remains excavated by Hurt (1960), which are still housed at the Museu Nacional do Rio de Janeiro (National Museum in Rio de Janeiro).[24] This collection is remarkable for having fragmentary skulls whose morphology is fairly uniform, with faces (male and female) that present extreme alveolar prognathism and long, low, dolichocranic neurocrania. While there are several Cerca Grande shelters, only Abrigos ("shelters") 6 and 7 date to the Early Archaic or terminal Pleistocene, the others (1–5) are Late Archaic (1200–1000 yr BP) in age. The radiocarbon ages from human bone collagen samples in Abrigo 6 remain ranged between 9028 and 9720 yr BP, with a median age of 9374 yr BP, and the median human bone collagen radiocarbon age for Abrigo 7 was 9130 yr BP (Hurt, 1960; Powell and Neves, 1999: table 1).

Southern Chile

Monte Verde

This is perhaps the most controversial Paleoindian site in South America, because of its purported pre-Clovis dates and unusual wooden artifacts and odd feature assemblage (mammoth skin huts). There are only fragmentary post-cranial human remains recovered from this site, but there is, however, an undeniable human footprint with easily identifiable plantar dermatoglyphs impressed in the wet sediments at Monte Verde (Dillehay *et al.*, 1992).

Patagonia

Fell's Cave, Chile

This is a large cave with charcoal-filled hearths on prehistoric living surfaces that date to $11\,000 \pm 170$ yr BP (Bird, 1938a; Roosevelt *et al.*, 2002; Turner and Bird, 1981: 1053). Bird (1938a) notes that during the terminal Pleistocene there was a massive roof collapse at Fell's Cave, probably brought about by the frequent seismic and volcanic activity that occurs in the Chico Basin of southern Patagonia (Bird, 1938b).[25] No human remains were discovered within Fells Cave, although some megafaunal remains, such as giant ground sloth (*Milodon tistai*) and American horse (*Parahipparlum saldasi*), were in the Late Pleistocene deposits, and appear to have been used as food resources (Bird, 1938a).

Cerro Sota Cave II, Chile

This Patagonian cave in the Chico basin near the Ultima Esperanza (final hope) inlet produced many Pleistocene-age faunal remains. It is a lava tube, 15 m in length, which is "poorly suited for human occupation" (Turner and Bird, 1981: 1053) as a result of a less than 1 m clearance from floor to roof, and is located 30 km from Fell's Cave.

At the rear of the lava tube, Bird located and excavated (at a depth of 1 m from the 1938 cave floor) a cremation feature that contained the charred bones and teeth of a minimum of seven individuals. Among these were teeth and bones from three older (50+ years of age at death) females, two young children (2–5 years of age), and two infants (0–2 years of age). The unusual demographics of this feature suggested that all of these people were killed in a single catastrophic event and that Cerro Sota Cave was a mortuary locale for the Fell's Cave occupants killed by the roof collapse. Bird (1938a) also suggested that the demographic composition of the cremation suggested that the deceased were those typically left behind at a forager base camp (the very old and very young) while gathering and hunting parties consisted of younger adult males and females and their older children. The pattern is consistent with ethnographic observations of modern forager hunting and gathering parties (Kelley, 1995). Unfortunately, "the skeletons were so badly burned and broken that ante-mortem injuries could not be assessed" (Turner and Bird, 1981: 1053). The complete cranium from this locality exhibits certain morphological features similar to other ancient New World skeletons and a few atypical features. The neurocranium of Cerro Sota 2 is extremely dolichocephalic, with a bulging occiput, a gracile supraorbital region, a gracile but wide face, and extreme orthognathism. The latter feature is atypical of other North and South American Paleoindians. Many of the above are characteristic of female crania. Turner and Bird's (1981) analysis of dental morphology was consistent with the northeast Asian Sinodont dental pattern, as is true with the remains at nearby Pali Aike Cave.

Pali Aike, Chile

This Patagonian cave is a remnant of the wall of an old volcano. Bird found the cave floor littered with ash and charcoal from numerous large hearth features scattered across the cave floor. Along with the hearth features, the cave floor was littered with "Period 1" (Paleoindian to Early Archaic) artifacts. Amidst the bones of horse, guanaco, and ground sloth was a scattered and disorganized cremation containing the charred remains of five individuals – two adults and one adolescent (10–15 years of age at death), all of indeterminate sex, along with remains of two 2–10-year-old children of indeterminate sex. Although these remains have no stratigraphic context, Turner and Bird (1981) assumed that the cremations and hearths were contemporaneous and dated them both with the 11 000 yr BP date from the hearths, which may or may not be a correct assumption. Based on the tooth crowns present in this cremation assemblage, Turner and Bird felt that there was adequate evidence to conclude that the Pali Aike individuals were all Sinodont and thus similar to the remains at Cerro Sota Cave. The pooled Pali Aike–Cerro Sota (Chilean) sample of Paleoindian teeth also suggested to Turner and Bird that these ancient people were likely to be the ancestors of "all modern Native peoples in the Americas" (Turner and Bird, 1981: 1054).

7.4 CONCLUSIONS

An interesting pattern emerges from the Paleoindian skeletons themselves. There seem to be First American skeleton recovery "hot spots" – Texas and the southern Plains (Shifting Sands, Horn Shelter, Midland, Wilson–Leonard, and Seminole Sink), southeastern Brazil (Lapa

Vermelha, Santana do Riacho, Cerca Grande Abrigos 6 and 7), north-west plateau (Buhl, Kennewick, and Stick), and central and southern Florida (Cutler Ridge, Warm Mineral Spring, Little Salt Spring, and Windover). Such regional clustering may reflect a wide range of factors, such as site visibility (rock art and huge shelters in Minas Gerais and Lagoa Santa), past environments that were attractive to the First American foragers and hunters, site taphonomy and preservation, and cultural beliefs (Florida Spring sites), as well as pure luck (Punin, Kennewick) and good science (AMS re-dating of suspected ancient remains, such as Wizards Beach and Spirit Cave). An alternative is that this part of Brazil has received more attention from archaeological surveys (1805–2003) and for a longer time than most regions of the country.

Many of the female Paleoindians so far found died in their late teens and early 20s, but because no infants were discovered lodged in their birth canals, there is no conclusive evidence that these represent childbirth-related deaths. Such younger females may also have died from uncontrolled post-partum bleeding or from a wide range of pathogenic causes. Many of the adult Paleoindians have Harris lines or enamel hypoplastic defects typically associated with periodic or seasonal stress or disease (Powell and Steele, 1993). Some of these First Americans died from accidental causes, as may be the case at the Cerro Sota site and Little Salt Spring. Pre-mortem inter-personal violence *may* have been a common occurrence among the First Americans, for example, Kennewick seems to have been the victim of both blunt and sharp trauma, while Spirit Cave Man has indications of blunt trauma to the skull.

Finally, and most importantly, is the observation by several independent researchers (Chatters *et al.*, 1999; Jantz and Owsley, 1997, 2001; Neves and Pucciarelli, 1991, 1998; Neves *et al.*, 1998, 1999a, 1999b; Powell and Neves, 1999; Steele and Powell, 1993; and many others) that few or no ancient American skeletons look like modern Native Americans. Many of the oldest crania and skulls are similar to one another, with strong lower facial (alveolar) prognathism and dolichocranic neurocrania (Wilson–Leonard, Buhl, Luzia, Santana do Riacho, Cerca Grande 6-VI) a combination of morphological features common among Upper Paleolithic peoples in eastern Europe, northern Egypt, and southern Asia (Hao São, Vietnam). This is not to say that they are Caucasoids, or Vietnamese, but that these groups tend to have some degree of facial narrowness (see Steele and Powell, 1992). They are also characterized as having dolichocranic neurocrania, much like ancient and modern Australians and Melanesians. Some ancient Americans (Luzia, Wilson–Leonard, Santana do Riacho) have broad noses like modern neotropical populations in Africa, Polynesia, and Southeast Asia. These commonalities may reflect adaptation, growth and development, other environmental effects (Powell, 1995), or new genes entering populations through mutation, through a distinct founder population at the initial human colonization of the Americas, or by in-migration from an external population, and subsequently increasing in frequency (Neves *et al.*, 1998).

In later chapters, I shall discuss how the First Americans express a dental morphological pattern intermediate between Sinodonts and Sundadonts. They all seem to have teeth with a unique dental morphological pattern specific to the first colonizers of the Americas (Powell, 1995; Powell and Neves, 1999).

Many First Americans are interred in or near permanent water sources, either by intent or accident. Most have ^{14}C ages corresponding to the sudden onset of an abrupt period of Late Pleistocene–Holocene cooling and aridity known as the Younger Dryas stadial (13 000–9000 yr BP), which may have affected nasal morphology through evolutionary processes. A certain number have grave goods or archaeological contexts of intentional burial (Anzick, Buhl, Browns Valley, Cerca Grande, Fells Cave, Gordon Creek, Lapa Vermelha, Pelican Rapids, Spirit Cave, Warm Mineral Spring, Wizards Beach, and, possibly, Kennewick). Many of the Paleoindian burial sites were reused by Archaic peoples during later periods (e.g. the Windover site, Little Salt Spring, Cerca Grande 6 and 7, and Santana do Riacho I are all Late Paleoindian or Early Archaic cemeteries). A high proportion of the Paleoindians found so far are also subadults (Dixon, 1999: table 5.1).

Most of the more recent Paleoindian skeletons seem to have belonged to individuals who had a lifestyle similar to the generalized foragers seen today (for example the !Kung San of the Kalahari desert, Ache of Paraguay, and some traditional Inuits and Australians) and do not seem to have lived as specialized hunters (Powell and Steele, 1993).

South American rock art panels dated to 10 000–9000 yr BP depict megafaunal hunting scenes, which constitute proof of the continued hunting of large prey at this time (Prous, 1994). This suggests, perhaps, that humans were the *coup de grâce* that led to the mass extinction of megafauna at the end of the Pleistocene, but not the primary cause (as suggested by Martin, 1973). Had overkill taken place for mammoths, we would expect to see kill sites for other megafauna such as glyptodonts, ground sloth, giant beavers, and other larger mammalian species that appear to go extinct simultaneously around the world during the terminal Pleistocene (for more on the debate over Pleistocene extinctions, see Martin, 1967, 1973, 1984).

Some analyses indicate that the First Americans have a degree of biological continuity with modern Native Americans, for example at Buhl (Green *et al.*, 1998) and Wizards Beach (Jantz and Owsley, 1997). However, the majority of analyses suggest a morphological difference between these and living groups in the Americas (Jantz and Owsley, 1997, 2001; Neves *et al.*, 1998, 2003; Powell and Neves, 1999; Steele and Powell, 1993, 1999, 2002).

Early skeletons (Punin) examined by Ernest Hooton and Sir Arthur Keith elicited suggestions that the skulls were morphologically most similar to Australian and Melanesian ("Australoid") skulls. This racial classificatory approach will be considered in full detail in Chapters 9 and 10. A pattern of morphological similarity to Old World Paleolithic populations has been detected in some analyses (Neves *et al.*, 1999a; Powell and Neves, 1999; Steele and Powell, 1992). The afore-listed researchers found that the First Americans were craniometrically intermediate between southern Asians and Europeans – what Brace *et al.* (2002) refer to as a "Eurasian population." Steele and Powell (1992) and Suzuki and Tanabe (1982) called such a group a "proto-Caucasoid" or "pre-Mongoloid" population (Kamminga and Wright, 1988; Neumann, 1952; Neves and Pucciarelli, 1989, 1991; Steele and Powell, 1992, 1993).

Despite all the media hype, Kennewick Man is not the oldest New World skeleton by far. That honor belongs to one or more of the following skeletons: Anzick, Arlington Springs, or Luzia (Lapa Vermelha).[26] Skeletons traced directly to the Late Pleistocene Clovis Culture Complex include only the two subadults at Anzick, Montana, whereas human remains of the Folsom Culture Complex and its Plainview, Firstview, or Midland variants include the subadults at Shifting Sands (Folsom), "Midland Woman," and "Wilson–Leonard Woman."

NOTES

1 Yes, this does seem to be a terminological oxymoron. Similar long wooden sticks are used by modern hunter-gatherers to kill small game (such as rabbits and other small mammals). Because these "rabbit sticks" are stabilized when thrown by a spiral, they are called boomerangs. They are not aerodynamic like the boomerangs used by Australian hunter-gatherers and are thus non-returning. Rock art panels in the Lower Pecos region of Texas depict similar nonreturning boomerangs in use by Archaic period peoples.

2 If the skeletal dates are correct, the man would have been alive at the terminus of the Younger Dryas (10 500–10 200 yr BP), a very dry period in Florida, with very cold and arid conditions that lasted nearly 350 years (based on pollen records).

3 Complete with stalactite formations about 6 to 12 m below the current surface.

4 The Black skull remains were, at the time of recovery, a relatively complete skeleton of an adult male, about 30 years of age, as described in an unpublished report by Morris (1975). When I examined the WMS assemblage (1994), most of this skeleton had been accidentally mixed with skeletal collections from other sites, and it was therefore not possible to verify Morris' findings.

5 This is the only archaeological site in which I ever swam. Swimming into the cave is not recommended by the spa owners, or the Florida state archaeologist and the Department of Historic Preservation.

6 These letters are in the archives of the Smithsonian Institution; Meltzer (1993b) has written that this debate structured all research on the First Americans and the peopling of the Americas from that time to the present.

7 This raised doubts about Jenks' other claims about the skeleton, especially its antiquity.

8 According to the analyses conducted by Steele and Powell (1992) and by Neves *et al.* (1999a), Jenks and Wilford's (1938) *Homo heidelbergensis* comparison is overstating the case a bit.

9 Here, Jenks aimed for a less widely read journal (at that time) than in the Pelican Rapids and Browns Valley cases, in the wake of his public rebuke by Hrdlička in 1937. Also note Jenks' shift to an unspecified sex by calling it the "Sauk Valley Skeleton" rather than "Sauk Valley Man," as he had mistakenly done for "Minnesota Man."

10 One calvarium fragment (the older child's?) exhibited some sunbleaching because the burial had been disturbed at one point. This cranium also produced several anomalous young dates that have been discredited as products of post-disturbance contamination by young carbon (Frison, 1990: 312).

11 Some authors described this assemblage as the single largest Clovis assemblage from a site (Jones and Bonnichsen, 1994).

12 The report of the results and site report (Owsley *et al.*) are housed as an unpublished manuscript in the archives of the Plains Anthropological Society, indexed at: http://www.usd.edu/library/special/aids/AidsHtml/PAS.htm.

13 Turner (1983b) modified Suzuki's description of northeast Asian (Sinodont) and Southeast Asian and Australian (Sundadont) tooth morphology in which the Sinodonts express features of robusticity such as incisor shoveling and double shoveling. Sundadonts express less robust and more generalized morphology. These patterns are discussed at length later in this volume.

14 These are based on the fact that the cremation was densely packed in the talus cone and must have been enclosed by some type of perishable container that left no physical evidence. Fawnskin pouches containing cremated subadult remains have been recovered at Fate Bell Shelter, very near to Seminole Sink.

15 Mr. Redder had discovered and excavated many of the sites in that part of central Texas within the limits of federal and state laws; unlike most other amateur archaeologists, Al was not a "pot hunter" digging in a haphazard manner merely to recover artifacts. He was a long-time member of the Texas Archaeological Society, and his work at Horn Shelter was described by one

academic archaeologist as "impeccably detailed and better quality than that of most professionals" (M. Collins, personal communication).

16 Entitled "Results of bioarchaeological assessments of human remains from Whitewater Draw, Arizona," archived at Texas A&M University, Department of Anthropology.

17 These are anomalous only because these skeletons were found in Holocene geo-archaeological context, and/or were re-dated in the 1980s and 1990s to produce Late- to Middle Archaic ^{14}C ages; see Taylor (1991: 89–91).

18 This skeleton is perhaps one of the oldest in North America, based on calibrated radiocarbon age ($>12\,500$ cal yr BP) and is, in fact, the skeleton of a female.

19 Human remains were assigned new catalogue numbers beginning with the letters AHUR (**A**rchaeological **Hu**man **R**emains).

20 Head lice eggs visible in macroscopic examination.

21 Fracture may be associated with a depressed feature (fracture) on the left parietal bone, according to Steele's analysis of the remains.

22 Dr. James Chatters kindly provided me, and several of my students, with a chance to examine his cast of the "Stick Man" calvarium; this was much appreciated.

23 The mine detector (*circa* WWII) was a primitive version of today's ground penetrating radar, used to find buried objects.

24 By kind permission of the curator of human remains, Dr. Ricardo Santos, whose assistance is much appreciated. This research was funded by a grant to W. A. Neves and J. F. Powell from the Foundation for Investigation and Research São Paulo (FAPESP).

25 The volcanism of southern Patagonia resulted in the Spanish name that Ferdinand Magellan gave to the region: "Tierra del Fuego" ("Land of Fire"). This activity is due to the movements of the Pacific and South American plate – which are also responsible for the uplifted formation on the western side of South America, called the Andes Mountains.

26 Assuming that the ^{14}C ages are correct.

8

Human variation in the Pleistocene

8.1 WESTERN OLD WORLD

Paleoindians represented by the Clovis and Folsom forms of Upper Paleolithic cultures are part of the long history of Upper or Terminal Pleistocene peoples from across the globe. The Upper Paleolithic is typified by subsistence strategies that emphasize large-mammal hunting with spear and dart technologies in which large, elaborately produced, bifacial stone projectile points; unifacial stone flakes; or microblade[1] play a key role.

There are many Late Pleistocene–Early Holocene human (*Homo sapiens sapiens*) skeletons in the Old World. In this chapter, a few better-known Upper Paleolithic skeletal specimens have been selected, which may or may not be representative of all 18 000–10 000 yr BP human remains in that part of the globe, but for the purposes of this book they will suffice.

Africa and Egypt

Lothagam 4b, West Turkana

The Lothagam fossil locality in West Turkana, East Africa has produced over 30 fully modern human skeletons dating from 6000 yr BP to 9000 yr BP. Between 1965 and 1975, crews from Michigan State University uncovered the Lothagam locality remains. Nearly all of the skeletons were discovered in good Early Holocene contexts. Angel *et al.* (1980) performed a reconstruction and analysis of the crania. The Lothagam (lo.4b) skull was the most complete in the sample, and is described here and by Larsen *et al.* (1991: 151). Based on the documentation, photographs, and illustrations of the skull, this individual appears to be a gracile adult female with indistinct supraorbital margins set over rectangular, slightly sloping orbits, with a tall, narrow, and extremely prognathic face, a tall and relatively narrow nose, and a low and long (dolichocranic) neurocranium. Overall, this individual presents morphological features consistent with other Upper Paleolithic and Early Holocene remains in the Old World.[2]

Afalou 13, Algeria

A terminal Pleistocene–Early Holocene (12 000–8000 yr BP) cemetery located near Oued Agrioun, Algeria was excavated in 1927-8 by a French expedition (Arambourg, 1929) to North Africa. This site produced 50 anatomically modern *Homo sapiens* (AMHS)[3] individuals and represents one of the largest Late Pleistocene skeletal populations north of the Sahara Desert. The Afalou individuals are thought to be the direct ancestors of modern tribes living in North Africa (Arambourg, 1929; Larsen *et al.*, 1991: 160). The Afalou 13 skull is robust, with a narrow, moderately short, orthognathic face[4] and reduced zygoma. It possesses a brachycranic brain case, as compared with other late Pleistocene humans in Africa (Larsen *et al.*, 1991: 160).

Wadi Halfa (6B 36) burial 25, Sudan

This locality was excavated in 1963–4 by the University of Colorado expedition to Nubian Sudan led by George Armelegos and colleagues (Ewing, Green, and Saxe). The site was a Late Pleistocene–Early Holocene hunter-forager cemetery related to Epi-Paleolithic cultures in Egypt and the rest of the Middle East. The cemetery yielded 40 human skeletons, of which several were in a fairly good state of preservation, including Wadi Halfa burial 25, a very complete male skeleton with an intact skull. Like most of the skeletons in the Wadi Halfa series, burial 25 was typified by a dolichocephalic neurocranium with a large projecting *inion*[5] on the occipital. The orbits of this skull are set low on the narrow, relatively short, and projecting face, and are somewhat rectangular in shape, with a moderate-sized browridge and a well-developed glabellar region. The teeth and jaws are robust, and exhibit alveolar prognathism. The very robust mandible is large, with a blunt, square chin and strong gonial eversion. The crania of the Wadi Halfa foragers are more robust and morphologically distinct from the gracile Late Holocene (3500 yr BP) agricultural peoples interred at the late Holocene cemetery at Kerma, located several kilometers south on the Nile River. Carlson and Van Gerven (1979) studied these morphological changes in Sudanese Nubian populations, and concluded that the gracility of the Kerma remains was due to adaptive changes brought on by the shift to an agricultural diet and lifeway.

Wadi Kubbaniya, Egypt

The Wadi Kubbaniya locality (20 000–8000 yr BP) is associated with the Afian cultural complex that stretched from the first cataract (Wadi Kubbaniya) of the Nile near Aswan to just north of the Qena bend to the site of Makhadma (Wendorf and Schild, 1986). Nilitic Pleistocene-age lithic industries are typified by unifacial flakes, blades, and micro-blades, with the Afian complex artifacts (12 500–11 600 yr BP) produced on fine-grained siliceous raw materials.[6] The Nile River Valley was a hot spot for late Pleistocene forager activity, with nearly 55 recorded sites dating to between 13 000 and 11 500 yr BP, including several human cemetery sites. Butzer (1980: 272) described the Nile River during this time as having been swiftly flowing in a down-cutting stage which created a braided and sediment-filled drainage called the "Wild Nile" (Butzer, 1980).

Human responses to Late Pleistocene environmental changes[7] included the collection of wild plants.[8] Dramatic environmental upheaval may have brought about the shift from highly mobile for-aging subsistence to more sedentary horticultural and agricultural subsistence adaptation (Wendorf and Schild, 1986: 817). The shift to a post-Pleistocene sedentary lifestyle is thought to have led to population growth and concomitant difficulties such as inter-personal or inter-group conflict – evidence for this kind of social upheaval in early Egyptian populations is observed in human remains from the cemetery at Jebel Sahaba (Wendorf, 1968). This pre-dynastic site contained 59 individuals, of which 24 (40.67%) presented evidence of blunt and sharp trauma (including unhealed longbone and cranial fractures, and deep cut marks on bone and stone tools imbedded in bones of the skull). Wendorf (1968) found that the traumatic injuries were present regard-less of the age or sex of the individual. Additional evidence for post-Pleistocene social upheaval is represented on the Narmer Palette from the site of Heirakanopolis near Luxor in the central Nile drainage. The palette depicts the violent unification of Upper and Lower Egypt, complete with 11 beheaded male figures.

The Wadi Kubbaniya crania, like the Lothagam remains, have faces with extreme alveolar (lower facial) prognathism. The faces of Wadi Kubbaniya people were shorter and broad, with flaring zygomatic bones and oval to circular orbits below robust supraorbital margins, flatter upper faces, and broader nasal apertures relative to the people at Lothagam. Wadi Kubbaniya skulls are similar in overall morphology to those from nearby Wadi Halfa.

The Middle East

Jebel Qafzeh, Israel

Qafzeh VI, an adult male, is one of 15 nearly complete AMHS recovered in the mid 1930s by R. Neuville and M. Steklis in a cave near Nazareth, Israel. The Qafzeh VI burial has a very robust supraorbital region and a large nasal aperture typical of more Archaic *Homo sapiens* forms, along with the high forehead of AMHS individuals. The somewhat intermediate craniofacial features provide support for the contemporaneity and possible admixture of AMHS and Archaic *Homo sapiens* (*Homo sapiens neanderthalensis*) in the Middle East. It most likely dates to the early part of the Middle Pleistocene (100 000–95 000 yr BP) and has been a key feature in the "Out of Africa" model of human emergence (Stringer, 1988).[9] The other remains from the site are probably Upper Pleistocene in age (50 000–20 000 yr BP) (Larsen *et al.*, 1991: 151). Qafzeh III and V are more gracile than Qafzeh VI. Radiometric ages, mostly electron spin resonance (ESR) or uranium series ages, consistently place the Jebel Qafzeh site and fossils in a range from 100 000 or 90 000 yr BP to 30 000 yr BP (Smith and Spencer, 1984).

Europe

Europe contains many human remains dating to the Middle to Late Pleistocene. Two such individuals are described below.

Cro-Magnon, France

The skeleton from this locality of Les Eyzies, Dordogne Province, France, is perhaps the best known Late Pleistocene-age (27 000–23 000 yr BP) skeleton. The cranial morphology is common to most Terminal Pleistocene–Early Holocene human remains in the Old and New World. Better known to paleoanthropologists as "the Old Man" of Cro-Magnon, the most striking features of this skull are his edentulous mandible and maxillae, which also have significant alveolar thinning, presumably due to extreme periodontal disease. The Old

Man's high vertical forehead and broad, high face are unmistakable signs of his taxonomic membership of *Homo sapiens sapiens*, as is his date range of 27 000–23 000 yr BP. According to Larsen *et al.* (1991: 162) Cro-Magnon also presents a nasal bone and nasal aperture configuration typical of western European Archaic *Homo* specimens (cf. La-Chapelle-aux-Saints).

Predmost 3, Czech Republic (formerly Czechoslovakia)

This 26 000 yr BP site produced 26 human skeletons during an 1894 excavation by K. J. Maska. The Predmost 3 skeleton possesses a skull with a very prognathic lower face; well-developed browridge; a robust and well-developed chin; a tall narrow face; horizontally oriented, sloping, rectangular orbits; a long, narrow (dolichocranic) neurocranium; and a high vault (Figure 8.1). The Predmost remains were destroyed by the Nazis along with Late Pleistocene remains from the Mladic fossil locality.

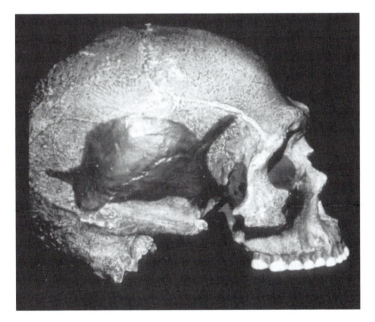

Figure 8.1 Lateral view of the Late Pleistocene Predmost 3 skull from the Czech Republic (formerly Czechoslovakia). Courtesy of Dr. Erik Trinkaus, Washington University.

8.2   EASTERN OLD WORLD

China

Lower Cave, Zhoukoudian I (Chokoutien I), Hopei Province

This fossil locality is a large rockshelter in the foothills of the Tai Hang Shan Mountains that was originally investigated by paleoanthropologist Franz Weidenreich (1943) (see also Woo, 1959; Wu and Lin, 1983). This site, and others in the area, contained remains of *Homo erectus* (Weidenreich, 1943), also called "Peking Man" (formerly *Sinanthropus pekinensis*). The Zhoukoudian remains date to between 460 000 and 23 000 yr BP (based on association with Riss-age fauna and stratigraphy). In the lower level of the site, workers discovered human remains corresponding to a minimum of 45 individuals, based on a skeletal assemblage represented by 15 neurocranial fragments, 6 sphlanchnocranial portions, 12 mandible fragments, over 150 teeth, and a variety of fragmentary post-cranial remains (Aigner, 1976). The importance of this site is that it verifies the presence of cold-adapted early *Homo* as far north and east as 40° north latitude and 135° east longitude. The Lower Cave remains were lost by the US Navy after the Japanese invasion of China in 1941, but Weidenreich (1943) sent detailed casts to the American Museum of Natural History in New York.

Liukang, China

The Liukang[10] skeleton was recovered in 1958 within a cave near Tongtianyan, Guangxi Zhuang Autonomous Region in far southern China by local farmers removing guano from the cave for use as a fertilizer. The Liukang remains include a complete skull and fragmentary post-cranial bones representing a middle-aged (40–45-year-old) "Australoid" male (Akazawa, 1999: 97). Liukang Man is morphometrically unlike the Upper Cave skeletons of China (see below) but is quite similar to the Minatogawa Man of Okinawa Island, Japan (see Akazawa, 1999: 97; Neves and Pucciarelli, 1998; Neves *et al.*, 1999a; and Suzuki and Tanabe, 1982).

Upper Cave (Shandingdong), China

Along with the *Homo erectus* remains from the lower deposits at Zhoukoudian I (Chokoutien I), Hopei Province, China, the so-called

Upper Cave (Shandingdong) produced Late Pleistocene-age (18 000–17 000 yr BP) remains of *Homo sapiens sapiens*. Aigner (1976) notes:

> Eight individuals are represented by several fragmentary skulls, teeth and other materials: two males (one old and one young), three females (two middle aged, one near twenty years), a youth, a child and an infant (0–1 years) or fetus (<0 years). Their cranial morphology and dentition are Mongoloid, according to most authorities. These remains present dolichocranic crania with a slight degree of mid-facial prognathism, but with Sinodont dental morphology. (Aigner, 1976: 31; see Weidenreich, 1943)

Other sites in China that produced Late Pleistocene human remains include Tingts'un (a 25 000-year-old adolescent, 12–13 years of age) (Aigner, 1976: 33) and Tzeyang (an extremely robust middle-aged male dated to 18 000–17 000 yr BP) (Aigner, 1976: 28).

Japan

Minatogawa 1

Assessments of this controversial skeleton from Gushikami, Okinawa Island, have been interpreted in a variety of ways. According to Akazawa (1999), some researchers have assessed the craniofacial morphology of Minatogawa 1 and concluded that this Upper Paleolithic skeleton, which has produced radiometric dates of $18\,250 \pm 650$ yr BP (TK-99) and $16\,600 \pm 300$ yr BP (TK-142), was clearly an ancestral Japanese person; others (Brace, 1982), see a Yayoi (agricultural) invasion from mainland China as a point of origin for the modern Japanese.

The Minatogawa site produced fragmentary remains for between five and nine individuals. The Japanese Paleolithic encompasses several lithic tool traditions (Akazawa, 1999: 96) including:

1. A core blank and core tool tradition (30 000–27 000 yr BP);
2. A flake, flake blank, prismatic core tools and modified blade tradition (27 000–15 000 yr BP);
3. A microblade tradition (15 000–10 000 yr BP).

The Minatogawa 1 remains are those of a short-statured (1.53 m), older adult male, who possessed a short, broad, orthognathic (flat) face, a short, extremely broad nose, with weak supraorbital margins atop sloping, oval orbits and a long, narrow (dolichocranic) brain case.

Other Pleistocene-age human remains include those from Yamashita, Okinawa, Mikkabi, and Hamakita of Honshu Island.

Southeast Asia

There are only a few Terminal Pleistocene occupation sites in Southeast Asia and even fewer that contain human skeletal remains. Most Late Pleistocene sites are found in southern Thailand and northern Vietnam, and most have little in the way of human remains; nearly all ancient sites in the country are located in the northern half of the country. Sites that have produced human remains include Tabon Cave, Philippines; Niah Cave, Malaysia; Moh Kiew Cave, Thailand; Hoa Binh rockshelter; Tham Khoung rockshelter; and Con Moong Cave, the latter producing solely Late Pleistocene human remains (Pookajorn, 1996).

Vietnam

A *Japan Times* article of March 30, 2001 reports that two sets of human remains associated with terminal Pleistocene deposits were discovered in a cave on the east slope of the Hang Saõ Mountains in Ninh Binh Province. The remains, complete skeletons of two adults and two children, all of unspecified sex, are dated to the 11 000–10 000 yr BP Hoabinhian[11] culture that spread through Southeast Asia in the terminal Pleistocene. The Hoa Binh type site is located in north-central Vietnam near the eastern Laotian border.

Thailand

Moh Kiew Cave, in the Palian district of Trang Province, Thailand, is a heavily disturbed Pleistocene rockshelter site that contains five main cultural levels. The third level dates from 8420 ± 90 yr BP (OAEP-1292) to $11\,020 \pm 150$ yr BP (OAEP-1284), with a median ^{14}C age of $10\,470 \pm 80$ yr BP (OAEP-1281). Three human burials were recovered from the third level of the site. Unfortunately, there is no readily available information about the morphological characteristics of the three Moh Kiew Cave skeletons. Pookajorn (1996: 205) notes that Burial 2 was a flexed skeleton interred with several bifacial and unifacial tools that link it culturally to Early Holocene Hoabinhian culture in Vietnam.

Australasia

Peter Brown (1987, 2003) and Alan Thorne's (1984) impressive body of work on ancient skeletons in Australia has quelled speculation about the taxonomic position and biological relationship, if any, between

Pleistocene skeletons in Australia, Java, and mainland Asia, and modern Australians and southeast Asians. "More than 50 terminal Pleistocene skeletons have been recovered from Australia" (Brown, 2003).

Wadjak 1, Java

In 1888, B. D. van Reitschoten discovered a nearly complete human cranium in a fissure on the slopes of Gunung Lawa, in central Java near Tulundagun, during a marble mining operation. In 1920, Eugene Dubois examined this cranium, known as Wadjak 1 and found it to be an anatomically modern *Homo sapiens sapiens*. Subsequent work by Weidenreich (1945a), and later by Wolpoff (1980) and Storm (1995) confirmed Dubois' (1922) taxonomic placement of the Wadjak remains. He continued his work with a scientific excavation in the area and removed a second skeleton, with a very fragmentary cranium, dubbed Wadjak 2, whose stratigraphic relationship to the first cranium is still unknown. Dubois (1922) conducted the first analyses of these remains and declared that they were clearly associated with now-extinct small mammals and must surely be of Terminal Pleistocene antiquity or Early Holocene at the very least (Dubois, 1922). Debate over the geological age of the Wadjak human skeletal material began after Dubois' 1922 publication in which he claimed a Late Pleistocene age for the remains; others (Wolpoff, 1980) have suggested Terminal Pleistocene or Early Holocene, or even Middle to Late Holocene (Storm, 1995). There are also doubts about the contemporaneity of the Wadjak 1 and Wadjak 2 remains. Storm's (1995) reanalysis included a bone apatite AMS radiocarbon age from Wadjak 1 and seems to settle the debate, placing Wadjak 1 squarely in the Middle Holocene with an age of 6560 ± 140 yr BP (Storm, 1995: 148); however, fauna from the site yielded a Terminal Pleistocene age, $10\,560 \pm 75$ (Storm, 1995: 148), an enigmatic result which may be due to contamination by either recent carbon or old carbon (depending on how one chooses to view this finding).

The Wadjak 1 cranium has been described as having a morphology intermediate between modern native Australians and Pleistocene Australians and Pleistocene Chinese (Dubois, 1922; Larsen *et al.*, 1991; Wolpoff, 1980) or as "Proto Australian" (Dubois, 1922). Others (Weidenreich, 1945a) felt that both Wadjak crania possessed craniofacial features linking them to modern Javanese and Australians. The cranium of Wadjak 1 is robust, with a large supraorbital region and oval-to-trapezoidal orbits that have a slight lateral slope. Wadjak 1 has a large face that exhibits moderate mid-facial and prominent alveolar prognathism; the mid-face is narrow, with a short and very broad nasal aperture and reduced nasal bones, relative to modern populations. The neurocrania are long, narrow, and high, with pronounced rounding in the occipital area. The sagittal region is prominent, but does not have a true torus. Wadjak 2 is missing the frontal bone and other upper facial bones; when the well-preserved jaws are in occlusion the Wadjak 2 lower face expresses extreme alveolar prognathism.

Despite the suggestions of Dubois (1922) and Weidenreich (1945a), Storm (1995) concluded that the Wadjak crania displayed Javanese features with hyper-robust morphology. Brown (1987) determined that the Wadjak crania had similarities to other Pleistocene and Early Holocene populations around the world, but differed in terms of their increased robusticity in morphology of the face and brain case relative to gracile modern humans. Pleistocene *Homo sapiens sapiens* has little in common morphologically with the crania of modern populations.[12]

Kow Swamp

The Kow Swamp fossil locality is one of several Terminal Pleistocene cemetery sites located in the central Murray River Valley of Victoria, Australia. Other Pleistocene cemeteries include nearby Cohuna (10 km to the southeast of Kow Swamp). The Kow Swamp remains were intensively studied by Thorne (1971, 1975, 1976; Thorne and Macumber, 1972) but were not described in great detail in those publications (Brown, 2003). Several years ago the entire Kow Swamp mortuary series of 22 individuals was reburied at the request of Aboriginal communities in northern Victoria (Brown, 2003). Dates for the burials and cemetery range from $13\,000 \pm 280$ yr BP (ANU1236) on shells marking the grave of KS5 to $10\,000 \pm 250$ (ANU603b) on bone apatite from burial KS10 to 6500 yr BP for KS16. Taylor (1987) found the potential for old carbon contamination to be so great that all three dates are suspect.

The 22 Kow swamp burials were very fragmentary, which would limit the ability of researchers to describe them. The descriptions given here are based, in part, on the work of Brown (1987, 2003), Thorne (1975), and Thorne and Macumber (1972), as well as on my own assessment of photographs and illustrations (Larsen *et al.*, 1991) of the skeletons, especially the well-preserved cranium of Kow Swamp Burial 1. Overall, many of the Kow Swamp burials, especially KS1, possess short, broad faces with varying degrees of mid-facial or lower-facial prognathism and very broad, U-shaped palates that contain huge teeth that express AMHS cuspal morphology. The very robust face of KS1 has horizontally oriented low-set orbits with sloping inferolateral margins. The nose is short and broad with flattened nasal bones. These phenotypic features make the KS1 cranium seem similar to modern native Australian Aborigines, although KS1 is much more robust than most Aboriginal peoples of Australia.

Despite some modern morphology, the KS1 cranium also presents several phenotypic features that are similar to Australasian *Homo erectus* fossils (Sangrian), such as a low and sloping frontal,[13] and an extremely robust supraorbital region that appears to be a supraorbital torus including a supraglabellar fossa. These features have been cited for taxonomic interpretation of regional evolutionary continuity (Weidenreich, 1945b; Wolpoff and Caspari, 1997), with a lineal connection from Archaic *Homo* to Early Holocene Australians to Late Holocene Australians (Thorne and Macumber, 1972; Thorne and Wolpoff, 1981; Wolpoff and Caspari, 1997).

Brothwell (1975), however, disagreed with the taxonomic assessments (Thorne, 1971, 1975; Thorne and Macumber, 1972) and stated that the morphology was the result of artificial cranial modification – especially in the case of Burial KS5 (Brothwell, 1975; Brown, 2003).

Siberia

Ushki Lake, Kamchatka, Russia

Five localities representing Pleistocene-age occupation sites were found to be situated on a southern shore secondary terrace of Ushki Lake in the Kamchatka River Valley of Siberia. Of these sites, Ushki locality 1 (Ushki 1) is perhaps of greatest interest. Dikov (1977) excavated large areas in each locality. Ushki 1 produced numerous unifacial and bifacial tools, including several stemmed and shouldered projectile points. These artifacts were concentrated in the lowest cultural level of the site (Level 7), which produced 14 conventional radiocarbon ages on organics (charcoal) dated within a range of $14\,300 \pm 200$ yr BP to $10\,360 \pm 220$ yr BP, with an average date of $13\,980 \pm 146$ yr BP, after excluding two anomalous dates (21 000 and 4700 yr BP). Ushki 1 contained a series ($n = 41$) of dwelling structures, consisting of partly subterranean floors (shallow depressions) with entrance corridors, and a central pit filled with burned loam and charcoal (a hearth within the dwelling). Other structures were circular or irregularly shaped dwellings with no entrance corridors but with central, rock-lined hearth features. Some of these features are similar in plan to pre-Puebloan pit houses, Navaho hogans, or Great Basin wikkiups. Some of the structures had floors smeared with charcoal and other burned organic matter and were unique in shape and size.

One ocher-floored structure held a 1.8 m diameter, 0.7 m deep pit feature that was filled with small stones, red ocher, 800 stone beads, several burin-like awls (probably bead-making equipment), and a poorly preserved human skeleton covered by a thick layer of charcoal. The poorly preserved bones from this ancient person were too badly decayed to provide detailed biological information such as age, sex, or biological affinity. Charcoal in the burial feature produced a conventional ^{14}C age of $13\,600 \pm 250$ yr BP. Several domesticated dogs were found buried in or near other Ushki 1 dwellings (Goebel and Slobodin, 1999: 130). The Ushki 1 grave offerings, use of a burial pit for interment, and use of red ocher have parallels with the oldest burials in the New World (Anzick and Lapa Vermelha, and Wilson–Leonard). Unfortunately, the poor preservation of the Ushki 1 remains prevents a comparison of the biology of ancient peoples in Siberia to those in the Americas.

Eastern Old World: summary and synthesis

Suzuki (1981) proposed that an Upper Paleolithic "Proto Mongoloid" population occupied southern China, the Indonesian archipelago, and, ultimately, the islands of Japan:

> The morphological position of the Minatogawa man, the Pleistocene man in Okinawa, is located much nearer to the Liukang man of South China than to the Upper Cave man of North China ... the Minatogawa man can possibly be regarded morphologically as one of the ancestors of Jomon-age man. Therefore, it will be possible to support the view in which Jomon people have a closer biological relationship with the southern Asian Minatogawa man and Liukang man than to the Upper Cave man. Consequently, so far as the available skeletal material is concerned, about 32 000 years ago, Pleistocene *Homo sapiens sapiens* on the Chinese continent, [sic] represented in the term "generalized proto-Mongoloid people" came to Japan. (Suzuki, 1981: 55–6)

Yamaguchi (1982) concurred that the phenotypes and "diminutive statures estimated for the early inhabitants in the Japanese islands suggest their possible relationship with the small-sized Upper Paleolithic population in the southeastern part of Asia, represented

by the Liukang Man of South China and Niah Cave Man from Borneo."
(Yamaguchi, 1982: 85). This expansion of humans out of Africa is
paralleled by the expansion of several species of elephant
(*Palaeoloxodon namadicus*, *Palaeoloxodon naumanni*, and *Mammuthus primi-
genius*) from East Africa (Akazawa, 1999: 97).

All Upper Paleolithic/Late Pleistocene crania in the Old World
seem to share a craniofacial *beau plane* or basal architecture (Neves and
Pucciarelli, 1991, 1998; Neves *et al.*, 1999a: 132; Steele and Powell, 1993:
140) with a narrow, tall face and long, low brain case, and fairly large
generalized dentition.

Akazawa (1999: 97; figure 2) presents a two-dimensional plot of his
factor analysis of modern and Pleistocene east Asian cranial data. His
multivariate assessments depict modern/historic Japanese grouped
together based on their values for the first factor (representing similar
cranial features). Jomonese samples form a cluster in the center of his
factor plot, while Pleistocene Japanese (Minatogawa) and southern
Chinese (Liukang) are adjacent to one another in the upper central area
of the factor plot. Contra Turner's (1985b: 52) placement of the Upper
Cave sample as ancestral to the First Americans, Akazawa's (1999: 97)
data for humans and fauna support an expansion from southern Asia to
Southeast Asia to Japan (Hokkaido), with a sea crossing to the islands
south of Kamchatka, then to the Aleutian Islands, then to the New World.

Neves and his coworkers (Neves and Pucciarelli, 1991, 1998; Neves
et al., 1998, 1999a) and others (Powell and Neves, 1998; Stringer, 1998)
have produced data and analyses to support the view that Late
Pleistocene peoples in east Asia were clearly non-Mongoloids (Neves
et al., 1999a). Neves *et al.*[14] (1999a) used published data on fossil and
modern populations for size-corrected multivariate descriptive analysis
based on plots of Principal Components Analysis scores from craniofacial
dimensions (Figure 8.2). All modern human populations (Australians,
Polynesians, Africans, Europeans, east Asians, and Native Americans)
are located in one area of the plot, which indicates the morphological
similarity of these samples for the variables employed. Around the
modern populations are the Late Pleistocene skeletons, which suggest
that all Terminal Pleistocene humans are craniofacially distinct from
their later "descendant" populations in the later Holocene. Neves *et al.*'s
(1999a: 132) conclusion, based on their two-dimensional plot (modified as
Figure 8.2) and other paleontological and archaeological data was:

> Modern humans evolved in Africa from Archaic forms of hominids
> around 120 000 years BP and soon spread to the Middle East. From this

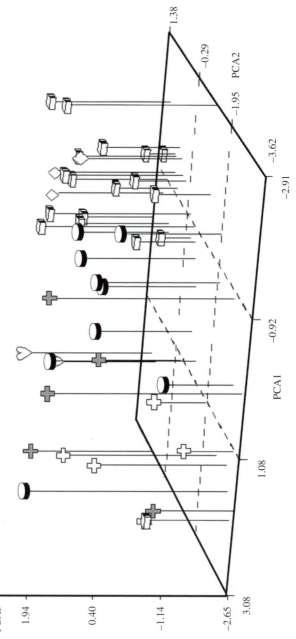

Figure 8.2 Principal components analysis (PCA) plots of Late Pleistocene east Asian humans based on cranial data, provided by W. A. Neves.

geographic region modern humans departed to East Asia, from which two divergent routes were taken: one southward that arrived around 60 000 years BP, if not earlier, and one northward that arrived in the Americas at 12 500 years BP, if not earlier. (Neves *et al.*, 1999a: 132)

Note that this is the exact same model presented by Akazawa (1999) based on his temporospatial series of archaeological evidence and fossil data (for *Homo* and two elephant genera – *Palaeoloxodon* and *Mammuthus*). These patterns and their evolutionary significance will be examined in greater detail in Chapters 10 and 11.

NOTES

1 Microblades have razor-sharp edges and were inserted into slotted bone or ivory dart points. The combination of flakes and slotted points creates a deadly weapon for hunting fast-moving prey like deer, elk, or other cervids. A modern parallel to the slotted bone point is the razor-tipped arrow used by some bow hunters to bring down fast-moving deer, elk, or moose. Such technologies kill prey by causing excessive internal and external tissue damage and bleeding without the need for a "kill shot" that kills by penetrating major organs.

2 The typical long, low skull with a narrow, tall face and nose and mid-to-lower facial prognathism is a feature found in Terminal Pleistocene humans around the globe, including the Americas (see Chapter 7 in this volume).

3 A designation that distinguishes modern humans from Archaic *Homo sapiens* such as *Homo sapiens neanderthalensis* (the Neanderthals).

4 The mid-facial region exhibits a slight degree of prognathism, a condition typical of *Homo sapiens neanderthalensis* (Larsen *et al.*, 1991).

5 *Opisthecranion* and *inion* are osteometric measurement landmarks on the most posterior aspect of the occipital bone.

6 With the exception of the later *Sebilian* industry (11 000 yr BP), centered on second cataract north of the Qena bend, but typified by the use of less fine-grained quarzitic sandstone or volcanic rocks used for the production of Lavallois-like discoid blanks.

7 Probably the changes associated with the Younger Dryas climate in the form of monsoonal weather patterns (Butzer, 1991), which led to a deeply entrenched Nile with little or no over-bank flooding, leading to a reduction in marsh environments and their associated abundant, predictable, resources.

8 Plants used include nut-grass tubers and possibly cereal grains.

9 New discoveries (2002) of apparent *Homo habilis* in the republic of Georgia at about 1.5 mya appear to deflate the "Out of Africa" model (Stringer, 1998) and strengthen the "trellis" model (Weidenreich, 1943) and multiregional evolution model (Wolpoff and Caspari, 1997), both of which depict regional evolution of modern human races from Archaic forms of *Homo sapiens*.

10 Transliterated from Chinese as either "Liukang" or "Liujang." I choose to use the older transliteration of Liukang, which may be more familiar for most readers.

11 The Hoabinhian cultural complex is typified by Late Pleistocene rockshelter and cave occupation sites in the northern parts of Thailand and Vietnam and open-air sites as far south as Sumatra. All sites contain typical Hoabinhian unifacial tools.

12 A hypothesis which will be examined in detail in Chapters 9 and 10 of this volume.

13 Described as "receding frontal squama" (Thorne and Macumber, 1972: 319).

14 The *et alia* in this case were J. F. Powell and E. G. Ozolins, both at the University of New Mexico.

PART III The First Americans, race and evolution

_____

9

Racial models of Native American origins

It is easier to find Australoid-looking dolichocephals in the more ancient burials in the New World than anything in the way of a skull that resembles a Mongoloid.

E. A. Hooton, 1933

I place all *post hoc* explanations of human biological variation such as population replacement by phenotypically different peoples, and colonization into the category of "typological assessments." However, they can also be called *model-free* methods (Relethford and Lees, 1982), because they have no underlying hypotheses to test. Typological approaches to prehistoric human variation do not attempt to understand the dynamic processes underlying the observed phenotypic differences (or similarities) in populations, except as the product of historical events, that is, population migration/colonization (Neves *et al.*, 1999b; Steele and Powell, 1992, 1993, 2002). The works of Blumenbach (1795), and Cuvier (1812) are by definition pre-evolutionary and thus racial–typological.[1]

9.1 MIGRATION, COLONIZATION, AND THE FIRST AMERICANS

Late nineteenth- and early twentieth-century researchers (Gladwin, 1947; Hooton, 1930; Morton, 1839; Neumann, 1952; Rivet, 1943; Oetteking, 1934) and some recent authors continue to place the First Americans within a racial–typological framework, although some migration/racial–typological models have components that appear evolutionary (Chatters, 1998; Chatters *et al.*, 1999; Greenberg *et al.*, 1986; Neumann, 1952; Neves and Pucciarelli, 1989; Neves *et al.*, 1996a, 1999a, 1999b, 2003; Steele and Powell, 1992, 1993; Turner, 1985a, 1990). These suggest some minimal role for microevolutionary processes, such as natural selection, genetic drift, and gene flow. Most migration models are based on racial–typological assessment, as well as on diffusionism, which is at odds with neo-Darwinian concepts of population variation through time and space (Lahr and Foley, 1998). Lahr and Foley (1998) have stated that migrationist racial–typological views "... have more in common with Elliot Smith's hyper-diffusionism than with modern evolutionary biology."

As noted in Chapter 6, the racial–typological views of amateur archaeologist and hyper-diffusionist Harold Gladwin (1947) envisioned at least six different migration events to accomplish the peopling of the Americas, each representing the arrival of a different racial "type." The racial "types" filling the prehistoric American melting pot were two Australoid migrations (Clovis and Folsom), followed by Algonquians, Eskimos, Mongoloids, and Polynesians.

G. K. Neumann's (1952) influential paper "Archeology and Race in the American Indian" classified North American Indians into ten varieties or "local races" that could be placed within two broader "types": the Paleoamerinds, whose craniofacial morphology was described as a dolichocephalic cranium with delicate facial features, and the Cenoamerinds whose members were brachycranic with a relatively more robust face when compared with the Paleoamerinds. From each of these two main racial types sprang at least ten varieties, or "local types," such as the Algonquian, Illinoisan, Siouxian, Athabaskan, Puebloan, and others. This is quite similar to the racial–typological construct framed by Ales Hrdlička.

Hrdlička's model

Ales Hrdlička's (1923) view of the peopling of the Americas has been echoed in other recent works (Greenberg *et al.*, 1986; Turner and Bird, 1981). Hrdlička (1923), like Acosta, considered that the route or routes of human entry to the New World may have been by land from Siberia to Alaska via the Bering Land Bridge or along the Aleutian chain by boat from Kamchatka. He recognized that the initial peopling of the Americas was not as a wave of people "flooding" into Alaska,[2] and then southward to warmer and more abundant areas of North America (Hrdlička, 1923: 492), but that:

> ... the newcomers though all belonging to the same main race were evidently not strictly homogeneous but represented several distinct

subtypes of the yellow-brown people, with differences in culture and language. The first of these subtypes was, according to many indications, the dolichocephalic Indian, represented in North America by the great Algonquian, Illinois, Sioux and Shoshonean stocks; farther south by the Piman-Aztec Tribes; and in South America ... by the so-called "Lagoa Santa Race." (Hrdlička, 1923: 493)

These racial subtypes were followed by a brachycephalic type described as "Toltec" by Morton and "Mound builder" by Hrdlička, and then by the late-entering Athabaskans, Eskimos, and Aleuts. The latter were described as having cranial features linking then to brachycephalic "Mongolian types" of Siberia and northeast Asia.

The tripartite model

The revised version of Hrdlička's (1923) multiracial assessment of prehistoric and other ancient human remains in the Americas is the commonly cited "tripartite" racial–typological scenario of the peopling of the New World, originally presented by linguist Joseph Greenberg (1985). He was later joined by dental anthropologist Christy Turner and geneticist Steven Zegura (see Greenberg *et al.*, 1986).

Based on linguistic, dental, and genetic evidence of varying quality, these researchers proposed that all linguistic and biological variation in Native Americans was the result of a series of migratory "waves" from northeast Asia. According to this model, all "Amerind" language speakers, or Amerindians[3] (a category that excludes *Aleuts*, *Eskimos*, and *Na-Dene* [Athabaskans]), are a linguistically, dentally, and genetically unified group descended from the initial wave of Siberian migrants who entered the New World approximately 15 000–12 000 years ago. These migrants swept from present-day Canada to the southern cone of South America in less than 2000 years. Today, their descendants are distributed throughout the Americas (Greenberg *et al.*, 1986).

Greenberg *et al.* (1986) used linguistic, dental, and genetic data from prehistoric (Late Holocene) and living North and South American peoples to suggest that these groups were, for the most part, biologically and linguistically homogeneous, a fact resulting from their common origin from the first wave of migration (Paleoindians) to the Americas. While this model has received strong support from archaeologists, many linguists reject it because of its relative simplicity and lack of historical approach. Furthermore, linguistic and biological data do not support the dental homogeneity of all living Amerindians. Despite these problems, the "tripartite" model continues to be the foundation for most current anthropological research on Native American origins and evolution.

One recent racial–typological assessment of the crania of the First Americans was published by Steele and Powell (1993). The authors presented a series of simple bivariate plots representing the average values of the cranial index (Figure 9.1) and facial index[4] (Figure 9.2). The pooled North American Paleoindian sample, along with several modern New World native groups, combined with Upper Paleolithic skull samples (Figure 9.1), are found below the lowest diagonal in the dolichocranic zone; those in the middle zone are mesocranic, while those above the upper line are brachycranic. The Upper Cave male and female skulls are the most extreme in cranial length, placing both sexes squarely in the dolichocranic zone. All of the Minatogawa skulls are mesocranic, while the pooled Paleoindian females are just inside the mesocranic zone. The mean Paleoindian male value is barely in the dolichocranic region. The Minatogawa male's neurocranial shape was similar to that of one modern Australasian sample and one Late Holocene European sample (Berg). The plots of facial breadth (ZYB) and height (NPH) in Figure 9.2 indicate that modern male and female Africans and Australasians have somewhat short and narrow faces, while prehistoric Aleuts, Eskimos, and Pleistocene Minatogawa males and females possess the shortest, broadest faces of any of the Old World populations used in the analysis. Paleoindians are once again closest to the modern Australians and southeast Asians. This bivariate study and a similar one preceding it (Steele and Powell, 1992), led these authors to support the findings of Brace and Tracer (1992), Kamminga and Wright (1988), and Neves and Pucciarelli (1989), which indicated the presence of a generalized *Proto Mongoloid* population in the far eastern Old World that was ancestral to the population of the New World and Australasia (Kamminga and Wright, 1988). The features used to characterize Mongoloids seem to be a post-Pleistocene biological phenomenon (Steele and Powell, 1993).

9.2   DENTAL AND CRANIAL PERSPECTIVES ON THE PEOPLING OF THE AMERICAS

Dental anthropological studies have been successfully applied to a number of questions regarding phylogeny and population history. Cusp patterns and crown morphology have been used to deduce phylogenetic relationships among mammals (Butler, 1939; Osborn, 1907) and to elucidate the origins of the Hominoidea, Hominidae, and

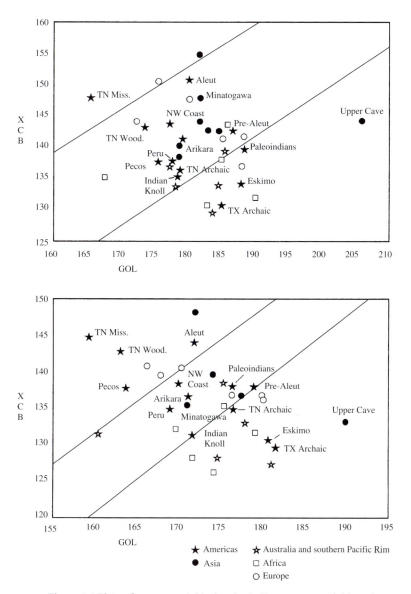

Figure 9.1 Plots of mean cranial index, including mean cranial length (GOL) and cranial breadth (XCB) for males (above) and females (below). Means were obtained from modern, prehistoric, and Paleoindians in the Americas, along with east Asian Late Pleistocene (Minatogawa, Upper Cave) samples. Lines (top to bottom) separate brachycranic, mesocranic, and dolichocranic samples. From Steele and Powell (1994).

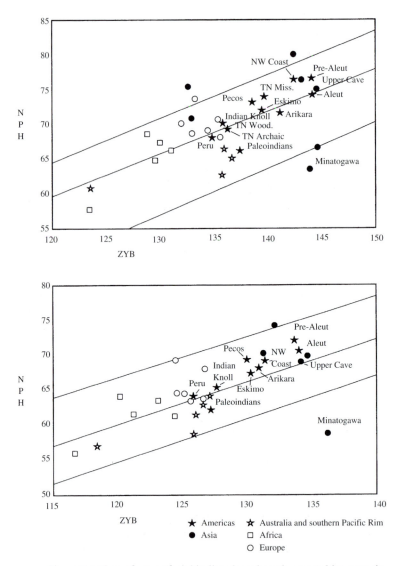

Figure 9.2 Plots of upper facial indices based on the mean bizygomatic breadth (ZYB) and upper facial height (NPH) for males (above) and females (below). Means were obtained from modern, prehistoric, and Paleoindians in the Americas, along with east Asian Late Pleistocene (Minatogawa, Upper Cave) samples. Lines separate leptene (narrow), mesene (intermediate), euryene (broad), and hypereuryene (very broad) faces. From Steele and Powell (1994).

Hominini (Dahlberg, 1991; Simons, 1971; Weidenreich, 1947). Intra-specific studies of dental morphology and size have also been broadly applied to primates in general and humans in particular. Aside from documenting the range of nonmetric and metric variation within human groups, anthropologists have had considerable success in using dental traits to reconstruct aspects of population history. Examples include work on the dispersal of human populations in Africa (Haeussler et al., 1989; Irish, 1993), Asia (Brace and Hunt, 1990; Brace and Nagai, 1982; Brace et al., 1989; Turner, 1979, 1985a, 1986b, 1990), and the Americas (Turner, 1971, 1983a, 1985a,b, 1986c; Turner and Bird, 1981), as well as to examine population structure and bio-logical affinity among living groups (Friedlander, 1975; Harris, 1977).

Native American dental variation

Given that teeth are useful in reconstructing population history, it is no surprise that numerous studies have utilized dental variation to explore questions of anthropological interest. Previous studies of Native American dental variation have been used to document the range of variation present in these populations (Dahlberg, 1949, 1968; Harris and Nweeia, 1980; Turner, 1971, 1983a, 1985a,b); to explain dental variation in terms of bioaffinity (Harris and Nweeia, 1980; Sciulli, 1979, 1990a,b; Scott and Dahlberg, 1982; Turner, 1985b), and to examine diachronic changes in tooth morphology and size (Perzigian, 1976, 1984; Sciulli and Mahaney, 1991; Scott, 1979). However, only a few researchers (Dahlberg, 1949, 1968; Powell, 1995; Powell and Steele, 1993; Turner, 1971, 1985b, 1994; Turner and Bird, 1981) have specifically examined dental variation in the context of Late Pleistocene New World colonization and subse-quent population dispersal.

Regardless of whether comparisons are made to other New World groups or to Old World populations, many investigators tend to view Native Americans as relatively homogeneous with regard to dentition, and interpret this homogeneity as a reflection of their com-mon descent from an ancestral Asian population. Teeth have provided the best evidence for Native American connections to Old World popu-lations and for the level of phenotypic variation present among pre-historic and modern populations in the New World. The most influential dental morphological assessments have been those of Dahlberg (1968, 1991), Turner (1985a,b), and K. Hanihara (1968).

Kazuro Hanihara (1968) examined dental morphological variation among modern Japanese, Ainu, and Native Americans, and found that these groups shared a number of dental traits, which he termed the "Mongoloid dental complex." Shared traits included high frequencies of upper central incisor (UI1) shoveling, and lower first molar (LM1) deflecting wrinkle, entoconulid, metaconulid, and protostylid, all characterizing populations in east Asia (Hanihara, 1968).

Dr. Christy G. Turner's (1983b) important and broad-ranging study of dental variation in Pacific Rim populations demonstrated that there was greater complexity in Native American teeth than could be accommodated in the "Mongoloid dental complex." Turner recorded data on nonmetric dental traits from over 15 000 individual dentitions from Africa, Europe, Asia, the Pacific, and the Americas (Turner, 1994). These data were used to derive general patterns of dental variation among world populations, based on the relative frequency of certain dental traits. In addition to describing and interpreting these general patterns, Turner employed the trait frequencies of various populations in a phenotypic distance statistic, C. A. B. Smith's mean measure of divergence (MMD) (Berry and Berry, 1967; Sjøvold, 1973). The MMD distances between populations were clustered using various computer algorithms and the overall pattern of clusters was interpreted as a reflection of population history, under the assumption that, in general, dental variation reflects genetic variation among populations.

This research, based on an extremely large sample and careful use of standardized recording methods, revealed that Hanihara's (1968) "Mongoloid dental complex" did not accurately describe the variation present among east Asians (Turner, 1990: 305). Instead, Asian populations were characterized by two major patterns of dental morphology, which Turner named Sinodonty and Sundadonty (Turner, 1983b, 1985b, 1990). Sundadonts, found primarily in southern Asia, are characterized by a less complex dental morphology that is thought to reflect the "primitive" or ancestral condition (Turner, 1985b, 1990).

Northern Asians, who diverged from their southern Asian ancestors at least 20 000 yr BP, developed a more complex dental morphology typified by an "intensification" of crown traits (Turner, 1985b). These Sinodont populations exhibit higher frequencies of several traits, such as incisor shoveling and enamel extensions of UM1, than southern Asian Sundadonts. Until recently, it has been difficult to determine exactly which traits best define the Sinodont pattern. Part of the problem stems from the fact that Sinodonty and Sundadonty were only defined through cluster analysis of trait frequencies. This was resolved in Turner's 1990 formal definition of Sundadont and Sinodont patterns, based on tests of trait frequency differences

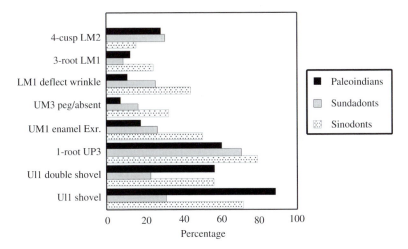

Figure 9.3 Dental discrete trait frequencies for Sinodont and Sundadont populations. Data from Turner (1990).

between populations. A total of eight nonmetric dental traits were found to differentiate northern and southern Asian populations at statistically significant levels: frequencies of shoveling and double shoveling of UI1, peg-shaped or absent UM3, enamel extensions and deflecting wrinkle of UM1, single-rooted UP3, three-rooted LM1, and four-cusped LM2 (Turner, 1990). Sinodont populations had higher frequencies of seven out of eight traits when compared with Sundadonts (Figure 9.3).

Because the Sinodont dental pattern contains a combination of traits that both strengthen (e.g. incisor shoveling) and weaken (e.g. single-rooted teeth) the dentition, Turner (1985b, 1990) felt that natural selection could not be responsible for the deviation of Sinodonts from the less complex ancestral condition found in Sundadonts. Turner (1985b: 317) also noted that many of the Sinodont dental traits are worn off by young adulthood, and are therefore less likely to be acted on by natural selection. He also felt that the absence of clinal distributions of dental nonmetric traits in Asia also supported this interpretation.

Cranial analyses of prehistoric and Native Americans

Principal components analysis (PCA) is a multivariate descriptive technique for ordination of observations and for the description of many variables as new functions of the total sample variation (e.g. "principal components" of cranial variation). In the analysis described here (Figures 9.4 and 9.5), two major worldwide comparative samples (those of W. W. Howells and T. Hanihara), both using similar measurement sets and collection methods, were pooled into a single comparative sample of $n = 9269$ individual crania for $t = 14$ (out of 82) craniofacial and neurocranial dimensions. The PCA produces variables that describe the total variation in the measurement data set by solving a simultaneous series of equations for the t original variables involved, so that a new set of t variables is created (the principal components) to describe the correlation and covariation of the original variables in a t-dimensional statistical hyperspace.[5]

The PCA scores displayed in Figure 9.4 and Figure 9.5 were subjected to a multiple analysis of variance (MANOVA) test for differences in regional sample means and differences by observer (Hanihara vs. Howells), and observer-by-region interaction were not significant at the 0.05 level (global $F = 0.5502$ at 9, 5268 d.f.; $p = 0.8384$) for the total model. After pooling the comparative data, each individual's values were corrected for size using the Darroch and Mosimann (1985) geometric-mean-size correction technique so that sexual dimorphism is eliminated and scaling within the variable set[6] does not play a role in driving the PCA. Body size differences between populations does not play a role after size correction of the data; the transformed variables can be considered to be residual variation, which is referred to as shape (Darroch and Mosimann, 1985; Jungers et al., 1995). This result allowed the two large comparative data sets to be used as a single sample for a model-free analysis.[7] The PCA employs the total sample variance–covariance matrix with no regard for the geographic origin of the comparative samples. The variance–covariance structure in the total data set (Howells + Hanihara) yields a new set of orthogonal vectors (or principal components) that can be used to plot individual observations in two or three dimensions. The plots show the position of Paleoindian individuals' cranial variation relative to that of all individuals in the Hanihara–Howells comparative data set (Figure 9.5).

Figure 9.4 and Figure 9.5 are good examples of why race is not a natural taxonomic category. The individual PCA scores for the first three principal components in Figure 9.4 (which summarize 52.1% of world craniofacial variation) are not clearly separated into races, with the possible exception of Australasians (Figure 9.4 [squares]). Even the 90% confidence ellipses of the individual PCA scores (Figure 9.5) show no significant separation of human skulls from different regions on the globe. The degree of phenotypic overlap is such that one of the Jomon

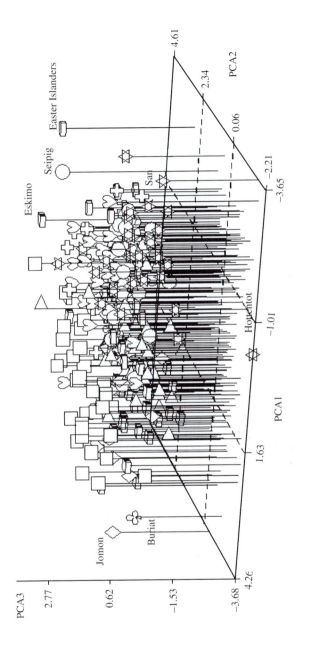

Figure 9.4 Plot of three principal components of craniofacial variation for a sample of Early and Late Holocene populations; based on data from W. Howells, T. Hanihara, and J. Powell and W. Neves.

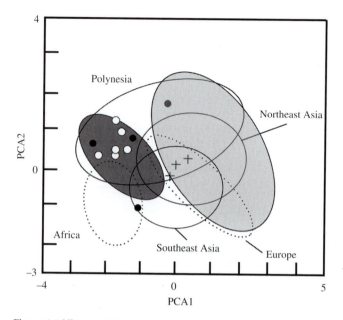

Figure 9.5 Ninety-eight percent confidence ellipses based on data from principal components of craniofacial variation for world populations (see Figure 9.4). Key: dark ellipse, Austro-melanesians; light gray ellipse, Native Americans; black dots, North American Paleoindians; white dots, South American Paleoindians; crosses, Ainu-Jomon.

samples falls within the range of four regional samples (European, New World, Polynesians, northeast Asians, and southeast Asians). All but two (Kennewick and Wilson–Leonard) of the First Americans are outside the Polynesian ellipse. North American Paleoindians display greater dispersion than do those of South America (Figure 9.5). The tight grouping of South American Paleoindians may relate their greater temporal and spatial proximity, compared with the spatiotemporal dispersion of Paleoindians in North America (Figure 9.5, Table 9.1). The Brazilian Luzia skeleton is well within both the Polynesian, Australasian, and African phenotypic ranges as observed by Neves *et al.* (1998). Only the Wizards Beach Paleoindian is squarely in the Native American phenotypic ellipse as well as the Polynesian ellipse (Figure 9.5). Does this mean that Kennewick Man is a Polynesian, as claimed by one South Pacific native leader,[8] or that Luzia is Australian? Not at all; the results simply indicate that those Paleoindians have craniofacial dimensions that are encompassed by three multivariate standard deviations of those particular groups. Because PCA is a descriptive method that tells us nothing about the genetic relationship of these individuals to

Table 9.1 Typicality probabilities for Paleoindians based on modern regional, Ainu, and Archaic reference samples.

Reference sample	La Brea	WMS	Wizards	Spirit	Sta. Riacho	Lapa Vermelha	CG 6A	CG 6B	CG 7A	CG 7B
Africa	0.0037	0.5388	0.1382	0.4390	0.5653	**0.9424**	**0.7998**	0.8622	0.1908	0.0011
Ainu–Jomon	0.0068	0.4892	0.7805	0.7555	0.1836	0.7547	0.6105	0.9586	0.0032	**0.0013**
America	0.0009	0.3972	**0.8045**	0.6148	0.0110	0.4202	0.2265	0.7983	0.0230	0.0000
Australasia	0.0016	0.3653	0.5633	**0.8854**	**0.6335**	0.9266	0.6973	0.7284	**0.2230**	0.0002
Europe	**0.0208**	**0.9183**	0.2099	0.7318	0.0819	0.7897	0.3255	0.8588	0.0298	0.0006
Indian Knoll	0.0002	0.0304	0.5796	0.3702	0.0653	0.3697	0.1225	0.6605	0.0975	0.0000
Northeast Asia	0.0100	0.4344	0.4219	0.4288	0.0235	0.5698	0.3936	0.9340	0.0000	0.0000
Polynesia	0.0003	0.3633	0.7601	0.5393	0.0310	0.4995	0.6449	**0.9835**	0.0286	0.0000
Southeast Asia	0.0016	0.3153	0.3517	0.3731	0.0256	0.5053	0.3209	0.8440	0.0215	0.0008
Windover	0.0003	0.7768	0.0019	0.2446	0.0000	0.1053	0.0788	0.1909	0.0000	0.0000

Based on ten variables; bold indicates highest typicality probability for a column.

Key to abbreviations: Warm Mineral Spring (WMS); Wizards Beach (Wizards); Spirit Cave (Spirit); Cerca Grande (CG).

others in the comparative sample, but may indicate a common adaptation to similar environments, diets, or even similar behaviors (such as head binding). Only a *model-bound* (i.e. evolutionary) analysis of these data will provide information on the causes of spatiotemporal variation among the First Americans.

Another approach to sorting out the relationships among Paleoindians is to calculate inter-individual distances using the Mahalanobis distance using the pooled (averaged) within-groups variance–covariance matrix from the Howells–Hanihara data (Figures 9.4 and 9.5).

Using this analysis, there is some grouping by continent, with South American Paleoindians forming a cluster just right of center, which again may be a function of either their stronger genetic relationship or geographic proximity, especially as regards diet, behavior, and environment. This plot (Figure 9.5) cannot be used to differentiate the cause of the morphological pattern observed here. Note that the two temporally and geographically proximate Paleoindians in North America (Wizards Beach and Spirit Cave) are not adjacent to one another in Figure 9.4. At best, we can calculate a typicality probability (Table 9.1) that indicates the probability that the individual belongs to each of the groups used in the comparison.

The typicality probabilities (Table 9.1) demonstrate that the Kennewick, La Brea, and Cerca Grande 7B skulls have a low probability of belonging to any of the modern reference samples.[9] Wizards Beach Man has an 80.45% probability of having a craniofacial phenotype that is typical of modern Native American populations, and a 76% probability of being typical of modern Polynesians. The other ancient Nevadan is 88.5% typical of modern Australasians (including Melanesians and Australians). Five of the First Americans have highest typicality values, placing them in either the modern Polynesian or Australian/ Melanesian Late Holocene samples.

Powell and Neves (1999) examined the distances (Table 9.2) used to generate Figure 9.5 and tested these for significance using the Defrise–Gussenhoven (1967) method, which provides the probability that the distances representing two individuals are sampled at random from the same biological population.[10] They obtained a result of $\sqrt{(2t-1)} = 5.1615$, which is significant at $p < 0.05$, meaning that the finding has only a 0.165 75 chance of being due to random errors. From the results for the ten variables presented in Table 9.1, it is clear that the La Brea woman is significantly separated from all other Paleoindians. Powell and Rose (1999) applied this technique to the Kennewick Man

Table 9.2 Mahalanobis' craniofacial shape distances for Paleoindians and modern regional populations including Ainu and Archaic reference samples.

	Southeast Asia	Aust	Amerind	Poly	NE Asia	Paleo	Europe	Ainu
Southeast Asia	0							
Aust	0.294989	0						
Amerind	0.181141	0.337261	0					
Poly	0.1125	0.285311	0.113652	0				
Northeast Asia	0.034711	0.304713	0.113748	0.117859	0			
Paleo	0.235731	0.162039	0.111963	0.12613	0.193073	0		
Europe	0.237831	0.314963	0.199303	0.274548	0.174487	0.200266	0	
Ainu	0.196533	0.198091	0.225958	0.2102	0.172096	0.08982	0.103096	0
Sum	1.293436	1.602378	0.764624	0.728737	0.539656	0.290086	0.103096	5.322013

0.147834 min Fst
0.239785 Fst (0.55)
0.331397 Fst (0.35)

skeleton, and obtained a result similar to that of La Brea woman ($p = 0.01$) for any North or South American comparative sample. As expected, the Lagoa Santa Paleoindian crania are all similar to one another, given their strong temporal and spatial proximity. The Wizards Beach skeleton is the only ancient American who has a high probability ($p = 80.45\%$) of belonging to the Holocene American sample, a result that may stem from his relatively more recent radiocarbon age, compared with other Paleoindians.

Powell and Neves (1999) tested for differences in means and variances between Paleoindian and Middle Archaic (8500–5000 yr BP) samples using a MANOVA procedure. They found that there was no significant difference (at $p = 0.05$) for any dimension except facial breadth (ZYB $F = 7.86$, $p = 0.0451$). The mean for this variable is greater within Archaic individuals, which suggests a modestly broader face in Middle Archaic samples, relative to the faces of Paleoindians. In a typological analysis, facial breadth is associated with Holocene northern Asian and Native American populations. A time-series analysis of the data indicated that faces became broader from the Early to Middle Holocene (Powell, 1999; Powell and Neves, 1999), but there is no model-free approach that tells us what factors may have led to this diachronic change in craniofacial shape.

The pattern of temporal change in dental nonmetric traits in Asia seems to provide support for the idea of considerable post-glacial biological change in Paleoindians and other Late Pleistocene human groups. Rather than invoking natural selection as a cause of variation among Asian groups, Turner hypothesized that these changes occurred when small populations in northeast Asia experienced genetic drift, resulting in a directional change from less complex to more complex morphology (Turner, 1990: 311). Such change appears to have occurred at some time between 20 000 and 40 000 yr BP (Turner, 1985b: 49), when anatomically modern humans were expanding into northeast Asia. The date of dental divergence between Sinodonts and Sundadonts is supported by the fossil record (Turner, 1985b) and by the "dento-chronology" method (Turner, 1986a).

Turner's research (Greenberg et al., 1986; Turner, 1983a, 1985a, 1986b,c, 1989, 1990, 1992a, 1994), like that of Dahlberg (1949, 1968), reveals that Native American populations shared a series of nonmetric dental traits. Specifically, all New World populations exhibited the Sinodont dental pattern. Turner felt that this was a direct reflection of Native American descent from Late Pleistocene populations in northeast Asia (Greenberg et al., 1986; Turner, 1983a, 1986c, 1990, 1994;

Turner and Bird, 1981). Although Native American samples differed slightly from northern Asian Sinodonts by exhibiting higher or lower frequencies of some Sinodont traits (Turner, 1990: 45) and stronger inter-trait correlations (Turner 1990: 311), they generally exhibit the Sinodont pattern. These results concur with earlier findings (Dahlberg, 1949, 1968; Hanihara, 1968; Hrdlička, 1920, 1923) that native populations of the New World were ultimately derived from a series of Late Pleistocene founding populations from Asia (Turner, 1971, 1983a, 1985a, 1989, 1990, 1992a; Turner and Bird, 1981).

Turner further suggested that "New World dental morphology as presently known shows much less variation than that of eastern Asia" (Turner, 1985a: 592), and that all New World populations resemble each other more closely than they do any Old World populations (Greenberg et al., 1986; Turner, 1983a, 1985a, 1986b,c, 1992b, 1994). The MMD values presented in Turner (1985a: 77) indicate that "Asian populations are more variable than are the four American regions [Arctic, Greater Northwest Coast, North America, South America] or Indians taken as a whole. Pan-Indians have less than half the average divergence of Northern Asians, and a quarter that of East Asians" (Turner, 1985a: 41). He also notes that "Within the New World, excepting the Greater Northwest Coast, there are no significant differences in the average regional divergence" (Turner, 1985b: 42). In almost all published dendrograms based on divergence (MMD) values, Native Americans form a distinct cluster among other populations (Figure 9.6). Turner and Bird (1981: 1054) used the minimal differences between Paleoindian dentitions and those of modern Amerindians (presumably the descendants of the Paleoindians) to support the idea that there has been very little dental microevolution in the Americas for the past 11 000 years (Turner, 1983a: 147, 1986b: 573). Brace (1964) proposed a slow evolution, the "probable mutation effect," which has a great deal in common with Kimura's neutral model of evolution via neutral mutations.

The assumption is that dental differences among populations are due to the steady accumulation of random changes over long periods of time rather than to major shifts in gene frequencies typical of natural selection. Thus, it was possible for a group like the Amerindians, who had occupied the New World for at least 11 000 years, to have experienced little dental change since their initial entry to the Americas.

The second important implication of limited New World dental variation is that the number of founding populations in the New World was assumed to be relatively limited. Turner (1990) hypothesized that founder effect was the most likely evolutionary

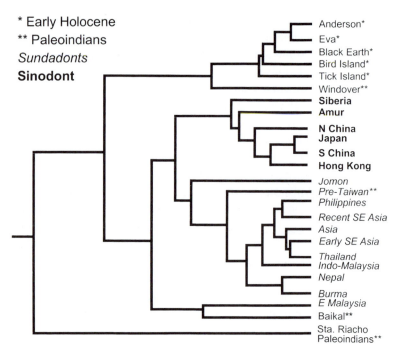

Figure 9.6 Cluster analysis of world populations based on mean measure of divergence values for dental discrete traits. Unweighted pair-group clustering of dental morphological data redrawn from Powell (1993, 1995).

mechanism accounting for the observed dental homogeneity of Native American populations:

- The greater dental homogeneity in the New World than in eastern Asia (Turner, 1985b) is consistent with a hypothesis of genetic drift or founder's effect being primarily responsible for Sinodonty. Turner felt that all Native Americans must be descended from the limited number of north China hunting bands that wandered into the harsh environs found in northeast Asia during the Late Pleistocene (Turner, 1990: 311).
- "Although biological diversity can easily be recognized in the Americas, its relatively limited amount indicates that the total number of colonists must have been very small" (Turner, 1992b: 43), a claim reiterated in other publications (Greenberg et al., 1986; Turner, 1985b Turner and Bird, 1981).

The above statement is supported by the fact that teeth from Pali Aike Cave, Chile, estimated to date to around 10 000 yr BP, exhibit the

Sinodont dental pattern (Turner and Bird, 1981). Greenberg *et al.* (1986: 480) note that the homogeneity of Native American phenotypes (Hrdlička, 1913), including dental phenotypes, indicates a common origin from a small northeast Asian founding group. One problem with the finding of Sinodonty in the Pali Aike remains (Turner and Bird, 1981) is that the tooth crowns of Pali Aike burials were badly fractured by the heat of cremation. This means that only root traits (based on the empty tooth sockets in mandibles) could be assessed, not the full suite of traits, so the completeness of the Paleoindian samples used may have skewed their finding towards Sinodonty. Other analyses of the First Americans (Powell, 1993, 1995, 1998; Powell and Neves, 1999; Powell and Rose, 1999; Powell *et al.*, 1998) and Archaic Americans (Haydenblit, 1993; Lahr, 1994, 1995; Powell, 1995) have found the Sundadont pattern among the oldest human teeth in the Americas, corresponding with the findings of craniofacial assessments of ancient Americans as having skulls similar to Polynesians, Australasians, and southeast Asians (all Sundadont populations). To be fair, Turner (2002) pointed out that these studies could have been affected by observer error caused by severe dental wear and subsequent erosion of features necessary to make a clear-cut assignment of individuals to either the Sinodont or Sundadont pattern. Powell *et al.* (1999), after eliminating teeth with severe attrition and wear, found that Paleoindians were intermediate in morphology between Sinodonts and Sundadonts. However, Paleoindians possess a higher frequency of UI1 shoveling compared with Sinodonts, as well as lower frequencies of single-rooted UP3, peg or absent UM3, and UM1 enamel extensions (Figure 9.3).

The biological relationship between Native Americans and Old World populations has also been explored using dental metric traits, though the inter-correlation of dental metric traits has presented some methodological difficulties (Harris and Nweeia, 1980; Harris and Rathbun, 1991). Most researchers have noted that rather large teeth (Brace and Hunt, 1990; Brace *et al.*, 1991; Dahlberg, 1968) characterize Amerindians and other Native American populations. Dahlberg (1968) noted the similarity between Greenland Eskimos, Amerindians, and Australians in overall tooth size and size apportionment. In particular, the size of the anterior teeth and the relative size of the premolars in the dental arcade were important in distinguishing Amerindians from other groups. He also noted the similarity in tooth size among Amerindian populations as compared with other geographic populations.

Brace *et al.* (1991) used summary tooth size[11] and cranial volume to rank modern human populations. They found that Native Americans had slightly smaller teeth than some African and Australian groups, but larger teeth than Asians and Europeans. Furthermore, cranial size was not directly related to tooth size, suggesting that body and tooth size had become "uncoupled" during recent human evolution. Brace *et al.* also suggested that tooth size similarities among humans may reflect similar adaptive responses and a reduction of selection pressure rather than direct phylogenetic relationships (Brace and Hunt, 1990; Brace *et al.*, 1991: 49).

In their analyses of tooth size and shape relationships among Upper Paleolithic, Middle Holocene, and living human populations (Harris and Nweeia, 1980; Perzigian, 1984), these researchers showed that phenotypic clusters based on tooth size did not reflect geographic relationships, while tooth shape did present plausible phylogenetic linkages. Tooth size similarities among geographically, genetically, and temporally varied populations reflect similarities in technology and culture rather than phylogenetic relationships, as Brace *et al.* (1991) later noted. In Perzigian's 1984 analysis, Native American populations clustered with modern and prehistoric Asians and Australo–Melanesians, indicating an Asian origin for these groups. Harris and Rathbun (1991) used PCA to examine tooth shape relationships among living and pre-historic populations. Using the principal component scores and score residuals, they found strong phenetic similarity between Asians, Melanesians, and Amerindians, again supporting the Asian affinity of Native Americans. Harris and Rathbun (1991) also found that tooth size apportionment within the dental arcade provided a better picture of taxonomic relatedness than raw size (cf. Dahlberg, 1968).

9.3   DENTAL EVIDENCE FOR AMERINDIAN HOMOGENEITY

Dental variation in the New World appears to be limited compared with the variation observed among Old World populations, in part because of the recency of human entrance to the Americas. There is, however, some internal diversity in nonmetric dental traits among Native American populations. Using the frequency of a single trait (three-rooted LM1), New World populations could be subdivided into three distinct and internally homogeneous subgroups: Aleut–Eskimos, Na-Dene, and all other North and South American Indians (called Macro-Indians or Amerindians in various publications) (Turner, 1971). This division of Native Americans neatly corresponds to the linguistic divisions presented by Greenberg (1987) and, along with the genetic data, forms the third line of evidence in the tripartite model (Greenberg *et al.*, 1986). In analyses subsequent to Turner's 1971 paper, the number of dental nonmetric traits used to delineate these three major New World subgroups was expanded from one to 28 key traits (Greenberg *et al.*, 1986; Turner, 1983a, 1985a,b, 1986a,b,c, 1992a, 1994). The clustering of published MMD values appears to support such a three-way partitioning of dental variation (Figure 9.6), as statistical tests for differences in trait frequencies and MMD values between pooled samples of Amerindians, Na-Dene, and Aleut–Eskimos revealed significant differences between these three subgroups (Turner, 1985b).

The tripartite subdivision of Native American dental variation was based primarily on patterns of trait frequency differences and the clustering of MMD values. Paleoindians and their direct descendants, the Amerindians, displayed increased dental robusticity and a limited amount of nonmetric dental variation because of the harsh environmental conditions and profound founder effect experienced by the first migrants. According to Turner (1985b), Amerindians can be distinguished from other Native American populations by higher frequencies of several nonmetric dental traits that might increase the durability of the teeth, such as incisor shoveling, despite previous claims that dental morphology is selectively neutral. Aleuts and Eskimos were dentally distinguished from other Native Americans by low frequencies of traits such as Carabelli's trait, UM2 hypocone, and high frequencies of three-rooted LM1s (Turner, 1985b). The observation of some low trait frequencies among Aleut–Eskimo groups suggested to Turner that "the Amur branch of the expanding Sinodonts might have met Southeast Asian Sundadonts (ancestral Jomonese) advancing northward in the Japanese islands" (Turner, 1985b: 52). Aleut–Eskimo populations formed a distinct cluster in MMD dendrograms and displayed "fewer traits that differ significantly in frequency from Northern Asians than do American Indians" (Turner, 1985b: 46). From these data Turner (1983a, 1985a, 1985b, 1986c, 1994) surmised that the Aleut and Eskimo populations represented a separate group of late-arriving Old World peoples, an interpretation also proposed by Laughlin (1967).

Nonmetric dental trait frequencies in Turner's "greater Northwest Coast" sample were intermediate between those observed in Aleut–Eskimos and those in Amerindians, and unweighted pair-group method using averages (UPGMA) clustering of biological distances revealed that the greater Northwest Coast formed a rather distinct cluster (Turner, 1985b). However, other publications show the Na-Dene to cluster with some Amerindian groups (Greenberg *et al.*, 1986: 484; Turner,

1986c: 41). This latter pattern was noted by Powell (1993) in his reanalysis of Turner's published data. Difficulties in the phylogenetic placement of Na-Dene populations have been attributed to possible mixing of Na-Dene and other Native American crania in skeletal series (Greenberg *et al.*, 1986: 383), inappropriate pooling of samples as a single unit (Meltzer, 1993b: 100; Szathmary, 1986), or the type of clustering algorithm used (Powell, 1993).

Assuming that dental evolution was slow and that genetic drift was the main evolutionary force responsible for dental morphological differences between populations, the significant differences in dental form between these groups could not have originated in the New World (Turner, 1986c: 44). If the Clovis-first chronology is correct, there was insufficient time for such *in situ* dental divergence. Instead, these significant differences must have occurred in the Old World (Turner, 1983a: 147), where low environmental productivity and differing habitats in sub-Arctic regions of northeast Asia kept population size to a minimum and favored both biological and cultural differentiation (Turner, 1985b). Small groups of Sinodont populations could then have experienced genetic drift, forming several biologically distinct groups in northeast Asia during the Late Pleistocene. Migration of each of these populations into the New World could then produce the observed differences among their descendants (Turner, 1983a, 1985a,b, 1986b,c). Such Old World differentiation is perhaps supported by the great time depth for mtDNA divergences (Ward *et al.*, 1993; Szathmary, 1993b), indicating that New World populations accumulated mtDNA differences over some 20 000–40 000 years. Assuming that the first human colonists in the New World did not arrive before this date, the differentiation of these groups must have occurred in the Old World. Subsequent migrant populations would therefore have brought their dental and mtDNA characteristics with them, rather than evolving their traits in the New World.

Nonmetric evidence of Amerindian homogeneity

Albert Dahlberg (1949, 1968), one of the pioneers of dental anthropology, systematically examined nonmetric dental variation among Amerindians in an evolutionary context. Although Dahlberg noted that Amerindian populations were "not a homogeneous representation of a homogeneous people" (1963: 149), he felt that they did share several dental characteristics as a result of their common descent from a Late Pleistocene Asian population as well as from other evolutionary processes such as selection and drift.[12] Shared traits included a high frequency of UI1 shoveling and winging, UI2 tuberculum dentale, protostylids, metacones, third molar agenesis, five-cusped LM1, and a low frequency of Carabelli's trait.[13]

Many of these traits add to the surface area of the tooth, or serve to buttress and reinforce the integrity of the crown. Dahlberg postulated that these traits might have had a selective advantage in environments where abrasive diets and nondietary use of teeth led to excessive wear, fracturing, and general tooth loss due to pulp exposure (Dahlberg, 1968: 172). Other traits probably had no particular adaptive value, and varied in frequency among Amerindians because of genetic drift. Overall, Dahlberg felt that the dentition of Amerindians and their earliest ancestors provided several adaptive advantages over the reduced and less specialized teeth of some Old World populations: "We may speculate whether the form and size of dentition in the early Asiatic immigrants was particularly well adapted to the rigors of conquering the New World. It seems unlikely that the teeth of, say, the peoples of the Eastern Mediterranean would have been so successful in the variety of new environments experienced by the 'first' Amerinds." (Dahlberg, 1968: 174) Holocene Amerindians share not only the Sinodont dental pattern, but form a dentally homogeneous subgroup within the New World, according to Turner (1971, 1983a,b, 1985a, 1985b, 1986c, 1994). Unlike the Aleut–Eskimos and Na-Dene, the Amerindians as a group exhibited high frequencies of several dental traits including winging, shoveling, double shoveling, interruption grooves, Carabelli's trait, UM1 enamel extensions, two-rooted UP3, and others (Turner, 1985b: 67, 1986a). Some Amerindians were also distinguished by the presence of the UP3 distosagittal ridge, or "Uto-Aztecan" premolar (Morris *et al.*, 1978). This trait, which is limited to Amerindian populations (Turner, 1985b), may be due to a mutation that arose in the Americas and was driven to higher frequencies through either selection or drift (Scott and Turner, 1988).

The analysis of dental trait frequencies and MMD values provided several results, which suggested that Amerindians were dentally homogeneous. First, UPGMA cluster analyses of the MMD values for Amerindians, Aleuts, Eskimos, and Na-Dene populations indicated that Amerindians could be distinguished from other groups. In most published studies based upon dental phenotypic data, North and South American populations formed a separate cluster from Arctic and sub-Arctic groups (cf. Turner, 1985b: 38).

Second, the UPGMA dendrograms published by Turner (1983a, 1985b, 1986b) were interpreted as lacking any internal or regional geographic clustering, suggestive of either regional dental variations or the process of natural selection:

> [T]here is generally no strong geographical clustering in the Americas. Tlatelolco (central Mexico) is more closely linked with Peru than with Coahuila (northern Mexico) or Panama. This lack of strict geographic or linguistic organization is taken to mean that there is marked odontological homogeneity in the Americas due to a limited number of Paleo-Indian founders with a small gene pool and to limited occupation of the Americas. In other words, there is as much convergence as there is divergence. (Turner, 1986b: 11)

Third, variation in MMD values was greater among Amerindian samples than among Na-Dene and Aleut–Eskimo groups. This result suggested that the Amerindian population had been in place in the New World for a greater period of time than the other groups and thus had experienced more *in situ* dental divergence (Turner, 1983a: 152, 1985b: 46). Furthermore, North American populations exhibited greater diversity in MMDs than South American populations (Greenberg *et al.*, 1986: 480), although "the average divergence is not significantly greater in the north" (Turner, 1985b: 42). This observation was interpreted as a reflection of the rapid north-to-south movement of a single founding population (Greenberg *et al.*, 1986: 480; Turner, 1986b: 11, 1986c: 37).

A fourth finding pointing toward Amerindian dental homogeneity was Turner's observation that regional descent groups remain more like temporally earlier regional samples than extra-regional groups (Turner, 1985b: 45), as shown by the increasing MMD distance between Paleoindians and, successively, North American populations (0.088), South American populations (0.101), greater Northwest Coast populations (0.107), Eskimo populations (0.132), and Aleut populations (0.184). Using univariate comparisons, Turner (1985b: 78) found that there were fewer significant trait differences between North and South American populations than between these groups as a whole and north Asians. These data suggest that the pattern of dental variation in Amerindians was stable over time, and that Amerindians, like the Na-Dene and Aleut–Eskimo samples, form an internally homogeneous dental subgroup within the Americas.

Biological variation in early human remains from South America

The South American Paleoindians present a unique dental pattern in terms of dental trait frequencies. Paleoindian samples have a frequency

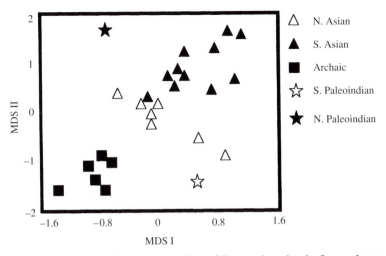

Figure 9.7 Multidimensional scaling of discrete dental traits for northeast Asian (Sinodont), southeast Asian (Sundadont), and American Paleoindians.

of incisor shoveling higher than that found in Sinodonts, and were intermediate between Sinodonts and Sundadonts for nearly all other dental discrete traits.

A principal components analysis of the craniofacial distances (Figure 9.4) revealed that early North and South American populations were different from Late Holocene Sinodonts and Sundadonts, contrary to the expectations of the tripartite model. The plot in Figure 9.5 shows the first three principal components, which explain 81.83% of the total variation in craniofacial dimensions among world samples.

Using a multidimensional scaling of dental discrete trait distances from South American Paleoindians and a detailed series of Sinodont and Sundadont populations obtained from Turner (1990), the Paleoindian sample shows as an outlier when compared with Archaic North Americans, Sinodonts, and Sundadonts (Figure 9.7). Southern Asian Sundadonts (such as east Malay and Thailand) are also separated from northern Asian Sinodonts (such as north China and Hong Kong). Early populations, including those from prehistoric Taiwan, Jomon, Baikal (neolithic Asians), and the North American Archaic (Black Earth, Anderson, Windover, Tick Island, and Bird Island sites) are also separated from modern groups. Furthermore, the oldest sample (Lagoa Santa pooled) is closest to the 8500 yr BP population from the site of Windover, Florida (Figure 9.4 and

Figure 9.5). Most importantly, the oldest American populations do not cluster with Sinodonts, as predicted by the tripartite model (Greenberg *et al.*, 1986).

An unweighted pair group method with arithmetic averages (UPGMA), clustering of biodistance data provides similar results (Figure 9.6). Using a 0.50 distance, five major clusters form, which can be divided into early samples (North American Archaic, South American Paleoindian sample [Lagoa Santa pooled], and Neolithic Lake Baikal) and modern samples (Sinodonts and Sundadonts). Again, early populations in the New World are not members of the Sinodont group. These results all show that early New World populations are dentally unique, and present a pattern of variation that is unlike modern Sinodont or Sundadont populations. The analyses also reveal a temporal trend in trait frequencies, with the oldest samples (Lagoa Santa, Windover, Baikal, Jomon, and prehistoric Taiwan) falling to the periphery of modern groups. These results are contrary to the claims of Turner and Greenberg *et al.*, in which all early New World populations represent a founding group of Sinodonts. Instead, I believe it is more likely that these populations represent a new pattern of dental variation that is unlike modern northeast Asians or modern Native American populations, and which may have been derived from a non-Mongoloid wave of migrants that first colonized the Americas.

NOTES

1 This is because they pre-date Darwinian thought, held to be the start of true evolutionary theory. The only construct available at that time was racial typology.
2 See Dietra Henderson's quotation about the cartoon Clovis-first model of migration in Chapter 7.
3 Some authors disagree with this usage (Campbell, 1986; Fox, 1996; Meltzer, 1993b; Szathmary, 1986).
4 The cranial index is Glabello-occipital length (GOL) relative to cranial breadth (XCB), initially used by Kemper, Blumenbach, and Morton. The facial index is the facial breadth/bizygomatic breadth (ZYB) relative to upper facial height/nasion–prosthion height (NPH).
5 For example, if we have $t = 3$ dimensions and GOL is positively correlated with maximum XCB, and both are negatively correlated with ZYB, the PC1 equation would look like this:

$$PC1 = 2.43\,(GOL) + 3.45\,(XCB) - 5.65\,(ZYB)$$

An individual's measurements are inserted for the GOL, XCB, and ZYB, and each is multiplied by a constant (an eigenvector) derived from the system of equations solution for three equations. Using these variables, the individual's PC score (eigenvalue) on the new variable (PC1) would be obtained.

There would be three PC scores for each observation (individual) because there are three variables and three simultaneous equations to solve in order to derive the eigenvectors from the data set.

6 Interorbital breadth (DKB) and ZYB are often proportional, but the DKB raw values are much smaller than those of ZYB. Size correction prevents either dimension from having undue weight in the generation of the PCs. It also eliminates sexual dimorphic variation, an uninformative source of variation in phenetic/phylogenetic studies.

7 Model-free analyses are usually in the form of racial–typological assessments of variation, rather than in the form of tests for population structure, as represented by the variation of the data.

8 Who laid his group's claim on Kennewick Man in court based on results of this PCA analysis.

9 Not an unexpected result, as they are not modern humans.

10 Given as $\sqrt{D^2}$ for a pair of individuals from a single population with distribution $\sqrt{(2t-1)}$, with $s^2 = 1$.

11 The sum of all tooth lengths (MD diameters) and breadths (BL diameters) in polar teeth for each individual in the data set.

12 Much of this work was undertaken by Al Dahlberg (1968: 149).

13 Carabelli's cusp is an accessory cusp on the mesiolingual cusp (protocone) of upper molars (usually the UM1).

10

Evolutionary models of Native American origins

One of the greatest faults and impediments of anthropology has always been and is largely to this day, in spite of ever-growing evidence to the contrary, the notion of the permanence of skull types, and their change-ability only through racial mixtures and replacements. It is time that this attitude be replaced by more modern and rational views on the subject, based on the steadily increasing knowledge of biological laws and pro-cesses, together with such powerful factors as segregation and isolation.

Hrdlička, 1935

10.1 EVOLUTION AND THE PEOPLING OF THE AMERICAS REDUX

Microevolutionary models

Boas (1912a,b), attempted to reconcile the migrationist approach of the racial–typologists with models of *in situ* biological change resulting from natural selection or genetic drift. He thought that Native Americans originated through one, or more migrations that intro-duced some variation to the New World (Boas, 1912a). However, once these populations settled in the Americas,

> ... the isolation and small number of individuals in each community
> gave rise to long-continued inbreeding, and with it, to a sharp
> individualization of local types. This was emphasized by subtle influences
> of natural and social environment. With the slow increase in numbers,
> these types came into contact; and through mixture and migration a new
> distribution of typical forms developed. Franz Boas (1912a,b)

This viewpoint was at odds with the traditional interpretations of biological variation within and among Native Americans. Although Boas recognized that migration and founder effect played a role in shaping the appearance of native populations, he also allowed that other evolutionary forces and environmental differences could addi-tionally bring about divergence. Most importantly, Boas (1912b) recognized that population growth and gene flow could also lead to homogeneity over time. Old World anthropologists "disavowed the notion that physical changes could have occurred among New World peoples" (Stewart and Newman, 1951: 21).

Templeton (1998b) and Karafet *et al.* (1999) have noted that population history and population structuring processes are not mutually exclusive, and both may have had a significant impact on the genetic structure of human populations. Most anthropologists dealing with phenotypic data of living native Americans tend to focus on historical aspects of variation, so that differences in modern groups can be interpreted as different historical events, such as "waves of migration" from Asia (Greenberg *et al.*, 1986; Neves *et al.*, 1996b; Turner, 1985b).

10.2   POINT OF ORIGIN FOR THE FIRST AMERICANS

A variety of data from past and present peoples in the Americas provide small clues about the Old World source for American humanity. These data range from discrete traits of the teeth to craniometric morphology to DNA evidence, all of which are presented in earlier parts of this volume and are reviewed here.

Nonmetric dental data and Old World relationships

Comparisons of Native American dental morphological variation to that of other populations all point to an Asian and *not* European origin for the First Americans. Hrdlička (1920) noted that Asian and Native American populations shared high frequencies of upper central incisor (UI1) and upper lateral incisor (UI2) shoveling, a finding supported by other investigators (Carbonell, 1963; Dahlberg, 1949, 1968; K. Hanihara, 1968; T. Hanihara, 1992; Turner, 1969, 1983b, 1986b, 1987, 1990). Kazuro Hanihara (1968) examined dental morphological variation among modern Japanese, Ainu, and Native Americans, and found that these groups shared a number of dental traits that he termed the "Mongoloid dental complex." Shared traits included high frequencies of UI1 shoveling and LM1 deflecting wrinkle, along with high frequencies of entoconulid, metaconulid, and protostylid (see Figure 9.3), all of which characterize populations of east Asia (Hanihara, 1968).

For the past three decades, Dr. Christy G. Turner II has conducted an important and broad-ranging study of dental variation in Pacific

Rim populations. He has found no evidence for a clinal distribution of dental traits in either Asia or the Americas, which he felt was evidence for a lack of natural selection in adult dental morphology.

One morphological trait in teeth, the distosagittal ridge UP3 (Moorrees *et al.*, 1963; Scott and Turner, 1988; Turner, 1985b), appears in both historic period and recent Amerindian speakers in the American southwest (mostly the Pima and Papago tribes of Arizona) at a frequency of 10.0%–11.0% (Moorrees *et al.*, 1963). This trait has its highest frequency among Paleoindian and Archaic populations (5%–18%), and gradually decreases over time to the present day (Powell, 1998). Presumably the decline over time represents the action of genetic drift on the distosagittal ridge, since Moorrees *et al.* (1963) and Turner (1985b) could find no selective advantage or disadvantage for this trait. The only other geographic area, besides North America, where the distosagittal UP3 has been recorded is Polynesia (Moorrees *et al.*, 1963). This may represent a potential southeast Asian prehistoric connection with the Americas, as suggested most recently by Brace *et al.* (2002).

Nuclear DNA

Kidd *et al.* (1998) tested for founder effects, and genetic bottlenecks, for 12 nuclear haplotypes. They also found that eight Amerindian language groups[1] had 5% lower overall heterozygosity (H^2) relative to the heterozygosity in Asian groups used for comparison. For single tandem repeats (STRs), Amerindians had lower heterozygosity and fewer alleles, but average $H^2 = 60\%$; east Asians also have considerable heterozygosity ($H^2 = 70\%$), making them similar to Native Americans for the 12 loci examined. Amerindians have subsets of alleles seen in Europe and Asia, and all Amerindian speakers share a subset of alleles rare or absent in east Asians – suggesting founder effect but no large genetic bottleneck (Kidd *et al.*, 1998).

Wright (1951) derived F_{st} values from pair-wise Mahalanobis' generalized distances (D^2) (Konigsberg and Blangero, 1993) obtained from craniofacial dimensions in Early ($n = 70$; Paleoindian and Archaic) and Late Holocene ($n = 650$) cranial samples in the Americas (Table 10.1). The total F_{st} for combined samples of Paleoindian/Archaic and Late Prehistoric American populations (total $n = 715$) was $F_{st} = 0.1547$, which is, as Powell and Neves (1999) note, well within the range of F_{st} values obtained from mtDNA variation in New World populations.[2]

Table 10.1 *Inter-individual Mahalanobis' D^2 distances for Paleoindian specimens*[a].

	K-Man	La Brea	CG 6A	CG 6B	WMS	WB	Spirit	LV
K-Man,	0							
La Brea	40.8785	0						
Cerca Grande 6A	21.1673	28.5956	0					
Cerca Grande 6B	13.8245	28.1190	3.7541	0				
Warm Mineral Spring (WMS)	35.31	26.8054	7.2639	8.5101	0			
Wizards Beach (WB)	7.8946	37.7262	8.9831	11.1791	22.1684	0		
Spirit Cave	27.1056	21.1060	5.8391	9.7502	6.3585	9.5726	0	
Lapa Vermelha (LV)	12.6391	24.9965	3.798	3.2441	6.0481	14.0533	5.8098	0

[a] Values based on individual dimensions, using the pooled within-groups covariance matrix for ten variables in the worldwide craniometric data. **Bold** indicates significance at $P \leq 0.05$ based on the criterion of Defrise-Gussenhoven (1967). See Table 9.1 for key to abbreviations.

Paleoindian trade networks and inter-regional gene flow

The great diversity of raw materials used to manufacture Clovis and Folsom points has suggested to some archaeologists that the Paleoindians wandered over fantastically huge ranges to collect raw materials. For example, Flint Ridge, Ohio, cherts are found as far afield as Washington state and New Mexico, while northern Texas alibates and central Texas Edwards cherts are found across America (Collins, 1999; Anderson and Sassaman, 1996).

An alternative hypothesis to the direct procurement model is one in which raw materials circulate among Paleoindian bands via exchange networks, so that exotic chert blanks move in a stepping-stone form, much in the same way as genes. In fact, ethnographic data on living !Kung San hunter-gatherers indicate that economic exchanges occur along the same lines as inter-group social inter-actions.[3] Marriage partners are exchanged along with material items, easing competition for limited resources (Braun and Plog, 1981; Wiessner, 1977). This process of exchange can be viewed as a series of random walks away from and back to an object's point of origin, so that the amount of a particular material in an archaeological assemblage is a function both of distance to source and time (Renfrew, 1973).

Gene flow (biological exchange) can also be modeled in this way. Konigsberg's (1987, 1990) model of *isolation by spatial and temporal distance* accounts for gene flow across time and space. Under this model, at any given time, populations that are geographically closer to each other should be genetically (and phenotypically) more similar due to the increased likelihood of gene flow between them. Over time, populations fixed at a given geographic distance should become increasingly similar owing to the continuous process of gene flow. Given that phenotypic variation is a general reflection of genetic variation, we would expect that skeletal series would be more similar within regions than between regions. Geographic and biological distances, *controlling for time*, should be positively correlated. In other words, two subpopulations, at a given point in time, are more likely to share more genes (and thus be pheno-typically more similar) when they are close to one another on the land-scape. The opposite is true when they are far apart on the landscape (i.e. they have a lesser chance of sharing genes) when separated by space at a given point in time because of isolation by distance. Temporal and biological distances, controlling for space, should be negatively correlated, because demes fixed on the landscape at a large geographic distance start off dissimilar (owing to isolation by distance) but, as time progresses, become more biologically similar to one another; bio-distances therefore decrease. In demes with small effective population sizes (N_e) the homogeneity created by gene flow and inter-marriage is balanced by genetic drift and loss of alleles via deme extinction and random events. The remains of Paleoindians at Marmes rockshelter (Washington state) and Patagonia's Fells Cave and Cerro Sota Cave (Bird, 1938b) are, perhaps, examples of random loss of alleles among victims of seismic activities, rockfalls, and avalanches (see Chapter 7).

The distribution of objects or raw materials (shell beads, jadeite pendants and other items of adornment, rare cherts, and obsidians, etc.), exchanged as marriage gifts or bride price, should exhibit the same patterns as genes represented by the biological distances; in other words, groups that regularly exchange marriage partners and genes also become similar. Carried out over a long time, this creates a pattern similar to a "down the line" circulation of exotic materials, and may better explain the presence of exotic items in the archaeological assemblages of distant Paleoindian groups.

Cranial evidence for microevolution in the Americas

The phenotypic inter-individual distances for Paleoindians (Table 10.1) were calculated by Powell and Neves (1999). Craniofacial distances were calculated within a sample of Paleoindians ($n = 8$), discussed in Chapter 7. The latitude and longitude values for each individual were used to calculate inter-individual geographic distances using a great circle distance formula.[4] Temporal distances were computed from differences in the median ^{14}C age of each Paleoindian skeleton from the data provided in Chapter 7. The initial matrix correlations were calculated from the phenotypic, geographic, and temporal distances using 1000 iterations of a Mantel permutation test to obtain random matrix correlations to determine the significance of the observed matrix correlations.

Only the phenotypic and geographic distance matrices exhibited significant positive correlation ($r = 0.4079$; $p = 0.0370$). None of the other matrices were significantly correlated, although phenotypic and temporal distances were negatively correlated but very close to 0 ($r = -0.0293$; $p = 0.4410$). Partial correlations accounting for time and space were generated from the method suggested by Konigsberg (1987, 1990):

$$r_{xy\,z} = \frac{r_{xy} - (r_{xz})(r_{yz})}{\sqrt{(1 - r_{xz}^2)}\sqrt{(1 - r_{yz}^2)}} \tag{10.1}$$

where x, y, and z represent variables and r is the correlation coefficient for the subscripted variables, and $xy.z$ is the partial correlation of x and y, taking into account the effect of z on the correlation of both.

The Lagoa Santa skeletons exhibit less phenotypic and cultural diversity than other groups. The results for the pooled North and South American Paleoindians indicated a weak negative partial correlation ($r = 0.0719$) between phenotypic distance and geographic distance, controlling for time, with a strong negative partial correlation ($r = -0.9161$) between phenotypic and temporal distance. These results are what would be expected if the North and South Americans sampled experienced relatively more genetic drift than gene flow over a given period of time. The large geographic distances between the North and South American Paleoindian remains most likely affect the results expected from this temporal–spatial analysis.

The model-free analyses depict a great degree of craniofacial similarity within the ancient South American remains, while their North American contemporaries exhibit craniofacial and dental heterogeneity (Jantz and Owsley, 1999; Powell, 1995; Powell and Neves, 1999; Powell and Rose, 1999; Steele and Powell, 1993). When the South American Paleoindian samples are removed from the analyses, a different picture emerges. The partial correlation of phenotypic and spatial distance (controlling for time) becomes strongly positive ($r = 0.9016$), while the phenotypic and temporal partial correlations (controlling for space) are negative ($r = -0.2773$), as predicted in Konigsberg's (1985) temporal–spatial stepping-stone migration model for inter-deme gene flow over time.

The model-free patterns and model-bound results may be indicative of a low level of inter-continental bioarchaeological interaction as suggested by the southern-most distribution of Clovis points in Panama and their absence in South America (Roosevelt et al., 2002). The development of unique point styles (fishtail) and sites (Monte Verde) in South America (Dillehay, 2000; Roosevelt et al., 2002) is also consistent with negligible biocultural interaction of Late Pleistocene populations between the two Americas.

A French connection? Probably not

As noted in Chapter 6, Straus (2000) presented several good archaeological and geoarchaeological reasons why a transatlantic migration of Solutrean peoples of Spain and France at the time of the last glacial maximum could never have occurred during the Late Pleistocene.

Similarly, Long *et al.* (1999) found no genetic evidence from analysis of direct admixture of pre-Columbian Americans and European DNAs based on evolutionary trees of several nuclear genes (nDNAs). Stone and Stoneking (1996) obtained similar results for a pre-Columbian Oneota skeletal population, using mtDNA markers.

Although a few of the Paleoindian crania had typicality probabilities (Table 9.1) greater than 50% for placement in the Howells–Hanihara European samples, only the Warm Mineral Spring "Brown" skull had a high probability ($P_t = 0.9183$) of being typical of the European comparative samples.

In addition to the above-listed genetic studies, Hammer *et al.* (1997) examined 12 nDNA loci and 2 Y-chromosome haplotype markers and found that haplotypes 1C and 1F are major New World founders, while 1B, 1I, and 1U are minor (or arrived via late admixture); 1G is a New World mutation. More than one paternal migration to the New World is needed to explain data – one from the homeland of Kets (1C) and another from Lake Baikal (1F). Brace *et al.* (2002) presented a compromise model, in which east Asia was occupied by a bioculturally admixed Eurasian population during the Late Pleistocene and Early Holocene, represented by Minatogawa, Upper Cave, and Jomon/Ainu skeletons, as well as by Late Holocene Native American evidence of Eurasian genes (Brown's X haplotype). This hypothetical population may have been a source of European/proto-Caucasoid (see Chatters *et al.*, 1999; Steele and Powell, 1993) phenotypes noted by some anthropologists (Chatters *et al.*, 1999; Stanford and Bradley, 2002).

Merriwether (2002) and Neel *et al.* (1994) argue, based on D-loop RFLPs of mtDNA, that only a single migration from Mongolia (or shared ancestors of Mongols and Amerindians) is needed to explain mtDNA diversity. Asian-specific X6 and X7 haplogroups are widely distributed in the New World at low frequency, and this will over-estimate gene flow between groups, thus making them all appear genetically similar, as if they were from a single founding migration to the Americas. Likewise, Merriwether *et al.* (1995) have used their four founding mtDNA lineages to indicate that all Native American DNAs are from a single founding/colonization event originating in Asia.

Nichols' (1995) historical linguistic examination of Pacific languages suggested that two or more migrations of coastally adapted Asian peoples to the Americas might have occurred 15 000–12 000 yr BP. Her Pacific Rim linguistic group is older than other groups that she has examined, and dates to before the last glacial maximum. The linguistic markers are widely distributed, suggesting inter-mingling of language families, and are closest first to other Amerindians, then to Australasians and populations in Southeast Asia. Languages suggest common ancestors for Australasians and SA Amerindians (which fits with Neves' data), with common ancestors feeding both populations.

O'Rourke et al. (1999) examined mtDNA from ancient skeletons (aDNA) and found that all mtDNA lineages seen among contemporary peoples were present in the ancient remains, that some rare or absent haplogroups in modern groups may have been present in higher frequency in the First Americans, and that regional patterns were established several thousand years ago, as noted by Powell (1995) for dental discrete traits and odontometric variation in ancient Americans. O'Rourke et al. (1999) found no evidence for a genetic bottleneck and no evidence for small, discrete migrations from Asia. They also found that population decline in the wake of European contact did not greatly affect mtDNA diversity in contemporary Native Americans.

Archaeological views

Goebel et al. (1997) argue that archaeological data from Siberia indicate no populations present before 25 000 yr BP, meaning that there was no colonization of Beringia until after the last glacial maximum at 18–15 kya, and, if entry was before 12 000 yr BP, it was by a coastal route. Rodgers et al. (1992) concur with Goebel et al. (1997), noting that ice-age geographic barriers structured patterns of linguistic and genetic variation in modern American Indians. They also noted that *in situ* population structure was a more parsimonious way to explain these data than multiple waves of migration (contra Greenberg et al., 1986).

Schurr et al. (1999) found that the mtDNA and Y-chromosome diversity of Siberian Chukchi populations suggest that there were multiple source populations in Asia (contra Kolman et al., 1996), and found no evidence for a single colonization of America from Siberia (contra Merriwether, 2002). Haplotype B is absent in Aleuts, Inuits (Eskimos), and Na-Dene populations, which provides limited support for the tripartite concept that states that these three Native American groups had a different origin from all other native peoples in the Americas (Amerindians). Schurr et al. (1999) state: "Paleoindian migration brought haplogroups A, C, and D into the New World *before* [italics mine] Beringian expansion." The Ainu and Itel'men of the Kamchatka Peninsula have a low frequency of B mtDNAs (Krasheninnkov, 1972, cited in Schurr et al., 1999). Schanfield et al. (1990) found that analysis of immunoglobulins (Km and Gm) supported four waves of population expansion (colonization) from east Asia. Overall, the colonization of the Americas and Siberia is much more complex than the multiple expansion model suggests.

10.3   MODEL-BOUND CRANIOMETRIC APPROACHES

Relethford–Blangero (1990) analysis

This model-bound approach to phenotypic variation employs the R matrix method of Harpending and Ward (1982), allowing for the assessment of genetic variation within and between populations via the distance measure F_{st} (Chapter 3, Equation 3.9). Phenotypic traits with estimated narrow-sense heritabilities are then substituted for the genetic data under the assumption that the genotypic variance is proportional to the phenotypic variance (Williams-Blangero and Blangero, 1989), so that:

$$G = h^2 P \tag{10.2}$$

For this method, the phenotypic data are converted to size-free shape variables either by centering the observations on the total sample mean or by using a Q-mode correction (Darroch and Mosimann, 1985). The Q-mode-corrected data are then converted to a g-by-t matrix of deviations (Δ) of the group means from the weighted total means. The method also requires an estimate of the narrow-sense heritability (h^2) for the trait. Devor (1987) obtained an average heritability for craniofacial dimensions of $h^2 = 0.55$, a value that has been used in numerous studies (Powell, 1995; Powell and Neves, 1999; Relethford, 1994, 1995; Relethford and Harpending, 1994). An average h^2 in the range of 0.33–9.00 for dental morphology and metrics is a fair estimate, with a median of $h^2 = 0.33$; given that $G = h^2 \times P$, a codivergence matrix C, can be computed as:

$$C = \Delta G^{-1} \Delta' \tag{10.3}$$

Here, the inverse of a t-by-t pooled within group additive genetic variance-covariance matrix is G^{-1}. The codivergence matrix is then averaged over all populations and weighted by population size (Blangero, 1990; Relethford and Blangero, 1990; Relethford and Harpending, 1994). The average codivergence over all t traits is (C/t), so that Wright's (1951) between-group variance measure F_{st}, then becomes the average genetic distance to the centroid:

$$F_{st} = \frac{\sum\limits_{i=1}^{g} w_i C_{ii}}{\left(2t + \sum\limits_{i=1}^{g} w_i C_{ii}\right)} \tag{10.4}$$

Low values of F_{st}, indicate limited between-group genetic variation with g subdivisions (demes), t traits, and w_i sample weights for each of the i samples from the g demes. Sample weights of $1/g$ can be used, but this assumes that all demes are of equal effective size, thus eliminating any possible effects from differences in long-term effective size (drift). The R matrix thus becomes:

$$R = \frac{C(1 - F_{st})}{2t} \tag{10.5}$$

The resulting diagonal elements, r_{ij}, of the R matrix are the genetic distances, d_{ij}, of each ith, jth deme to a regional centroid (Harpending and Jenkins, 1973). The genetic distance between demes i and j becomes:

$$d_{ij} = r_{ii} + r_{jj} - 2r_{ij} \tag{10.6}$$

Cranial dimensions for pooled samples representing Greenberg *et al.*'s (1986) Amerindians ($n = 11$ demes), Na-Dene ($n = 2$ demes), and Eskimos ($n = 2$ demes) were tested using the Relethford–Blangero method (1990), under the assumption that all groups (demes) have similar or equal long-term effective sizes using a relative weight of 1 for each sample. This assumes that any structure reflected in the genetic distances is due to gene flow (migration), selection, or mutation.

Genetic, and thus phenotypic, diversity via drift and migration are functions of inter-deme distance as well as deme effective size (N_e). The result of this assumption is presented in Figure 10.1a. Note that the North and South American Paleoindians are strongly differentiated in the principal coordinate plot of genetic distances in the Relethford–Blangero analysis of craniofacial dimensions, and that they are a biologically different population from late Holocene Native Americans. Also note that each of the two Aleut–Eskimo (solid squares in Figure 10.1) and Na-Dene (open circles in Figure 10.1) samples are grouped together, suggesting genetic similarity and, for Aleut–Eskimos, their clear separation from sub-Arctic native peoples in North America. The deviation of North and South American Paleoindians from the Late Holocene samples (Figure 9.7) has been observed in many model-free, racial–typological studies and has been interpreted as a result of multiple colonization/migration to the Americas (Brace *et al.*, 2002;

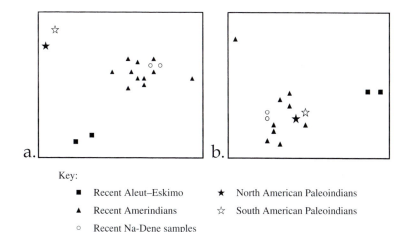

Key:

■ Recent Aleut–Eskimo   ★ North American Paleoindians

▲ Recent Amerindians   ☆ South American Paleoindians

○ Recent Na-Dene samples

Figure 10.1 Principal coordinates ordination based on **R** matrix analysis of New World craniofacial data from the Relethford–Blangero analysis. (a) All populations given equal weight: $N_e = 3$ for all groups (i.e. no drift effect); (b) Paleoindians given lower weight: $N_e = 1$ for Paleoindians, $N_e = 3$ for all other groups (to account for the smaller population size of Paleoindians).

Chatters *et al.*, 1999; Greenberg *et al.*, 1986; Steele and Powell, 1992, 1993, 2002; Turner, 1985b) or as a replacement of an earlier founding population, by late-arriving Mongol hordes (Chatters, 1998; Chatters *et al.*, 1999). An alternative to a *post hoc* typological approach is to test specific hypotheses, as demonstrated in the next section.

Genetic drift

Evidence for genetic drift as a factor explaining biological variation among populations is found in DNA sequence data, as well as in dental morphology, in the form of a possible founder effect (a special type of drift). The assumption of equal long-term effective size for the populations used in the analysis (Figure 10.1b) may not be acceptable, given what is known about past and present forager demography and subsistence. Steele *et al.* (1998) provided environment-specific simulation of Paleoindian migration to the Americas. They found that to colonize all of North and South America in a Clovis-first time frame would yield a population density of 0.023 persons per km^2, given the productivity of environmental megapatches exploited by Paleoindians over a period of 3000 years (13 000–10 000 yr BP).

This suggests that Paleoindian population densities were low (as previously assumed by archaeologists), and implies that the average N_e for Late Pleistocene and Early Holocene foragers was small. Assuming that 5000 Paleoindian bands were scattered across North America, the Steele *et al.* (1998) density estimate results in a short-term effective size in the range of $N_e = 36–100$ persons per deme (Powell and Neves, 1999).

Based on the estimated N_e, a reanalysis was undertaken using a reduced weight (w_i) of 0.30 for Paleoindians, rather than a weight of 1, and a weight of 1 for all other groups (Figure 10.1a). Such values of demographic weight account for a smaller deme size in Paleoindian hunter-gatherers, relative to more sedentary Middle and Late Holocene Native American groups, and result in a reduced distance from the Late Holocene comparative samples (Figure 10.1a). This result indicates that the phenotypic variance among the First Americans is a function of their small population and subpopulation sizes, as opposed to the huge populations implied in Clovis-first megafaunal overkill models (Martin, 1973, 1984). This would imply that genetic drift must have been an important factor in the structure of early populations in the Americas, resulting in a genetic and phenotypic deviation from later populations.

I (Powell, 1997) performed a series of genetic variance simulations to predict what might have occurred as a result of a Clovis-first colonization with an initial effective population of $N_e = 50$ for a relatively monomorphic phenotypic trait[5] in the founder population, controlled by ten underlying genetic loci. Given these conditions, the effective population sizes for Paleoindian groups must have been quite large to prevent genetic drift from occurring: a viewpoint consistent with population size predictions used in the Clovis megafaunal overkill models of Martin (1967, 1984). A human population growth rate of the order of $r = 0.40$ would be needed to prevent population structuring through random genetic drift. This high population growth rate has only been observed during the Industrial Revolution ($r = 0.44$) and in some modern developing nations ($r = 0.38$) (Weiss, 1973).

The drift hypothesis appears to account for the observations of phenotypic craniofacial and dental diversity in ancient humans in the Americas without the need to fall back on population replacement (Chatters *et al.*, 1999) and multiple migration models (Greenberg *et al.*, 1986). Genetic drift could also account for the dramatic phenotypic heterogeneity (see Figure 8.2) among the First Americans, as depicted in model-free typological analyses (Figures 9.4 and 9.5) used to interpret the phenotypic uniqueness of many Late Pleistocene skeletons in the Americas (i.e. Kennewick, Wilson–Leonard, and La Brea, to name a few). In my opinion, the use of nineteenth-century typological models provides less satisfactory results than do models that rely on evolutionary mechanisms.

The Relethford–Blangero (1990) model is used here to detect deviations from an equilibrium between gene flow and genetic drift derived from observed $(\bar{v}_i)$ and expected $[E(\bar{v}_i)]$ values of within-group phenotypic variance. Residual within-group variances were calculated as

$$R(\bar{v}_i) = \bar{v}_i - E(\bar{v}_i) \tag{10.7}$$

Standard errors for residuals were obtained by jackknifing across the t variables. The residual divided by its standard error is distributed as a t-statistic with $t-1$ degrees of freedom. Positive residuals for this model can represent either:

1. higher rates of gene flow between the groups under examination;
2. very high long-distance mutation rates in one of the g groups in the analysis;
3. larger effective population size (N_e) in one of the groups Relethford and Harpending, 1990,
4. different timing of population growth relative to the other groups; or
5. nonrandom sampling effects or population pooling that artificially increases the within-group variance.

The North and South American composite samples of Paleoindians both have significantly ($p = 0.00$ to 0.02) greater observed craniofacial variation than expected in equilibrium conditions. This suggests that the modern American comparative groups might have larger population size, as demonstrated in Figure 10.1. Alternatively, it is just as likely that the Paleoindian skeletal samples are a nonrandom assortment of ancient Americans. The latter is often questioned by critics of Paleoindian bioarchaeological research. Of course, it does stretch credibility to believe that the small numbers of ancient remains currently known represent an actual population, but as is the case in the analyses of other fossil material, they are all that we have, which may explain the ferocity with which the Kennewick plaintiffs attacked the government's decision and final report.[6] In using such remains in these analyses, the assumption that they are a random collection of Late Pleistocene and Early Holocene individuals must be made, just as archaeologists must assume that the stone tools they discover are representative of the kinds of stone objects used by people in pre-historic cultures. It is true that, once in a while, a new find (like Kennewick, Prince of Wales Island, and Arlington Springs), can turn our view of past peoples and past lifeways upside down. The initial **R** matrix indicates that if Paleoindian effective population sizes were small, this probably affected their genetic and phenotypic variation, through the evolutionary process of genetic drift. Several of the studies presented here indicated that drift was a likely factor in causing the observed patterns of inter-individual variation among the First Americans. If genetic drift occurred in a polymorphic founding popula-tion (or populations) isolated by eco-geographic barriers (Rodgers *et al.*, 1992; Szathmary, 1993b) or simply by distance (Powell, 1995, 1997), it may have resulted in the extreme morphological diversity of Paleoindians relative to Late Holocene natives (see Figure 9.4).

NOTES

1 *Sensu* Greenberg *et al.* (1986).
2 New World Alu insertion data for mtDNAs by Novick *et al.* (1998).
3 A practice called !*Hraxo*, which has some similarities to the payment of bride price, found in some horticultural societies in the South Pacific.
4 This distance, rather than straight-line equations, accounts for the curved surface of the Earth.
5 An example might be upper-incisor shoveling.
6 Because adding one new sample to your data set can make a big difference to your results.

11

The First Americans: Native American origins

11.1 TRADITIONAL VIEWS OF THE PEOPLING OF THE AMERICAS

Most researchers studying the peopling of the Americas are presented with a simple explanation for how humans came to the Americas from east Asia. At first, like most who hear the story, I was a true believer and never doubted the veracity of this traditional anthropological tale, which is still taught to university undergraduates and anthropology graduate students around the world:

All Native Americans trace their biological and cultural roots to one or more groups of Late Pleistocene (Upper Paleolithic) hunters from northeast Asia who migrated to North America across the Bering Land Bridge in pursuit of giant mammals that provided their sustenance. Once in Alaska, these intrepid hunters rushed south through an Ice-Free Corridor between two massive ice sheets, and in the process created a new set of stylized tools, later to be called Clovis, Fishtail, and later, Folsom. The hunters then spread across the whole of North and South America and hunted their prey to extinction. These ancient hunters left behind descendants who learned to cultivate plants, and build towns, cities, chiefdoms, and kingdoms, which then collapsed in the wake of European contact and colonization. The descendants of the ancient hunters were greatly reduced in number by epidemic disease, but now number in the millions. They were pushed off their traditional homelands and were forced onto reserves and often forced to accept new languages, religious beliefs, and cultural practices.

This story has been passed, in a variety of forms, from teachers to students for nearly two centuries, with very little alteration. In the last 20 or so years it appears that certain parts of the story are being re-cast in light of new discoveries, new methods, new theories, and new attitudes.

Because some Native Americans have faces that appear similar to some northeast Asians and share certain soft-tissue features such as skin

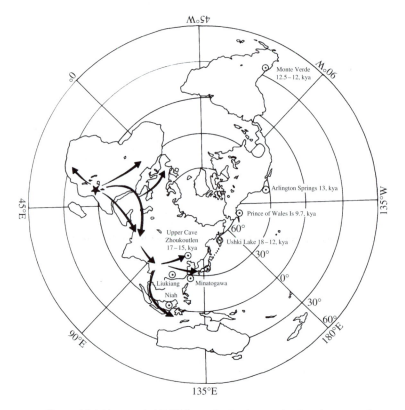

Figure 11.1 Akazawa's (1999) hypothesized coastal migration route for the peopling of the Americas. Note, in this model Paleoindians would be derived from Late Pleistocene peoples of southeast Asia and Japan, as well as Jomon and Ainu peoples.

color and epicanthic fold around the eye (which gives the eye an "almond-shaped" appearance), early observers assumed that northeast Asians were the ancestors of all New World native peoples. This paradigm was staunchly supported by Hrdlička and other American physical anthropologists. To date, the data supporting this traditional scientific view of Native American origins are scanty, conflicting, and confusing. New techniques are pointing toward different dates and modes of entry for the First Americans. It is true that there was a "land bridge" between the Old and New World, as predicted by José de Acosta in the fifteenth century (see the Prologue and Chapter 1). Moreover, the evidence for the occupation of Beringia by humans and their mammalian prey during periglacial periods is well documented. However, the Ice-Free Corridor has been less productive in terms of archaeological evidence of a human presence. Since the 1970s scholars have looked to the seashores of the Pacific Rim (Figure 11.1) as a possible route into the New World (Akazawa, 1999; Dixon, 1999; Fladmark, 1978).

As noted by Dixon (1999), human remains have now been found (see Neves *et al.*, 1999a, 1999b) that pre-date the 11 000 yr BP opening of the "Ice-Free" (McKenzie) Corridor between the Laurentide and Cordilleran ice sheets, which suggests that these intrepid explorers must have used some route other than this corridor to enter subglacial North America. Dixon (1999), Fladmark (1978), and Mandryk (1990) have produced new evidence to discount the likelihood of colonization of the Americas via an "Ice-Free Corridor." The former two authors have proposed an alternative route along the Pacific coasts of east Asia and North America (see also Akazawa, 1999). A coastal route by boat would have humans entering the North American continent just below the Cordilleran ice sheet, then moving into the continental interior. The recent critics of the Ice-Free Corridor route of entry have generally been met in kind by the "true believers," who take the Ice-Free Corridor to be an undeniable scientific fact.

Another critical issue arises when the Ice-Free Corridor model is referred to as an *event* that implies nearly instantaneous American occupation. The peopling of the New World was not a series of migration "events," it was a time-transgressive process of demographic expansion into an unknown territory not previously occupied by humans (Powell and Neves, 1999: 158).

11.2   AN ALTERNATIVE VIEW OF HUMAN OCCUPATION IN THE AMERICAS

The peopling of the Americas was a very complex process, leaving behind complex evidence. Skeletons found thus far represent persons drawn from a presumably small group, so sampling effect is a major problem in terms of the postulation of patterns and their causes.

As people and animals adapted to new environmental conditions in the New World, these adaptations may have made it possible for a group of pre-Clovis colonists to enter America; these were followed by Clovis peoples during the very latest Pleistocene period. These ancient explorers lived, died, and left behind a rich and interesting archaeological record that included the mortal remains of their dead.

Racial–typological analyses find Paleoindians (or Paleoamericans, as some may prefer) to have a skeletal morphology similar to that of modern Southeast Asians and other Pacific Rim groups (Neves *et al.*, 1998; Powell and Rose, 1999; Steele and Powell, 1999). Nichols' (1995) most recent linguistic analysis of Pacific Rim languages points toward a southern Asian origin for some American languages. This finding is concordant with the craniofacial morphology of the First Americans assessed in Chapters 9 and 10, and may indicate that early groups in coastal Asia and the Americas share common ancestors (Akazawa, 1999; Brace *et al.*, 2002; Neves *et al.*, 1998, 1999a). However, to interpret this as evidence of a separate wave of migration into the Americas suggests that post-colonization processes had little effect on the structure of populations. Genetic data and model-bound (i.e. evolutionary) analysis of craniodental phenotypes argue otherwise. Cavalli-Sforza *et al.* (1994) found a Polynesian–coastal Pacific American genetic connection based on their synthetic nDNA maps and trees, but posit this pattern to a Late Holocene Polynesia–South America direct contact (cf. Thor Heyerdahl, 1950). Although Heyerdahl's model was debunked in the 1960s, other data do support a connection between the South Pacific and the Americas. For example, HLA genetic data find seven HLA allotypes common to Australia, Micronesia, Melanesia, Western Polynesia, and America (Figure 11.2).

As previously noted, Nichols' linguistic analysis finds a connection between Native American languages and those of Australasia (Nichols, 1990, 1995, 2002). This linguistic connection supports both the typological and evolutionary results presented in this book that also note a Southeast Asian connection. This linguistic connection has been heavily criticized by the so-called "Clovis Mafia" (i.e. those for whom the Clovis-first story and a northeast Asian origin are inalienable and literal truths). A linguistic connection between Southeast Asia and the Americas completely flies in the face of the Clovis-first linguistic analysis of Greenberg (1985) and does not indicate a northeast Asian origin for Paleoindians or for their presumed Native American descendants.

When compared with modern Native Americans, Paleoindians can be excluded (with 95% confidence) from modern Amerindians and Europeans (Figure 9.5); this result was noted in work by Neves (Neves and Pucciarelli, 1989; Neves *et al.*, 1998, 1999a, 1999b) and Powell (Powell, 2002; Powell and Neves, 1999; Powell and Rose, 1999; Steele and Powell, 1999).

There is no evidence for a European component of craniofacial variation (Chatters, 1998, 2000; Chatters *et al.*, 1999), but similarities with the Ainu (whom some refer to as "Caucasoids") are evident (Brace *et al.*, 2002). Similar results from nDNA were found by Long *et al.* (1999) and O'Rourke *et al.* (1999), who found no European admixture before AD 500 and high DNA diversity in ancient remains. The dental pattern of Paleoindians is unique – they are intermediate in trait frequencies

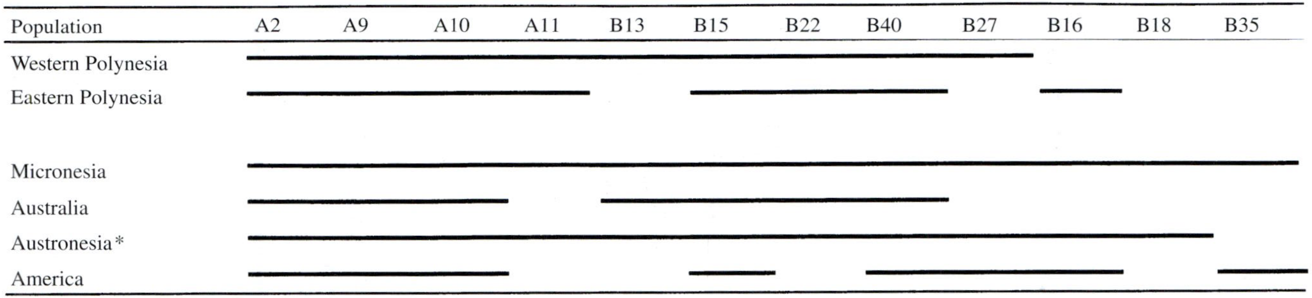

Population	A2	A9	A10	A11	B13	B15	B22	B40	B27	B16	B18	B35
Western Polynesia												
Eastern Polynesia												
Micronesia												
Australia												
Austronesia *												
America												

* Austronesian-speaking Melanesians.

Figure 11.2 Presence of A and B HLAs for Pacific Rim populations.

between the Sinodont and Sundadont pattern. However, they express rare and unique traits, and a high degree of dental developmental problems typical of the effects of genetic drift and/or inbreeding.[1]

The racial–typological analyses of Paleoindian crania in Chapter 9 indicate the First American remains to be completely different from their presumed Late Holocene descendants now living throughout the Americas. Evolutionary analyses using the F_{st} statistic provide a testable alternative to *ad hoc* racial typologies. On the whole, it seems that DNA and evolutionary analyses of ancient craniofacial features point toward a Southeast Asian (Sundadont) origin for the point of origin for the first peoples to colonize the Americas. Several new lines of evidence also support this viewpoint, such as new genetic and linguistic analyses (Brace *et al.*, 2002; Dixon, 1999; Nichols, 2002).

There is higher cranial and dental diversity within Paleoindian and Archaic New World groups than within modern Native Americans, a finding consistent with several typological studies (Jantz and Owsley, 2001; O'Rourke *et al.*, 1996; Steele and Powell, 1994). This is perhaps due to the genetic structure and effective population size of the First Americans (Powell and Neves, 1999).

F_{st} (as discussed in Chapters 3 and 10) is a measure of between-group genetic variation relative to the total genetic variation present in a population; it is also a measure of genetic distance that provides an evolutionary (contra typological) measure of how different two groups are based on their genetic structure, as determined from their pheno-types, (see Box 3.1 and Relethford and Blangero, 1990), so that low values represent groups that are genetically more similar and therefore less distant from one another. Powell and Neves (1999) found that Amerindians and Paleoindians produced an F_{st} of 0.174 ± 0.01, which is just outside the range of F_{st} values for modern worldwide human craniofacial variation: F_{st} range $= 0.065$–0.085 (Relethford, 1994). These results indicate that, for the dimensions under study, there is sufficient divergence to consider the First Americans to be *completely* separated from modern worldwide human variation, including that of native peoples of North America. This should come as no surprise, since Paleoindians are ancient and *not* modern people, as is also the case with other Late Pleistocene and Early Holocene humans. This may help to explain why Kennewick Man, Luzia, and more well-known ancient skeletons present unusual phenotypes.[2]

A similar pattern was noted by Weidenreich (1947), who used the cranial index to compare Late Pleistocene skulls in Asia and Europe with those of Late Holocene peoples in the same region, respectively, which may indicate selection, drift, or other evolutionary or adaptive forces operating on some of these cranial features throughout the Holocene. Facial dimensions and vault chords of ancient and modern peoples in the Americas display a consistent F_{st} pattern, suggesting that there has been less change in this area of the skull than in the brain case during the Holocene.

A trait-by-trait F_{st} analysis indicated that Paleoindians and modern Native Americans differ most in their neurocranial breadths, heights, and lengths (the average F_{st} is close to 0.1543). Paleoindian remains clearly deviate from the modern condition for these vault dimensions. This pattern has been observed for Late Pleistocene and modern populations in Asia, Europe, and parts of Africa, which to this author is a good indication that there was a worldwide change in craniofacial morphology during the Holocene. Similar results were obtained by Wendorf and Schild (1986, 1996), who suggested that the differences represent craniofacial adaptation to a horticultural/ agricultural diet and lifeway during the environmental changes and human population growth of the Middle- to Late Holocene.

The great American anthropologist Ales Hrdlička (1935) said it best when comparing the explanatory power of race and evolution, as attested by the opening quote in Chapter 10, which I paraphrase less elegantly here:

The concept that variation comes only from "mixtures or replacements" is based on the assumption of the permanence of skull types, while evolutionary models that employ "biological laws and processes" such as "segregation" of alleles and "isolation" (i.e. genetic drift) are much more "powerful" as explanatory tools with which to examine human variation anywhere, but especially in the Americas.

Evidence for ancient population structure from teeth, among Middle Holocene North Americans (Powell, 1995), includes a pattern of correlations of phenotypic distances with time and space distances among Archaic populations (Powell, 1998). These results are suggestive of the actions of regional population structuring via the action of intra- or inter-regional gene flow and genetic drift on a small colonizing population. Early American remains exhibit rare features and phenotypes seen to a lesser degree in modern Amerindians,[3] suggesting that founder effect followed by random drift and/or migration over the past 10 000 to 12 000 years might best explain the variation within, and differences between, ancient and contemporary peoples in the Americas – without resorting to racial–typological multiple migration schemes.

The number of Amerindian-founding Asian lineages (e.g. "migrations") in typological assessments is still an unanswered question – there may have been two or more, but at present the possibility of a single founding event during the Late Pleistocene cannot be ruled out, with considerable microevolutionary change from gene flow, drift, and natural or sexual selection. Clearly, *in situ* drift, including founder effect, would have occurred if colonizing groups were relatively small, as illustrated by the results of the Relethford–Blangero analysis presented in Chapters 3 and 10. This is a model that I favor, rather than a multiple migration/colonization model (cf. Brace *et al.*, 2002; Gladwin, 1947; Greenberg, 1985; Greenberg *et al.*, 1986; Neves and Pucciarelli, 1998; Neves *et al.*, 2003; Turner, 1985b).

This book has been couched in terms of racial typology vs. evolutionary assessments. The racial approach is based on a historical concept in which phenotypically different groups (races) separately contribute to the colonization and peopling of the Americas. It is unlikely that migration alone or evolution alone can adequately explain the patterns of biological and cultural variation seen among ancient and modern peoples in the Americas. However, a evolutionary approach provides a better way of assessing the limited data obtained from the physical remains of the First Americans.

NOTES

1 These have quite similar effects on genotypic frequencies.
2 And why do we expect ancient peoples to look modern? They are not modern – we should not expect them to remain unchanged over such a vast amount of time (10 000–12 000 years).
3 The Uto-Aztecan premolar (UP3) is a good example; this trait occurs in 10% of Uto-Aztecan-speaking natives in the American southwest but in 17.3% of Paleoindians in the Americas (especially in Brazil). See Powell and Neves (1998).

References

Abbott, C. C. (1876a). Antiquity of man in America. *American Naturalist*, **10**, 51–2.

Abbott, C. C. (1876b). Indications of the antiquity of the Indians of North America: derived from a study of their relics. *American Naturalist*, **10**, 65–72.

Acosta, J. (1590). *Historia natural y moral de las Indias*. Sevilla: En Casa de Juan de León. (Reprinted by the Spanish National Library, 1940.)

Adovasio, J. M. and Pedler, D. R. (1997). Monte Verde and the antiquity of humankind in the Americas. *Antiquity*, **71**, 573–80.

Adovasio, J. M., Donahue, J., and Stuckenrath, R. (1990). Meadowcroft rockshelter radiocarbon chronology, 1975–1990. *American Antiquity*, **55**, 348–54.

Aigner, J. S. (1976). Early Holocene evidence for the Aleut maritime adaptation. *Arctic Anthropology*, **13**(2), 32–45.

Akazawa, T. (1999). Pleistocene peoples of Japan and the peopling of the New World. In *Ice Age Peoples of North America: Environment, Origins, and Adaptations of the First Americans*, ed. R. Bonnichsen and K. L. Turnmire. Center for the Study of the First Americans. Corvallis, OR: Oregon State University Press, pp. 95–103.

Alvesalo, L. and Varrela, J. (1991). Taurodontism and the presence of an extra Y chromosome: study of 47 XYY males and analytical review. *Human Biology*, **63**, 31–8.

Alvim, M. C. M. (1977). Os antigos habitantes da área arqueológica de Lagoa Santa, MG. *Arquivos do Museu de História Natural da UFMG*, **2**, 119–74.

Anderson, D. C. (1966). The Gordon Creek burial. *Southwestern Lore*, **32**, 1–9.

Anderson, D. G. and Hanson, G. T. (1989). Early Archaic settlement in the southeastern United States: a case study from the Savannah River valley. *American Antiquity*, **53**, 262–86.

Anderson, D. G. and Sassaman, K. E. (1996). *The Paleoindian and Early Archaic Southeast*. Tuscaloosa, AL: University of Alabama Press.

Anderson, J. E. and Wendorf, F. (1968). Late Paleolithic skeletal remains from Nubia. In *The Prehistory of Nubia*, ed. F. Wendorf. Dallas, TX: Southern Methodist University Press, pp. 167–75.

Angel, J. L., Phenice, T. W., Robbins, L. H., and Lynch, B. M. (1980). Late stone age fishermen of Lothagam, Kenya. National Anthropological Archives, Smithsonian Institution, Part 3.

American Anthropological Association (AAA) (2000). Statement on "Race." (1998 original.) Available at http://www.aaanet.org/race/.

Arambourg, C. (1929). Dé courverte d'un ossuaire humain du paléolithique supérieur in Afrique du Nord. *L'Anthropologie*, **39**, 219–21.

Armelagos, G.J., Carlson, D.S., and Van Gerven, V.P. (1982). The theoretical foundations and development of skeletal biology. In *A History of American Physical Anthropology, 1930–1980*, (ed.) F. Spencer. New York, NY: Academic Press, pp. 305–28.

Bada, J.L. and Protch, R. (1973). Racemization reaction of aspartic acid and its use in dating fossil bones. *Proceedings of the National Academy of Science*, **70**, 1331–4.

Bada, J.L., Schroeder, R.A. and Carter, G.F. (1974). New evidence for the antiquity of man in North America deduced from aspartic acid racemization. *Science*, **184**, 791–3.

Bailliet, G., Rothhammer, F., Carnese, F.R., Bravi, C.M., and Binachi, N.O. (1994). Founder mitochondrial haplotypes in Amerindian populations. *American Journal of Human Genetics*, **54**, 27–33.

Baker, B.W. (1998). The Pleistocene and early Holocene fauna of east central Texas: zooarchaeology of the Wilson-Leonard Site. Unpublished Master's thesis, Texas A&M University.

Ballinger, S.W., Schurr, T.G., Torroni, A. *et al.* (1992). Southeast Asian mitochondrial DNA analysis reveals genetic continuity of ancient Mongoloid migrations. *Genetics*, **130**, 139–52.

Barker, P., Ellis, C. and Damadio, S. (2000). Determination of cultural of ancient human remains from Spirit Cave, Nevada. US Bureau of Land Management, Nevada State Office, July 26, 2000.

Bar-Yosef, O. (1996). The impact of late Pleistocene–early Holocene climatic changes on humans in southwest Asia. In *Humans at the End of the Ice Age: The Archaeology of the Pleistocene–Holocene Transition*, ed. L.G. Straus, B.V. Eriksen, J.M. Erlandson and D.R. Yesner. New York, NY: Plenum Press pp. 78–91.

Begley, S. and Muir, A. (1999). The first Americans. *Newsweek*, **83**(17), 50–7.

Berger, R. (1975). Advances and results in radiocarbon dating: early man in the New World. *World Archaeology*, **7**, 174–84.

Beriault, J., Carr, R., Stipp, J., Johnson, R., and Meider, J. (1981). The archaeological salvage of the Bay West site, Collier County, Florida. *Florida Anthropologist*, **34**, 39–58.

Berry, A.C. and Berry, R.J. (1967). Epigenetic variation in the human cranium. *Journal of Anatomy*, **101**, 361–79.

Biasutti, R. (1959). *Le Razze e i Popoli Della Terra. Con la collaborazione dei professori Raffaello Battaglia*. Unione Tipografico-Editrice Torinese, 1st edn.

Bird, J. (1938a). The Fell's Cave in Patagonian Chile. *Geographical Review*, **28**, 250.

Bird, J. (1938b). The antiquity and migrations of the early inhabitants of Patagonia. *Geographical Review*, **28**(2), 250–75.

Bird, J. (1951). South American radiocarbon dates. In *Radiocarbon Dating*, Memoirs of the Society of American Archaeology, 8. *American Antiquity*, **17**(1), part 2, pp. 37–49.

Birdsell, J.B. (1951). The problem of the early peopling of the Americas as viewed from Asia. In *The Physical Anthropology of the American Indian*, ed. W.S. Laughlin. Ann Arbor, MI: Edwards Brothers, pp. 1–68.

Blangero, J. (1988). The selective neutrality of dermatoglyphic variation. *International Journal of Anthropology*, **3**, 289–99.

Blangero, J. (1990). Population structure analysis using polygenic traits: estimation of migration matrices. *Human Biology*, **62**, 27–48.

Blangero, J. and Konigsberg, L.W. (1991). Multivariate segregation analysis using the mixed model. *Genetic Epidemiology*, **8**, 229–316.

Blumenbach, J.F. (1775). *De generis humani variate nativa*. Goettingen: University of Goettingen.

Blumenbach, J. F. (1795). *On the Natural Varieties of Mankind*, 3rd edn. (1969, New York, NY: Bergmann). Translated by T. Bendyshe. Originally published for the Anthropological Society of London, 1865.

Boas, F. (1895)

Boas, F. (1912a). Migrations of Asiatic races and cultures to North America. *Scientific Monthly*, **28**, 110–17.

Boas, F. (1912b). The history of the American race. *Annals of the New York Academy of Sciences*, **21**, 117–83.

Boas, F. (1969). 1895 letter from the Northwest coast to the Smithsonian Institution. *The Ethnography of Franz Boas Written on the Northwest Coast from 1886–1931*, edited and compiled by R. P. Rohener, translation by H. Parker. Chicago: Chicago University Press.

Bonnichsen, R. (1978). Critical arguments for Pleistocene artifacts from the Old Crow Basin, Yukon: a preliminary statement. In *Early Man from a Circum-Pacific Perspective*, ed. A. L. Bryan. Occasional papers No. 1 of the Department of Anthropology, University of Alberta. Edmonton Alberta, Canada: Archaeological Researches International, pp. 102–18.

Bonnichsen (1990)

Borrero, L. A. (1996). The archaeology of the far south of America – Patagonia and Tierra del Fuego. In *Ancient Peoples and Landscapes*, ed. E. Johnson. Lubbock, TX: Museum of Texas Tech University, pp. 207–15.

Bousman, C. B., Collins, M. B., Goldberg, P. *et al.* (2002). The Palaeoindian-Archaic transition in North America: new evidence from Texas. *Antiquity*, **76**, 980–90.

Boyd, W. C. (1950). *Genetics and the Races of Man*. Boston, MA: Heath.

Brace, C. L. (1964). The probable mutation effect. *American Naturalist*, **98**, 453–5.

Brace, C. L. (1982). The roots of the race concept in American anthropology. In *A History of American Physical Anthropology*, *1930–1980*, ed. F. Spencer. New York, NY: Academic Press, pp. 11–29.

Brace, C. L. and Hunt, K. D. (1990). A nonracial craniofacial perspective on human variation: A(ustralia) to Z(uni). *American Journal of Physical Anthropology*, **82**, 341–60.

Brace, C. L. and Nagai, M. (1982). Japanese tooth size, past and present. *American Journal of Physical Anthropology*, **59**, 399–411.

Brace, C. L. and Tracer, D. P. (1992). Craniofacial continuity and change: a comparison of late Pleistocene and recent Europe and Asia. In *The Evolution and Dispersal of Modern Humans in Asia*, ed. T. Akazawa, K. Aoki and T. Kimura. Tokyo: Hukusen-Sha Publishing Co., pp. 439–79.

Brace, C. L., Shao, X., and Zhang, Z. (1984). Prehistoric and modern tooth size in China. In *The Origins of Modern Humans: A World Survey of the Fossil Evidence*, ed. F. H. Smith and F. Spencer. New York, NY: Alan R. Liss, pp. 485–516.

Brace, C. L., Brace, M. L., and Leonard, W. R. (1989). Reflections on the face of Japan; a multivariate craniofacial and odontometric perspective. *American Journal of Physical Anthropology*, **78**, 93–113.

Brace, C. L., Smith, S. L., and Hunt, K. D. (1991). What big teeth you had Grandma! Tooth size, past and present. In *Advances in Dental Anthropology*, ed. M. A. Kelley and C. S. Larsen. New York, NY: Wiley-Liss Inc., pp. 33–57.

Brace, C. L., Nelson, A. R., Seguchi N. *et al.* (2002). Old World sources of the first New World human inhabitants: a comparative craniofacial view. *Proceedings of the National Academy of Sciences*, **98**(17), 10017–22.

Braun, D. P. and Plog, S. (1981). Evolution of "tribal" social networks: theory and prehistoric North America. *American Antiquity*, **47**, 504–25.

Breternitz, D. A., Swedlund, A. C., and Anderson, D. C. (1971). An early burial from Gordon Creek Colorado. *American Antiquity*, **36**, 170–82.

Brothwell, D. R. (1963). *Dental Anthropology*. Oxford: Pergamon.

Brothwell, D. R. (1975). Possible evidence of a cultural practise affecting head growth in some late Pleistocene East Asian and Australasian populations. *Journal of Archaeological Science*, **2**, 75–7.

Brown, M. D., Hosseini, S. H., Torroni, A. *et al.* (1998). MtDNA haplogroup X: an ancient link between Europe/Western Asia and North America? *American Journal of Human Genetics*, **63**, 1852–61.

Brown, P. (1987). Pleistocene homogeneity and Holocene size reduction: the Australian human skeletal evidence. *Oceania*, **22**, 41–71.

Brown P. (2003). Peter Brown's Australian and Asian Palaeoanthropology. Available at http://www-personal.une.edu.au/~pbrown3/palaeo.html

Bryan, A. L. (1969). Early man in America and the late Pleistocene chronology of western Canada and Alaska. *Current Anthropology*, **10**(4), 55–69.

Buffon, G. L. L. (1788). *Histoire naturelle, generale et particuliere*. Paris: Imprint Royale.

Buikstra, J. E., Frankenberg, S. R., and Konigsberg, L. W. (1990). Skeletal biological distance studies in American physical anthropology: recent trends. *American Journal of Physical Anthropology*, **82**, 1–7.

Butler, P. M. (1939). Studies of the mammalian dentition: differentiation of the post-canine dentition. *Proceedings of the Zoological Society, London*, **109**, 1–36.

Butzer, K. W. (1980). Ice ages: solving the mystery. *Geographical Review*, **70**, 244–5.

Butzer, K. W. (1991). An Old-World perspective on potential mid-Wisconsinan settlement of the Americas. In *The First Americans: Search and Research*, ed. T. D. Dillehay and D. J. Meltzer. Boca Raton, FL: CRC Press, pp. 137–58.

Cadien, J. D., Harris, E. F., Jones, W. P. and Mandarino, L. J. (1974). Biological lineages, skeletal populations, and microevolution. *Yearbook of Physical Anthropology*, **18**, 194–201.

Calcagno, J. M. and Gibson, K. R. (1988). Human dental reduction: natural selection or the probable mutation effect? *American Journal of Physical Anthropology*, **77**, 505–17.

Calcagno, J. M. and Gibson, K. R. (1991). Selective compromise: evolutionary trends and mechanisms in hominid tooth size. In *Advances in Dental Anthropology*, ed. M. A. Kelley and C. S. Larsen. New York, NY: Wiley-Liss, pp. 59–76.

Campbell, L. (1986). Comment on "The settlement of the Americas: a comparison of the linguistic, dental, and genetic evidence." *Current Anthropology*, **27**, 488.

Cann, R. L. (1994). MtDNA and Native Americans: a southern perspective. *American Journal of Human Genetics*, **55**, 7–11.

Carbonell, V. M. (1963). Variations in the frequency of shovel-shaped incisors in different populations. In *Dental Anthropology*, ed. D. R. Brothwell. Oxford: Pergamon Press, pp. 211–34.

Carlson, D. S. and Van Gerven, D. P. (1977). Masticatory function and post-Pleistocene evolution in Nubia. *American Journal of Physical Anthropology*, **46**, 495–506.

Carlson, D. S. and Van Gerven, D. P. (1979). Diffusion, biological determinism and biocultural adaptation in the Nubian corridor. *American Anthropologist*, **81**, 561–80.

Cavalli-Sforza, L. L., Menozzi, P., and Piazza, A. (1994). *The History and Geography of Human Genes*. Princeton, NJ: Princeton University Press.

Chakraborty, R. (1990). Quantitative traits in relation to population structure: why and how are they used and what do they imply? *Human Biology*, **62**, 147–62.

Chakraborty, R. and Nei, M. (1982). Genetic differentiation of quantitative characters between populations or species. I. Mutation and random genetic drift. *Genetic Research*, **39**, 303–14.

Chatters, J. C. (1998). Encounter with an ancestor. *American Anthropological Association Newsletter* (January), 9–10.

Chatters, J. C. (2000). The recovery and first analysis of an early Holocene human skeleton from Kennewick, Washington. *American Antiquity*, **65**, 291–316.

Chatters, J. C., Neves, W. A., and Blum, M. (1999). The Kennewick Man: a first multivariate analysis. *Current Research in the Pleistocene*, **16**, 87–90.

Chauchat, C. and Dricot, J. M. (1979). Un nouveau type humain fossile en Amérique du Sud: l'Homme de Paijan (Perou). *Comptes rendus Académie des Sciences Paris, Série D*, **289**, 387–9.

Cheverud, J. M. (1988). A comparison of genetic and phenotypic correlations. *Evolution*, **42**, 958–68.

Cheverud, J. M. and Buikstra, J. E. (1978). A study of intragroup biological change induced by social group fission in *Macaca mulatta* using discrete cranial traits. *American Journal of Physical Anthropology*, **49**, 41–6.

Cheverud, J. M. and Buikstra, J. E. (1981). Quantitative genetics of skeletal non-metric traits in the Rhesus Macaques on Cayo Santiago I: single trait herit-abilities. *American Journal of Physical Anthropology*, **54**, 43–9.

Clausen, C. J., Brooks, H. K., and Wesolowsky, A. B. (1975). The early man site at Warm Mineral Springs, Florida. *Journal of Field Archeology*, **2**, 191–213.

Clausen, C. J., Cohen, A. D., Emiliani, C., Holman, J. A., and Stipp, J. J. (1979). Little Salt Spring, Florida: A unique underwater site. *Science*, **203**, 609–14.

Cleland, C. E. (1976). The focal-diffuse model: an evolutionary perspective on the prehistoric cultural adaptations of the eastern United States. *Midcontinental Journal of Archaeology*, **1**, 59–76.

Collins, M. B. (1999). *Clovis Blade Technology*. Austin, TX: University of Texas Press.

Colón, C. (1969). The letter of Christopher Columbus describing the results of his first voyage. In *The Journal of Christopher Columbus*, ed. L. A. Vigneras. New York, NY: Albert and Charles Bondi.

Coon, C. S. (1950). *The Mountains of Giants*, PMP Series **23**(3).

Coon, C. S. (1954). *The Story of Man*. New York, NY: Knopf.

Coon, C. S. (1957). *The Seven Caves*. New York, NY: Knopf.

Coon, C. S. (1962). *The Origin of Races*. New York, NY: Knopf.

Coon, C. S. (1965). *The Living of Races of Man*. New York, NY: Knopf.

Coon, C. S. (1968). Comment on "Bogus science." *Journal of Heredity*, **59**, 275.

Cotter, J. L. (1991). Update on Natchez Man. *American Antiquity*, **56**, 36–9.

Crawford, M. H. (1992). When two worlds collide. *Human Biology*, **64**(3), 271–9.

Crawford, M. H. (1998). *The Origins of Native Americans: Evidence from Anthropological Genetics*. Cambridge, England: Cambridge University Press.

Crow, J. F. and Kimura, M. (1970). *An Introduction to Population Genetics Theory*. Minneapolis, MN: Burgess.

Cunha, E. M. S. and Mello e Alvim, M. C. (1971). Contribuição conhecimento da morfologia das populções indígenas daGuana bara. Notas sobre a população do sitio arqueológico Cabeça de Índio. In *O Homem Antigo na América*. São Paulo, Brazil: Instituto de Pré-histôna, Universidade de São Paulo, pp. 21–4.

Custer, J. F. (1990). Early and Middle Archaic cultures of Virginia: cultural change and continuity. In *Early and Middle Archaic Research in Virginia: A Synthesis*, ed. J. M. Wittkofski and T. R. Reinhart. Council of Virginia Archeologists and Archeological Society of Virginia Special Publication No. 22. Richmond, VA: Deitz Press, pp. 1–60.

Cuvier, G. (1812). *Recherches sur les ossements fossiles*. Paris.

Dahlberg, A. A. (1949). The dentition of the American Indian. In *The Physical Anthropology of the American Indian*, ed. W. S. Laughlin. New York, NY: Viking Fund, pp. 138–76.

Dahlberg, A. A. (1968). Analysis of the American Indian dentition. In *Dental Anthropology*, ed. D. R. Brothwell. Oxford: Pergamon Press, pp. 149–77.

Dahlberg, A. A. (1991). Historical perspective of dental anthropology. In *Advances in Dental Anthropology*, ed. M. A. Kelley and C. S. Larsen. New York, NY: Wiley-Liss, pp. 7–11.

Darroch, J. N. and Mosimann, J. E. (1985). Canonical and principal components of shape. *Biometrika*, **72**, 241–52.

Darwin, C. (1859). *On the Origin of Species by Means of Natural Selection, or the Preservation of Favoured Races in the Struggle for Life*. London, England: John Murray.

Darwin, C. (1871). *The Descent of Man and Selection in Relation to Sex*. London, England: John Murray.

Davies, D. M. (1978). Some observations on the Otavalo skeleton from Imbabura province, Ecuador. In *Early Man from a Circum-Pacific Perspective*, ed. A. L. Bryan. Occasional Papers No. 1, Department of Anthropology, University of Alberta. Edmonton, Alberta, Canada: Archaeological Researches International, p. 273.

Defrise-Gussenhoven, E. (1967). Generalized distance in genetic studies. *Acta genetico medica gemellologie*, **17**, 275–88.

Dettwyler, K. A. (1994). *Dancing Skeletons: Life and Death in West Africa*. Prospect Heights, IL: Waveland Press.

Devor, E. J. (1987). Transmission of human craniofacial dimensions. *Journal of Craniofacial Genetic and Developmental Biology*, **7**, 95–106.

Dewar, E. (1999). *Bones: the Search for the First Americans*. New York, NY: Random House.

Diamond, J. (1994). Race without color. *Discover*, November, 83–9.

Dickel, D. N. (1980). An investigation of the association of nonmetric and metric variation of the skull. Ph.D. thesis, University of California.

Dickel, D. N. (1990). Maxillary anterior attrition (AMA) and molar lingual root polish (LRP) from the Florida early Archaic. *American Journal of Physical Anthropology*, **81**, 215.

Dickel, D. N. and Doran, G. H. (1989). Severe neural-tube defect syndrome from the early Archaic of Florida. *American Journal of Physical Anthropology*, **80**, 325–34.

Dickel, D. N., Aker, C. G., Barton, B. K., and Doran, G. H. (1989). An orbital floor and ulna fracture from the early Archaic of Florida. *Journal of Paleoanthropology*, **2**, 165–70.

Dikov, N. N. (1977). *Arkheologicheshie pamyatniki Kamchctiki i Verkhnej Kolymy* (Archaeological Monument of Kamchatka, Chukota and the Upper Kolyma). Moscow: Nauka.

Dillehay, T. (1999). The late Pleistocene cultures of South America. *Evolutionary Anthropology*, **7**, 206–16.

Dillehay, T. D. (1989). *Monte Verde: A Late Pleistocene Settlement in Chile*. Vol. I: *Paleoenvironment and Site Context*. Washington, DC: Smithsonian Institution Press.

Dillehay, T. D. (2000). *The Settlement of the Americas: A New Prehistory*. New York, NY: Basic Books.

Dillehay, T. D. and Meltzer, D. J. ed. (1991). *The First Americans: Search and Research*. Boca Raton, FL: CRC Press.

Dillehay, T. D., Ardila, G., Politis, G., and Beltrão, M. C. (1992). Earliest hunters and gatherers of South America. *Journal of World Prehistory*, **62**, 145–204.

Dillehay, T. D., Collins, M. B., Pino, M. *et al.* (1999). Monte Verde revisited: reply to Fiedel, Part I. *Scientific American Discovering Archaeology*, November/December, 12–14.

Dixon, E. J. (1983). Pleistocene proboscidean fossils from the Alaskan continental shelf. *Quaternary Research*, **20**, 113–19.

Dixon, E. J. (1999). *Bones, Boats and Bison*. Albuquerque, NM: University of New Mexico Press.

Dixon, E. J., Heaton, T. H., Fifield, T. E., Hamilton, T. D., Putnam, D. E., and Grady, F. (1997). Late quaternary regional geoarchaeology of southeast Alaska karst: a progress report. Special issue: geoarchaeology of caves and cave sediments. *Geoarchaeology: An International Journal*, **12**(6), 689–712.

Dong, X. (1989). *Homo erectus* in China. In *Early Humankind in China*, ed. R. Wu, X. Wu and S. Zhang., Beijing: Science Press, pp. 9–23.

Doran, G. H. (1992). Problems and potential of wet sites in North America: the example of Windover. In *The Wetland Revolution in Prehistory*, ed. B. Coles. Exeter, England: University of Exeter, pp. 125–34.

Doran, G. H. and Dickel, D. N. (1988a). Multidisciplinary investigations at the Windover archaeological site. In *Wet Site Archaeology*, ed. B. Purdy. Caldwell, NJ: Telford, pp. 263–89.

Doran, G. H. and Dickel, D. N. (1988b). Radiometric chronology of the archaic Windover archaeological site (8BR246). *Florida Anthropologist*, **41**, 365–80.

Doran, D. H., Dickel, D. N., Ballinger, W. E. Jr., Agee, G. F., Laipis, P. J., and Hauswirth, W. W. (1986). Anatomical, cellular, and molecular analysis of 8000 year old human brain tissue from the Windover archaeological site. *Nature*, **323**, 803–6.

Dubois, E. (1922). The proto-Australian fossil man of Wadjak, Java. *Koninklijke Akademie van Wetenschappen te Amsterdam*, **B 23**, 1013–51.

Easton, R. D., Merriwether, D. A., Crews, D. W., and Ferrell, R. E. (1996). MtDNA variation in the Yanomami: evidence for additional New World founding lineages. *American Journal of Human Genetics*, **59**, 213–25.

Elias, S. A., Short, S. K., and Phillips, R. L. (1992). Paleoecology of Late Glacial peats from the Bering land bridge, Chukchi Sea Shelf Region, northwestern Alaska. *Quaternary Research*, **38**, 371–8.

Endler, J. A. (1986). *Natural Selection in the Wild*. Princeton, NJ: Princeton University Press.

Erlandson, J. M. (1996). Asia and Australia during the Pleistocene transition. In *Humans at the End of the Ice Age: The Archaeology of the Pleistocene–Holocene Transition*, ed. L. G. Straus, B. V. Eriksen, J. M. Erlandson and D. R. Yesner. New York, NY: Plenum Press.

Erlandson, J. M. and Moss, M. L. (1996). The Pleistocene–Holocene transition along the Pacific coast of North America. In *Humans at the End of the Ice Age: The Archaeology of the Pleistocene–Holocene Transition*, ed. L. G. Straus, B. V. Eriksen, J. M. Erlandson and D. R. Yesner. New York, NY: Plenum Press, pp. 277–301.

Estes, A. M. (1988). Non-invasive investigations of skeletal stress markers in an Archaic population from central Florida (Br246). Unpublished Master's thesis, Florida State University.

Estes, A. M. and Dickel, D. N. (1989). Computed tomography and cortical thickness is an early Archaic archaeological sample from Windover. *Supplement to the American Journal of Physical Anthropology* (published abstract).

Fagan, B. M. (1987). *The Great Journey: The Peopling of Ancient America*. London, England: Thames and Hudson.

Falconer, D. S. (1989). *Introduction to Quantitative Genetics*, 3rd edn. Essex, UK: Longman Scientific and Technical.

Faught, M. K. and Anderson, D. G. (1996). Across the straits, down the corridor, around the bend, and off the shelf: an evaluation of Paleoindian colonization models. Presented at the 61st Annual Meeting of the Society for American Archaeology, New Orleans, April, 1996.

Fenton, T. W. and Nelson, A. R. (1998). Biological affinities of the Buhl Woman: one of the two oldest Paleoindian skeletons. *American Journal of Physical Anthropology Supplement*, **26**, 81–2.

Fidel, S. (1996). Letter. *Science*, **274**, 1823–4.

Fix, A. G. (1999). *Migration and Colonization in Human Microevolution*. Cambridge, England: Cambridge University Press.

Fladmark, K. R. (1978). The feasibility of the Northwest coastal migration routes for early man. In *Early Man in America from a Circum-Pacific Perspective*, ed. A. L. Bryan. Occasional Papers No. 1, Department of Anthropology. Edmonton, Alberta, Canada: University of Alberta, Archaeological Researches International, pp. 119–28.

Fladmark, K. R. (1983). Times and places: environmental correlates of mid-to-late Wisconsin human population expansion in the Americas. In *Early Man in the New World*, ed. R. Shutler. Beverly Hills, CA: Sage Publications, pp. 13–42.

Fladmark, K. R. (2002). Routes revisited: a reassessment of how and when North Americans moved south of Beringia during the late Pleistocene. Paper presented at the 17th Biennial Meeting of the American Quaternary Association (AMQUA), University of Alaska, Anchorage, AK, August 9, 2002.

Fox, C. L. (1996). Mitochondrial DNA haplogroups in four tribes from Tierra del Fuego–Patagonia: inferences about the peopling of the Americas. *Human Biology*, **68**, 855–71.

Franciscus, R. G. (1995). Later Pleistocene nasofacial variation in western Eurasia and Africa and modern human origins. Ph.D. thesis, University of New Mexico.

Franciscus, R. G. and Long, J. C. (1992). Variation in human nasal height and breadth. *American Journal of Physical Anthropology*, **85**, 419–27.

Friedlander, J. S. (1975). *Patterns of Human Variation: The Demography, Genetics and Phenetics of Bougainville Islanders*. Cambridge, MA: Harvard University Press.

Frison, G. (1990). Clovis, Goshen and Folsom: lifeways and cultural relationships. In *Megafauna and Man: Discovery of America's Heartland,* ed. L. D. Agenbroad, J. I. Mead and L. W. Nelson. Scientific Papers Volume 1, the Mammoth Site of Hot Springs, pp. 100–8.

García, G. (1607) *Origen de los Indios de el Nuevo Mundo, e Indias Occidentales*, ed. A. González de Barcia Carballio y Zuniga. Madrid: Fracisco Martínez Abad (reprinted 1729).

Genovés, S. C. (1967). Some problems in the physical anthropological study of the peopling of America. *Current Anthropology*, **8**, 297–312.

Gill, G. W. (2000). "Race": a proponent's view. http://www.pbs.org/wgbh/nova/first/gill.html.

Gill, G. W. and Rhine, S. (1990). *Skeletal Attribution of Race: Methods for Forensic Anthropology*. Anthropological Papers No. 4, Maxwell Museum of Anthropology, Albuquerque, University of New Mexico.

Gladwin, H. S. (1947). *Men out of Asia*. New York, NY: McGraw-Hill, Inc.

Gloger, C. W. L. (1833). *Das Abändern der Vogel durch Einfluss des Klimas*. (The Effect of Climatic Change on Birds). Breslau: A. Schulz. (In German).

Goebel, F. E., Powers, R., and Bigelow, N. (1991). The Nenana Complex of Alaska and Clovis origins. In *Clovis: Origins and Adaptations*, ed. R. Bonnichsen and

D. G. Steele. Corvallis, OR: Center for the Study of the First Americans, pp. 49–79.

Goebel, T. and Slobodin, S. B. (1999). The colonization of western Beringia: technology, ecology, and adaptations. In *Ice Age People of North America: Environments, Origins, and Adaptations*, ed. R. Bonnichsen and K. L. Turnmire. Corvallis, OR: Oregon State University Press, Center for the Study of the First Americans, pp. 104–55.

Goebel, T., Powers, R. Bigelow, N. H. and Higgs, A. S. (1997). Walker Road. In *American Beginnings: The Prehistory and Palaeoecology of Beringia*, ed. F. H. West. Chicago, IL: University of Chicago Press, pp. 356–63.

Goggin, J. M. (1962). Recent developments in underwater archaeology. *Southeast Archaeology Conference News*, **8**, 77–88.

Goodall, J., Pusey, A., and Williams, J. (1996). The influence of dominance rank on the reproductive success of female chimpanzees. *Science*, **277**, 828–31.

Goodman, A. (1997). Racializing Kennewick Man. *Anthropology Newsletter*, October, 3–5.

Goodman, A. (1998). Archaeology and human biological variation. *Conference on New England Archaeology Newsletter*, **17**, 1–8.

Goodman, A. H. and Armelagos, G. J. (1989). Disease and death at Dr. Dickson's Mound. In *Applying Anthropology: An Introductory Reader*, ed. A. Podolefsky and P. J. Brown. Mountain View, CA: Mayfield Publishing Company, pp. 91–5.

Goodyear, A. (1999). The early Holocene occupation of the southeast United States: a geoarchaeological summary. In *Ice Age People of North America: Environments and Adaptations*, ed. R. Bonnichsen and K. L. Turnmire. Corvallis, OR: Oregon State University Press, Center for the Study of the First Americans, pp. 432–81.

Gould, S. J. (1981). *The Mismeasure of Man*. New York, NY: Norton.

Green, J. H. (1987). *Language in Americas*. Palo Alto, CA: Stanford University Press.

Green, T. J., Cochran, B., Fenton, T. W. *et al.* (1998). The Buhl burial: a Paleoindian woman from southern Idaho. *American Antiquity*, **63**, 437–56.

Greenberg, J. H., Turner, C. G. II, and Zegura, S. L. (1986). The settlement of the Americas: a comparison of the linguistic, dental, and genetic evidence. *Current Anthropology*, **27**, 477–97.

Greenman, E. (1960). The North Atlantic and Early Man in the New World. *Michigan Archaeologist*, **6**(2), 19–39.

Greenman, E. (1963). The Upper Paleolithic and the New World. *Current Anthropology*, **4**, 41–91.

Gruhn, R. (1988). Linguistic evidence in support of the coastal route of earliest entry into the New World. *Man* **23**, 77–100.

Gruhn, R. (1994). The Pacific coastal route of entry: an overview. In *Method and Theory for Investigating the Peopling of the Americas*, ed. R. L. Bonnichsen and D. G. Steele. Corvallis, OR: Oregon State University Press, Center for the Study of the First Americans, pp. 249–56.

Haeussler, A. M., Irish, J. D., Morris, D. H., and Turner, C. G. II (1989). Morphological and metrical comparison of San and central Sotho dentitions from southern Africa. *American Journal of Physical Anthropology*, **78**, 115–22.

Hall, D. A. (1998). Coastal-entry model gains support as Ice-Free Corridor theory fades: the coastal-route theory is "in." *Mammoth Trumpet*, **13**(3).

Hall, R. L. (1996). Who WERE the first Americans? An interview with a specialist in human diversity (Marta Lahr). *Mammoth Trumpet*, **11**(3).

Halladay, A. (2001). Skin and eye color may have evolved as beauty traits. Wonderquest science column. *USA Today* (August 15, 2001) http://www.usatoday.com/new . . . e/wonderquest/2001-08-15-skin-color.htm

Hammer, M. F., Spurdle, A. B., Karafet, T. *et al.* (1997). The geographic distribution of human Y chromosome variation. *Genetics*, **145**, 787–805.

Hanihara, K. (1968). Mongoloid dental complex in the permanent dentition. In *Proceedings of the VIIIth International Congress of Anthropological and Ethnological Sciences,* Volume 1, Anthropology. Tokyo: Science Council Japan, pp. 298–300.

Hanihara, T. (1992). Negritos, Australian aborigines, and the "proto-Sundadont" dental pattern: the basic populations in East Asia, V. *American Journal of Physical Anthropology*, **88**, 183–96.

Hanke, L. U. (1937). Pope Paul III and the American Indians. *Harvard Theological Review*, **30**, April, 65–102.

Hantman, J. L. (1990). The early and middle Archaic in Virginia: a North American perspective. In *Early and Middle Archaic Research in Virginia: A Synthesis*, ed. J. M. Wittkofski and T. R. Reinhart. Council of Virginia Archeologists and Archeological Society of Virginia Special Publication No. 22. Richmond, VA: Deitz Press, pp. 133–53.

Harding, R. M., Healy, E., Ray, A. J. *et al.* (2000). Evidence for variable selective pressures at MC1R. *American Journal of Human Genetics*, **66**, 1351–61.

Harpending, H. C. and Jenkins, T. (1973). Genetic distance among Southern African populations. In *Methods and Theories of Anthropological Genetics*, ed. M. H. Crawford and P. L. Workman. Albuquerque, NM: University of New Mexico Press.

Harpending, H. C. and Ward, R. H. (1982). Chemical systematics and human populations. In *Biochemical Aspects of Evolutionary Biology*, ed. M. H. Nitecki. Chicago, IL: University of Chicago Press, pp. 213–56.

Harper, A. B. and Laughlin, W. S. (1982). Inquiries into the peopling of the New World: development of ideas and recent advances. In *A History of American Physical Anthropology 1930–1980*, ed. F. Spencer. New York, NY: Academic Press.

Harris, E. F. (1977). Anthropologic and genetic aspects of the dental morphology of Solomon Islanders. Ph.D. thesis, Arizona State University.

Harris, E. F. and Bailit, H. L. (1980). The metaconule: a morphological and familial analysis of a molar cusp in humans. *American Journal of Physical Anthropology*, **53**, 349–58.

Harris, E. F. and Nweeia, M. T. (1980). Tooth size of Ticuna Indians, Columbia, with phonetic comparisons to other Amerindians. *American Journal of Physical Anthropology*, **53**, 81–9.

Harris, E. F. and Rathburn, T. A. (1991). Ethnic differences in the appointment of tooth sizes. In *Advances in Dental Anthropology*, ed. M. A. Kelley and C. S. Larsen. New York, NY: Wiley-Liss, pp. 121–41.

Hartl, D. L. and Clark, A. G. (1989). *Principles of Populations Genetics*. Sunderland, MA: Sinauer Associates.

Hauser, G. and De Stefano, G. F. (1989). *Epigenetic Variants of the Human Skull.* Suggart: Verlag.

Hauswirth, W. W., Dickel, C. D., Doran, G. H., Laipis, P. J., and Dickel, D. N. (1991). 8000-year-old brain tissue from Windover archaeological site: anatomical, cellular and molecular analysis. In *Humans Paleopathology: Current Syntheses and Future Options*, ed. D. J. Ortner and A. C Aufederheide. Washington, DC: Smithsonian Institution Press, pp. 60–72.

Hauswirth, W. W., Dickel, C. F., Rowold, D. J., and Hauswirth, M. A. (1994). Inter- and intrapopulation studies of ancient humans. *Experientia (Basel)*, **50**, 585–91.

Haydenblit R. (1993). Variation in dental formation patterns among indigenous American populations. Paper presented at the 13th International Congress of Anthropological and Ethnological Sciences, Mexico City (published abstract).

Haydenblit, R. (1996). Dental variation among four prehispanic Mexican populations. *American Journal of Physical Anthropology*, **100**, 225–46.

Haynes, C. V. (1964). Fluted points: their age and dispersion. *Science*, **145**, 14098–113.

Haynes, C. V. (1992). Contributions of radiocarbon dating to the geochronology of the peopling of the New World. In *Radiocarbon After Four Decades*, ed. R. E. Taylor and A. Long. New York, NY: Springer-Verlag, pp. 355–74.

Heaton, T. H. (2002). The vertebrate paleontology and paleoecology of Prince of Wales Island, southeast Alaska over the last 50 000 years. *American Quaternary Association Programs and Abstracts of the 17th Biennial Meeting*, pp. 54–6.

Hemphill, B. E., Lukacs, J. R., and Kennedy, K. A. R. (1991). Biological adaptations and affinities of Bronze Age Harrapans. In *Harrapa Excavation 1986–1990: A Multidisciplinary Approach to Third Millenium Urbanism*, ed. R. Meadows. Madison, WI: Prehistory Press, pp. 137–82.

Henderson, D. L. (1998). Ancient bones seem to say Kennewick Man was a homicide victim. *Seattle Times*, March 27.

Heyerdahl, T. (1950). *Kon-Tiki: Across the Pacific by Raft*. Chicago: Rand-McNally.

Hofman, J. L. (1992) Recognition and interpretation of Folsom technological variability on the Southern Plains. In *Ice Age Hunters of the Rockies*, ed. D. J. Stanford and J. S. Day. Denver, CO: Denver Museum of Natural History, pp. 193–224.

Holliday, V. T. (1995). Stratigraphy and paleoenvironments of Late Quaternary. *Quaternary Research*, **28**, 238–44.

Holliday, V. T. (1997). *Paleoindian Geoarchaeology of the Southern High Plains*. Austin, TX: University of Texas Press.

Holliday, V. T. (1998)

Holliday, V. T. and Meltzer, D. J. (1996). Geoarchaeology of the Midland (Paleoindian) site, Texas. *American Antiquity*, **61**(4), 755.

Holmes, W. H. (1892). Modern quarry refuse and the Paleolithic Theory. *Science*, **20**, 295–7.

Holmes, W. H. (1910)

Hooton, E. A. (1930). *The Indians of Pecos Pueblo*. New Haven, CT: Yale University Press.

Hooton, E. A. (1933). Racial types in America and their relation to Old World types. In *The American Aborigines*, ed. D. Jenness. New York, NY: Russell and Russell, pp. 131–63.

Hooton, E. A. (1946). *Up from the Ape*, 2nd edn. New York, NY: Macmillan.

Hopkins, D. M. (1967). *The Bering Land Bridge*. Stanford, CA: Stanford University Press.

Hopkins, D. M. (1982). Aspects of the Paleogeography of Beringia during the Late Pleistocene. In *Paleoecology of Beringia*, ed. D. M. Hopkins, J. V. Matthews, Jr., C. E. Schweger, and S. B. Young. New York, NY: Academic Press, pp. 3–28.

Horai, S., Kondo, R., Nakagawa-Hattori, Y., Hayashi, S., Sondona, S., and Tajima, K. (1993). Peopling of the Americas, founded by four major lineages of mitochondrial DNA. *Molecular Biological Evolution*, **10**, 23–47.

Horai, S., Kondo, R., Sonoda, S., and Tajima, K. (1996). The first Americans: different waves of migration to the New World inferred from mitochondrial DNA sequence polymorphisms. In *Prehistoric Mongoloid Dispersals*, ed. T. Akazawa and E. J. E. Szathmary. Oxford: Oxford University Press, pp. 270–83.

Hossani, A. A. and Allison, M. J. (1976). Paleoserologic studies: ABO and histocompatibility antigens in mummified American Indians. *MCV Quarterly*, **12**, 67–73.

Hrdlička, A. (1902). The crania of Trenton, New Jersey and their bearing upon the antiquity of man in that region. *American Museum of Natural History Bulletin*, **316**, 23–62.

Hrdlička, A. (1907). Skeletal remains suggesting or attributed to early man in North America. *Bureau of American Ethnology Bulletin*, **33**, 1–113.

Hrdlička, A. (1913). A search in eastern Asia for the race that peopled America. *Smithsonian Miscellaneous Collection*, **60**, 10–13.

Hrdlička, A. (1917). Preliminary report on finds of supposedly ancient human remains at Varo, Florida. *Journal of Geology*, **25**, 43–51.

Hrdlička, A. (1918). Recent discoveries attributed to early man in America. *Bureau of American Ethnology Bulletin*, **66**, 1–67.

Hrdlička, A. (1920). Shovel-shaped teeth. *American Journal of Anthropology*, **3**, 429–65.

Hrdlička, A. (1923). The origin and antiquity of the American Indian. In *Annual Report of the Board of Regents of the Smithsonian Institution*. Washington, DC: US Government Printing Office, pp. 481–93.

Hrdlička, A. (1928). The origin and antiquity of man in America. *New York Academy of Medicine Bulletin*, **4**(7), 802–16.

Hrdlička, A. (1930). Anthropological survey in Alaska. In *The Forty-Sixth Annual Report of the Bureau of American Ethnology*. Washington, DC: US Government Printing Office.

Hrdlička, A. (1935). Melanesians and Australians and the peopling of America. *Smithsonian Miscellaneous Collection*, **94**, 1–58.

Hrdlička, A. (1937). Early man in America: what have the bones to say? In *Early Man as Depicted by Leading Authorities at the International Symposium at the Academy of Natural Sciences, Philadelphia, March 1937*, ed. G. G. MacGurdy. Philadelphia, PA: J. B. Lippincott, pp. 93–104.

Huddleston, L. E. (1967). *Origins of the American Indians: European Concepts, 1492-1729*. Latin American Monographs, No. 11. Institute of Latin American Studies, University of Texas. Austin, TX: University of Texas Press.

Hurt, W. R. (1960). The cultural complexes from the Lagoa Santa region, Brazil. *American Antiquity*, **62**, 569–85.

Irish, J. D. (1993). Biological affinities of Late Pleistocene through modern African aboriginal populations: the dental evidence. Ph.D. thesis, Arizona State University.

Jablonski, N. G., ed. (2002). *The First Americans: The Pleistocene Colonization of the New World*. San Francisco, CA: Memoirs of the California Academy of Sciences, No. 27.

Jantz, R. L. and Owsley, D. W. (1997). Pathology, taphonomy, and cranial orphometrics of the Spirit Cave Mummy (AHUR 2064). *Nevada Historical Society Quarterly*, **40**(1), 62–84.

Jantz, R. L. and Owsley, D. W. (2001). Variation among early American crania. *American Journal of Anthropology*, **114**, 146–55.

Jelinek, A. J. (1971). Early man in the New World: a technological perspective. *Arctic Anthropology*, **8**, 15–21.

Jenks, A. E. (1936). *Pleistocene Man in Minnesota: A Fossil* Homo Sapiens. Minneapolis, MN: University of Minnesota Press.

Jenks, A. E. (1937). *Minnesota's Brown Valley Man and Associated Burial Artifacts*. Memoirs of the American Anthropological Association, No. 49. Menasha, WI: American Anthropological Association.

Jenks, A. E. and Wilford, L. A. (1938). The Sauk Valley skeleton. *Bulletin of the Texas Archaeology and Paleontological Society*, **10**, 162–3.

Johnson, J. (2001). California – Arlington Springs remains: an informal update. (Online) *Friends of America's Past* (posted 7/31/2001). Available at http://www.friendsofpast.org/earliest-americans/california.html/.

Johnson, W. A. (1933). Quaternary geology of North America in relation to the migration of man. In *The American Aborigines: Their Origins and Antiquity*, ed. D. Jenness. A collection of papers published for presentation at the Fifth Pacific Scientific Congress. Toronto, Ontario, Canada: The University of Toronto Press, pp. 9–46. (Reprinted 1973).

Johnson, J. *et al* (2000)

Jones, S. and Bonnichsen, R. (1994). The Anzick Clovis burial. *Current Research in the Pleistocene*, **11**, 42–3.

Jowett, B. (1911). Introduction to the Phaedo. In *The Dialogues of Plato*, Vol. 1. New York, NY: Charles Scriber's Sons, pp. 364–81.

Jungers, W. L., Falsetti, A. B., and Wall, C. E. (1995). Shape, relative size, and size adjustments in morphometrics. *Yearbook of Physical Anthropology*, **38**, 137–61.

Kamminga, J. and Wright, R. S. V. (1988). The upper cave at Zhoukoudian and the origins of the Mongoloids. *Journal of Human Evolution*, **17**, 739–67.

Karafet, T. M., Zegura, S. L., Posukh, O. *et al.* (1999). Ancestral Asian source(s) of New World Y-chromosome founder haplotypes. *American Journal of Human Genetics*, **64**, 817–31.

Keith, A. (1911). *Ancient Types of Man*, 1st edn. New York, NY: Harper.

Keith, A. (1949). *A New Theory of Human Evolution*, 2nd edn. New York, NY: Harper.

Kelley, R. L. (1995). *The Foraging Spectrum: Diversity in Hunter-Gatherer Lifeways*. Washington, DC: Smithsonian Institution Press.

Kelley, R. L. and Todd L. C. (1998). Coming into the country: early Paleoindian hunting and mobility. *American Antiquity*, **53**(2), 231–44.

Key, P. J. (1983). Craniometric relationships among Plains Indians: culture-historical and evolutionary implications. Ph.D. thesis, University of Tennessee.

Kidd, K. K., Morar, B., Castiglione, C. M. *et al.* (1998). A global survey of haplotype frequencies and linkage disequilibrium at the DRD2 locus. *Human Genetics*, **103**, 211–27.

Kieser, J. A. (1990). *Human Adult Odontometrics: The Study of Variation in Adult Tooth Size*. Cambridge, England: Cambridge University Press.

Kieser, J. A., Groeneveld, H. T., and Preston, C. B. (1985). An odontometric analysis of the Lingua Indians dentition. *Human Biology*, **57**, 611–20.

Kimura, M. and Weiss, G. H. (1964). The stepping-stone model of population structure and the decrease of genetic correlation with distance. *Genetics*, **49**, 561–76.

Kolman, C. J., Sambuughin, N., and Bermingham, E. (1996). Mitochondrial DNA analysis of Mongolian populations and implications for the origins of New World Founders. *Genetics*, **142**, 1321–34.

Konigsberg, L. W. (1985)

Konigsberg, L. W. (1987). Population genetics models for interpreting prehistoric intracemetery biological variation. Ph.D. thesis, Northwestern University.

Konigsberg, L. W. (1988). Migration models for interpreting post-marital residence. *American Journal of Anthropology*, **77**, 471–82.

Konigsberg, L. W. (1990). Analysis of prehistoric biological variation under a model of isolation by geographic and temporal distance. *Human Biology*, **62**, 49–70.

Konigsberg, L. W. and Blangero, J. (1993). Multivariate quantitative genetic simulations in anthropology with an example from the South Pacific. *Human Biology*, **65**, 897–915.

Konigsberg, L. W. and Ousley, S. D. (1993). Multivariate quantitative genetics of anthropometrics from the Boas data. *American Journal of Anthropology Supplement*, **16**, 127–8.

Kottak, C. (2000). *Anthropology: The Exploration of Human Diversity*, 8th edn. New York, NY: McGraw-Hill Companies.

Krafet (1999)

Krasheninnkov, S. (1972). *A Description of the Kanchatka Region, 1735–1741*, ed./transl. E. A. P. Crownhart-Vaughn. Portland, OR: Oregon Historical Society.

Kroeber, A. L. (1962). The Rancho La Brea skull. *American Antiquity*, **27**, 416–17.

Kutzbach, J. E. and Webb, T. III (1993). Conceptual basis for understanding late-Quaternary climates. In *Global Climates Since the Last Glacial Maximum*, ed. H. E. Wright Jr., J. E. Kutzbach, T. Webb III, W. F. Ruddiman, F. A. Street-Perrott and P. J. Bartlein. Minneapolis, MN: University of Minnesota Press, pp. 5–11.

Lahr, M. M. (1994). The multiregional model of modern human origins: a reassessment of its morphological basis. *Journal of Human Evolution*, **26**, 23–56.

Lahr, M. M. (1995). Patterns of modern human diversification: implications for Amerindian origins. *Yearbook of Physical Anthropology*, **38**, 163–98.

Lahr, M. M. (1996). *The Evolution of Modern Human Diversity: A Study of Cranial Variation*. Cambridge Series in Biological Anthropology, **18**. Cambridge, England: Cambridge University Press.

Lahr, M. M. (1997). History in the bones. *Evolutionary Anthropology*, **6**, 2–6.

Lahr, M. M. and Foley, R. A. (1998). Towards a theory of modern human origins: geography, demography, and diversity in recent human evolution. *Yearbook of Physical Anthropology*, **41**, 137–76.

Laming-Emperaire, A. (1979). Missions archéologiques franco-brésiliennes de Lagos Santa, Minas Gerais, Brésil: le grand abri de Lapa Vermelha P. L. *Revista de Pré-história*, **1**, 53–89.

Laming-Emperaire, A., Prous, A., Moraes, A. V., and Beltrão, M. C. M. C. (1975). Grottes et abris de la région de Lagoa Santa, Minas Gerais, Brésil. *Cahiers d'archéologie d' Amérique du sud*, **1**.

Lande, R. (1976). Natural selection and random genetic drift in phenotypic evolution. *Evolution*, **30**, 314–34.

Lande, R. (1988). Quantitative genetics and evolutionary theory. In *Proceedings of the Second International Conference on Quantitative Genetics*, ed. B. S. Weir, E. J. Eisen, M. M. Goodman and G. Namkoong. Sunderland, MA: Sinauer Associates, pp. 71–84.

Larsen, C. C. S., Matter, R. M., and Gebo, D. L. (1991). *Human Origins: The Fossil Record*. Prospect Heights, IL: Waveland Press.

Laughlin, W. S. (1967). Human migration and permanent occupation in the Bering area. In *The Bering Land Bridge*, ed. D. M. Hopkins. Stanford, CA: Stanford University Press, pp. 409–50.

Lawlor, D. A., Dickel, C. D., Hauswirth, W. W., and Parham, P. (1991). Ancient HLA genes from 7500-year-old archaeological remains. *Nature*, **349**, 785–8.

Lawson 1994

Lawson, W. (1999). Skeletons in the closet: thousands of Indian skeletons may never return to tribes. ABC News.com, May 22. Available at http//:www.abc-news.com/wlawson.052299/skeleton.

Leclerc, G. L. (1749)

Lees, F. C. and Relethford, J. H. (1982). Population structure and anthropometric variation in Ireland during the 1930s. In *Current Developments in Anthropological Genetics*, Vol. 2: Ecology and Population Structure, ed. J. H. Mielke and M. H. Crawford. New York, NY: Plenum Press, pp. 385–428.

Lepper, B. (2001). Plains Anthropological Society (PAS) papers, 1947–2000. I. D. Weeks Library, Archives and Special Collections, University of South Dakota. Available at http://www.usd.edu/library/special/aids/AidsHtml/PAS.htm

Lewontin, R. C. (1972). The apportionment of human diversity. In *Evolutionary Biology*, Vol. 6, ed. T. H. Dobzhansky, M. K. Hecht and W. C. Steere. New York, NY: Appleton-Century-Crofts, pp. 381–98.

Linnaeus, C. V. (1907)[1735]. *Systema naturæ*. Facsimile reprint. Stockholm: Generalstabens Litografiska Anstalt.

Livingston, F. B. (1962). On the non-existence of human races. *Current Anthropology*, **33**, 279–81.

Long, J. C., Urbanek, M., Romero, F. C., and Goldman, D. (1999). DNA marker analysis for evidence of European contributions to Native American gene pools before and after Columbus. *American Journal of Physical Anthropology Supplement*, **28**, 186.

Lorenzo, J. L. (1978). Early man research in the American hemisphere: appraisal and perspectives. In *Early Man from a Circum-Pacific Perspective*, ed. A. L. Bryan. Occasional Papers No. 1 of the Department of Anthropology, University of Alberta, Archaeological Researches International, Edmonton, Alberta, Canada, pp. 2–9.

Lorenzo, J. L. and Miriambell, L. (1999). The inhabitants of Mexico during the upper Pleistocene. In *Ice Age Peoples of North America*, ed. R. Bonnichsen. Center for the Study of the First Americans. Corvallis, OR: Oregon University Press.

Lukacs, J. R. and Hemphill, B. E. Odontometry and biological affinity in south Asia: analysis of three ethnic groups from northwest India. *Human Biology*, **65**(2), 279–325.

Lynch, T. F. (1990). Glacial man in South America? A critical review. *American Antiquity*, **55**, 12–36.

Malêcot, G. (1959). Les modèles stochastiques en genétique de population. *Public Institute of Statistics, University of Paris*, **8**, 173–210.

Mandryk, C. A. (1990). Could humans survive in the ice-free corridor? Late Glacial vegetation and climate in West Central Alberta. In *Megafauna and Man: Discovery of America's Heartland*, ed. L. D. Agenbroad, J. Mead and S. L. Nelson. The Mammoth Site of Hot Springs Inc. Scientific Papers, Vol. 1. Hot Springs, SD, pp. 67–79.

Mandryk, C. A. (2002). Humans in the Ice Free Corridor? Paper presented at the 17th Biennial Meeting of the American Quaternary Association (AMQUA), University of Alaska, Anchorage, AK, August 9, 2002.

Martin, P. S. (1963). *Animal Species and Evolution*. Cambridge, MA: Harvard University Press.

Martin, P. S. (1967). Prehistoric overkill. In *Pleistocene Extinctions: The Search for a Cause*, ed. P. S. Martin and H. E. Wright. New Haven, CT: Yale University Press, pp. 75–120.

Martin, P. S. (1973). The discovery of America. *Science*, **179**, 969–74.

Martin, P. S. (1984). Prehistoric overkill: the global model. In *Quaternary Extinctions: A Prehistoric Revolution*, ed. P. S Martin and R. G. Klein. Tucson, AZ: University of Arizona Press, pp. 354–403.

Martin, P. S., and Klein, R. G. (eds.) (1989). *Quaternary Extinctions: A Prehistoric Revolution*, Tuscon, AZ: University of Arizona Press.

McAvoy, J. M. and McAvoy, L. D. (1997). *Archaeological Investigations of Site 44SXS202, Cactus Hill, Sussex County, Virginia*. Virginia Department of Historic Resources, Research Report Series No. 8. Sandston, VA.

McManamon, F. (1997). Federal judge criticizes Army Corps's handling of Kennewick Man. Tri-City Herald Kennewick Interpretive Center. Available at http://www.kennewick.com/story/07-97/.

McManus, D. A., Creager, J. S., Echols, R. J., and Holmes, M. L. (1983). The Holocene transgression of the Arctic flank of Beringia: Chukchi Valley to Chukchi Sea. In *Quaternary Coastlines and Marine Archeology*, ed. P. M. Masters and M. C. Flemming. New York, NY: Academic Press, pp. 365–88.

Meltzer, D. J. (1991). On "paradigms" and "paradigm bias" in controversies over human antiquity in America. In *The First Americans: Search and Research*, ed. T. D. Dillehay and D. J. Meltzer. Boca Raton, FL: CRC Press, pp. 13–49.

Meltzer, D. J. (1993a). Pleistocene peopling of the Americas. *Evolutionary Anthropology*, **1**, 157–69.

Meltzer, D. J. (1993b). *Search for the First Americans*. Montreal, Quebec, Canada: St. Remy Press.

Meltzer, D. J. (1994). The discovery of deep time: a history of views on the peopling of the Americas. In *Method and Theory for Investigating the Peopling of the Americas*, ed. R. Bonnichsen and D. G. Steele. Corvallis, OR: Oregon State University, pp. 7–26.

Meltzer, D. J. (2001). What do you do when no one's been there before? Thoughts on the exploration and colonization of new lands. In *The First Americans: The Pleistocene Colonization of the New World*, ed. N. G. Jablonski. San Francisco, CA: Memoirs of the California Academy of Sciences, No. 27, pp. 25–56.

Meltzer, D. J. and Smith, B. D. (1986). Paleoindian and early Archaic subsistence strategies in eastern North America. In *Foraging, Collecting, and Harvesting: Archaic Period Subsistence and Settlement in the Eastern Woodlands*, ed. S. W. Neusis. Occasional Paper No. 6. Carbondale, IL: Center for Archaeological Investigations, pp. 3–31.

Meltzer, D. J., Grayson, D. K., Ardila, G. *et al.* (1997). On the Pleistocene antiquity of Monte Verde, Southern Chile. *American Antiquity*, **62**(4), 659–63.

Merbs, C. F. and Clausen, C. J. (1981). The people of Little Salt Spring. Presented at the 46th Annual Meeting of the Society for American Archaeology, San Diego, CA.

Merriwether, D. A. (2002). A mitochondrial perspective on the peopling of the New World. In *The First Americans: The Pleistocene Colonization of the New World*, ed. N. G. Jablonski. San Francisco, CA: Memoirs of the California Academy of Sciences, No. 27, pp. 295–310.

Merriwether, D. A, Rothhammer, F., and Ferrell, R. E. (1995). Distribution of the four founding lineage haplotypes in North Americans suggests a single wave of migration for the New World. *American Journal of Anthropology*, **98**, 411–30.

Milanich, J. T. and Fairbanks, C. H. (1980). *Florida Archaeology*. New York, NY: Academic Press.

Minthorn, A. (1996). Human remains should be reburied. Confederate Tribes of the Umatilla Indian Reservation. Available at http://www.umatilla.nsn.us/kennmn.html.

Mizoguchi, Y. (1985). *Shoveling: A Statistical Analysis of its Morphology*. Tokyo: University of Tokyo.

Mochanov, Y. A. (1978). Stratigraphy and absolute chronology of the Paleolithic of northeast Asia. In *Early Man in America from a Circum-Pacific Perspective*, ed. A. L. Bryan. Edmonton, Alberta, Canada: Archaeological Researches International, pp. 54–66.

Mochanov, Y. A. (1992). The earliest Paleolithic of northeastern Asia and the problem of an extratropical cradle of man. Presented at the 45th Annual Northwest Anthropological Conference, Burnaby, British Columbia, Canada.

Monsalve, M. V., de Restrepo, H. G., Espinel, A., Correal, G., and Devine, D. V. (1994). Evidence of mitochondrial DNA diversity in South American aboriginals. *Annals of Human Genetics*, **58**, 265–73.

Moorrees, C. F. A., Fanning, E. A., and Hunt, E. E. Jr. (1963). Formation and resorption of three deciduous teeth in children. *American Journal of Physical Anthropology*, **21**, 205–13.

Morell, V. (1998). Kennewick Man: more bones to pick. *Science*, **279**, 25–6.

Morris, D. H., Hughes, S. G., and Dahlberg, A. A. (1978). Uto-Aztecan premolar: the anthropology of a dental trait. In *Development, Function, and Evolution of Teeth*, ed. P. M. Butler and K. A. Joysey. New York, NY: Academic Press, pp. 69–79.

Morton, S. G. (1839). *Crania americana*. Philadelphia, PA: Dobson.

Morton, S. G. (1844). *Crania egyptica*. Philadelphia, PA: Penington.

Mosch, C. and Watson, P. J. (1997). The ancient explorer of Hourglass Cave. *Evolutionary Anthropology*, **5**(4), 111–15.

Munford, D., Zanini, M. C., and Neves, W. A. (1995). Human cranial variation in South America: implications for the settlement of the New World. *Brazilian Journal of Genetics*, **18**, 673–88.

Myster, S. M. T. and O'Connell, B. (1997). Bioarchaeology of Iowa, Wisconsin, and Minnesota. In *Bioarchaeology of the North Central United States*, ed. D. W. Owsley and J. C. Rose. Fayetteville, AR: Arkansas Archeological Survey, pp. 147–239.

Neel, J. V., Salzano, F. M., and Lingoes J. C. (1974). The genetic structure of a tribal population, the Yanomamö Indians. X. Agreement between representations of village distance based on different characteristics. *American Journal of Human Genetics* **26**, 281–303.

Neel, J. V., Biggar, R. J., and Sukernik, R. I. (1994). Virological and genetic studies relate Amerind origins to the indigenous people of Mongolia/Manchuria/ Southeastern Siberia. *Proceedings of the National Academy of Sciences USA*, **91**, 10 737–41.

Nei, M. (1973). Analysis of gene diversity in subdivided populations. *Proceedings of the National Academy of Sciences USA*, **70**, 3321–3.

Nei, M. (1977). F-statistics and analyses of genetic diversity in subdivided populations. *Annals of Human Genetics*, **41**, 225–33.

Nelson, A. R. (1998). A craniofacial perspective on North American Indian population affinities and relations. Unpublished Ph.D. thesis, University of Michigan.

Nelson, N. C. (1933). The antiquity of man in America in the light of archaeology. In *The American Aborigines: Their Origin and Antiquity*, ed. D. Jenness. A Collection of Papers by Ten Authors Assembled and Edited by Diamone Jenness. Published for presentation at the Fifth Pacific Science Congress, Canada, 1973. New York, NY: Cooper Square Publishers, pp. 85–130.

Neumann, G. K. (1952). Archeology and race in the American Indian. In *Archeology of the Eastern United States*, ed. J. B Griffin. Chicago, IL: University of Chicago Press, pp. 13–43.

Neves, W. A. and Blum, M. (2000). The Buhl burial: a comment on Green *et al*. *American Antiquity*, **65**(1), 191–3.

Neves, W. A. and Pucciarelli, H. M. (1989). Extra-continental biological relationships of early South American human remains: a multivariate analysis. *Ciência e cultura*, **41**, 566–75.

Neves, W. A. and Pucciarelli, H. M. (1991). Morphological affinities of the first Americans: an exploratory analysis based on early South American human remains. *Journal of Human Evolution*, **21**, 261–73.

Neves, W. A. and Pucciarelli, H. M. (1992)

Neves, W. A. and Pucciarelli, H. M. (1998). The Zhoukoudien Upper Cave skull 101 as seen from the Americas. *Journal of Human Evolution*, **34**, 219–22.

Neves, W. A., Meyer, D., and Pucciarelli, H. M. (1996a). Early skeletal remains and the peopling of the Americas. *Revista de antropologia*, **392**, 121–39.

Neves, W. A., Munford, D., and Zanini, M. C. (1996b). Cranial morphological variation and the colonization of the New World: towards a Four Migration Model. *American Journal of Anthropology Supplement*, **22**, 176.

Neves, W. A., Powell, J. F., Prous, A., and Ozolins, E. G. (1998). Lapa Vermelha IV, Hominid I: morphological affinities of the earliest known American. *American Journal of Anthropology Supplement*, **26**, 169.

Neves, W. A., Powell, J. F., and Ozolins, E. G. (1999a). Modern human origins as seen from the peripheries. *Journal of Human Evolution*, **37**, 129–33.

Neves, W. A., Powell, J. F., and Ozolins, E. G. (1999b). Extracontinental morphological affinities of Palli Aike, southern Chile. *Interciéncia* (Venezuela), **24**, 258–63.

Neves, W. A., Prous, A., González-Jose, R., Kipnis, R., and Powell, J. (2003). Early Holocene human skeleton remains from the Santana do Riacho, Brazil: implications for the settlement of the New World. *Journal of Human Evolution*, **45**, 19–42.

Nichol, C. R. (1989). Complex segregation analysis of dental morphological variants. *American Journal of Physical Anthropology*, **78**, 37–59.

Nichols, J. (1990). Linguistic diversity and the first settlement of the New World. *Language*, **66**, 475–521.

Nichols, J. (1995). The spread of language around the Pacific Rim. *Evolutionary Anthropology*, **3**(6), 205–15.

Nichols, J. (2002). The first American languages. In *The First Americans: The Pleistocene Colonization of the New World*, ed. N. Jablonski. San Francisco, CA: Memoirs of the California Academy of Sciences, No. 27, pp. 273–93.

Novick, G. E., Novick, C. C., Yunis, J. *et al.* (1998). Polymorphic Alu insertions and the Asian origin of Native American populations. *Human Biology*, **70**, 23–39.

Oetteking, B. (1934). Anthropomorphologische Beziehungen zwischen der Osterinsel und America. *Eugen Fischer Festband Zeitsch Morphol Anthropol*, **34**, 303–13.

Oetting, B. (2002). Coat color genes. International Federation of Pigment Cell Societies (April, 2002). Available at http://cbc.umn.edu/ifpcs/micemut.html.

d'Orbigny, A. (1839). *L'homme américain (de l'Amérique méridionale), considéré sous ses rapports physiologiques et moraux*, Vol. 1. Paris: Pitois-Levrault.

O'Rourke, D. H., Carlyle, S. W., and Parr, R. L. (1996). Ancient DNA: methods, progress and perspectives. *American Journal of Human Biology*, **8**, 557–71.

O'Rourke, D. H., Carlyle, S. W., and Hayes, M. G. (1999). Ancient DNA patterns and the peopling of the Americas. *American Journal of Physical Anthropology Supplement*, **28**, 214.

Orr, P. C. (1956). Pleistocene Man in Fishbone Cave, Pershing County, Nevada. *Nevada State Museum Bulletin*, Department of Anthropology, Carson City, NV, **2**, 1–20.

Orr, P. C. (1962). The Arlington Springs site, Santa Rosa Island, California. *American Antiquity*, **27**, 417–19.

Orr, P. C. (1965). Radiocarbon age of a Nevada mummy. *Science*, **148**, 1466–7.

Orr, P. C. (1968). *Prehistory of Santa Rosa Island*. Santa Barbara, CA: Santa Barbara Museum of Natural History.

Osborn, H. F. (1907). *Evolution of Mammalian Molar Teeth to and from Triangular Type*. New York, NY: Macmillan.

Ossa, P. (1978). Paijan in early Andean prehistory: the Moche Valley evidence. In *Early Man in America from a Circum-Pacific Perspective*, ed. A. Bryan. Edmonton, Alberta, Canada: Archaeological Researches, pp. 290–5.

Ousley, S. D. (1985). Relationships between Eskimos, Indians, and Aleuts: old data, new perspectives. *Human Biology*, **67**, 427–58.

Owen, R. C. (1984). The Americas: the case against an ice-age human population. In *The Origins of Modern Humans: A Survey of the Fossil Evidence*, ed. F. H. Smith and F. Spencer. New York, NY: Alan R. Liss Publishing, pp. 517–63.

Owsley, D. W. (1999). From Jamestown to Kennewick: an analogy based on early Americans. In *Who Were the First Americans?* Proceedings of the 58th Annual Biology Colloquium, Oregon State University, ed. R. Bonnichsen. Corvallis, OR: Center for the Study of the First Americans, Oregon State Univeristy, pp. 127–40.

Owsley, D. W. and Hunt, D. R. (2001). Clovis and Early Archaic period crania from the Anzick site (24PA506), Park County, Montana. *Plains Anthropologist*, **46**(176), 312.

Pääbo, S., Gifford, J. A., and Wilson, A. C. (1988). Mitochondrial DNA sequences from a 7000-year-old brain. *Nucleic Acid Research* **16**, 9775–87.

Pääbo, S., Higuchi, R. G., and Wilson, A. C. (1989). Ancient DNA and the polymerase chain reaction: the emerging field of molecular archaeology. *Journal of Biological Chemistry*, **264**(17), 97009–12.

Pääbo, S., Dew, K. Frazier, B. S., and Ward, R. H. (1990). Mitochondrial evolution and the peopling of the Americas. *American Journal of Physical Anthropology*, **81**, 277.

Perzigian, A. J. (1976). The dentition of the Indian Knoll skeletal population: odontometrics and cusp number. *American Journal of Physical Anthropology*, **44**, 113–22.

Perzigian, A. J. (1984). Human odontometric variation: an evolutionary and taxonomic assessment. *Anthropologie*, **22**, 193–7.

Petit, C. E. (1998). Rediscovering America: The New World may be 20,000 years older than experts thought. *US New & World Report*, **125**(4), 56–64.

Pookajorn, S. (1996). Human activities and environmental changes during the late Pleistocene to middle Holocene in southern Thailand and southeast Asia. In *Humans at the End of the Ice Age: The Archaeology of the Pleistocene–Holocene Transition*, ed. L. G. Straus, B. V. Eriksen, J. M. Erlandson and D. R. Yesner. New York, NY: Plenum Press, pp. 201–13.

Powell, J. F. (1993). Dental evidence for the peopling of the New World: some methodological considerations. *Human Biology*, **65**, 799–819.

Powell, J. F. (1995). Dental variation and biological affinity among Middle Holocene human populations in North America. Ph.D. thesis, Texas A&M University.

Powell, J. F. (1997). Variação dentária nas Américas: uma visão alternativa. *Revista USP*, **34**, 82–95.

Powell, J. F. (2002). The peopling of the Americas: a view from the north Pacific. Paper presented at the 17th Biennial Meeting of the American Quaternary Association (AMQUA), Anchorage, AK, August 9, 2002.

Powell, J. F. and Neves, W. A. (1998). Dental diversity of early New World populations: taking a bite out of the tripartite model. *American Journal of Anthropology Supplement*, **26**, 179–80.

Powell, J. F. and Neves, W. A. (1999). Craniofacial morphology of the first Americans: pattern and process in the peopling of the Americas. *Yearbook of Physical Anthropology*, **42**, 153–88.

Powell, J. F. and Rose, J. C. (1999) *Report on the Osteological Assessment of the "Kennewick Man" Skeleton (CENWW.97.Kennewick)*. US Department of the Interior Report. Available at http://nps.aad.kennewick.org/kennewick.

Powell, J. F. and Steele, D. G. (1993). A multivariate craniometric analysis of North American Paleoindian remains. *Current Research in the Pleistocene*, **9**, 59–61.

Powell, J. F. and Steele, D. G. (1994). Diet and health of Paleoindians: an examination of early Holocene human dental remains. In *Paleonutrition: The Diet and Health of Prehistoric Americans*, ed. S. D. Sobolik. Center for Archaeological Research Occasional Papers Series. Carbondale, IL: Center for Archaeological Research, Southern Illinois University, pp. 176–90.

Powell, J. F., Neves, W. A., Ozolins, E., and Pucciarelli, H. M. (1999). Afinidades biológicas extra-continentales de los dos esqueletos más antiguos de América: implicaciones para el poblamiento del Nuevo Mundo. *Antropologia fisica Latinoamericana*, **IIIb**, 114–27.

Preston, D. (1997). The lost man. *The New Yorker*, June 16, 1997, p. 70.

Prous, A. (1980). Fouilles du grand abri de Santana do Riacho Minas Gerais, Brésil. *Journal de la Societé des Américanistes*, **67**, 163–83.

Prous, A. (1986). L'Archéologie au Brésil. 300 siècles d'occupation humaine. *L'Anthropologie*, **90**, 257–306.

Prous, A. (1991). *Arqueologia brasileira*. Brasilia: Editora UNB.

Prous, A. (1994). L'art Rupestre du Brésil in Préhistoroire Ariégeoise. *Bulletin de la Société Préhistorique Ariége-Pyrenées*, **44**, 77–144.

Purdy, B. A. (1991). *The Art and Archaeology of Florida's Wetlands*. Boca Raton, FL: CRC Press, Inc.

Radosavljevich, P. R. (1911). Professor Boas' new theory of the form of the head: a critical contribution to school anthropology. *American Anthropologist*, **13**, 394–433.

Relethford, J. H. (1991). Genetic drift and anthropometric variation in Ireland. *Human Biology*, **63**, 155–65.

Relethford, J. H. (1994). Craniometric variation among modern human populations. *American Journal of Anthropology*, **95**, 53–62.

Relethford, J. H. (1995). Genetics and modern human origins. *Evolutionary Anthropology*, **4**, 53–63.

Relethford, J. H. and Blangero, J. (1990). Detection of differential gene flow from patterns of quantitative variation. *Human Biology*, **62**, 5–25.

Relethford, J. H. and Harpending, H. C. (1994). Craniometric variation, genetic theory, and modern human origins. *American Journal of Anthropology*, **95**, 249–70.

Relethford, J. H. and Harpending, H. C. (1995). Ancient differences in population size can mimic a recent African origin of modern humans. *Current Anthropology*, **36**, 667–74.

Relethford, J. H. and Lees, F. C. (1982). The use of quantitative traits in the study of human population structure. *Yearbook of Physical Anthropology*, **25**, 113–32.

Renfrew, C., ed. (1973). *The Explanation of Culture Change: Models in Prehistory*. London: Duckworth Press.

Rhine, S. (1990). Nonmetric skull racing. In *Skeletal Attribution of Race*, ed. G. W. Gill and S. Rhine. Maxwell Museum Occasional Papers No. 4, University of New Mexico, pp. 9–20.

Riberio-Dos-Santos, A. K. C., Santos, S. E. B., Machado, A. L., Guapindaia, V., and Zago, M. A. (1996). Heterogeneity of mitochondrial DNA haplotypes in Pre-Columbian natives of the Amazon region. *American Journal of Physical Anthropology*, **101**, 29–37.

Rivet, P. (1943). *Les origins de l'homme americaine*. Montreal, Quebec, Canada: Les Edition l'Abre.

Rodgers, R. A., Rodgers, L. A., and Martin, L. D. (1992). How the door opened: the peopling of the New World. *Human Biology*, **64**, 281–302.

Rogan, P. K. and Salvo, J. J. (1990). Study of nucleic acids isolated from ancient remains. *Yearbook of Physical Anthropology*, **33**, 195–214.

Rogers, J. L., Almasy, L., Commuzie, A. G., Blangero, J., and Mahaney, M. C. (1999). Quantitative trait linkage mapping in anthropology. *Yearbook of Physical Anthropology*, **39**, 127–51.

Roosevelt, A., da Costa, M. L., Machado, C. L. *et al.* (1996). Paleoindian cave dwellers in the Amazon: the peopling of the Americas. *Science*, **272**, 373–84.

Roosevelt, A. C., Douglas, J., and Brown, L. (2002). The migrations and adaptations of the first Americans: Clovis and pre-Clovis views from South America. In *The First Americans: The Pleistocene Colonization of the New World*, ed. N. G. Jablonski. San Francisco, CA: Memoirs of the California Academy of Sciences, No. 27, pp. 159–223.

Salzano, F. M. and Callegari-Jacques, S. M. (1988). *South American Indians: A Case Study of Evolution*. Oxford: Oxford University Press.

Sauer, N. J. (1992). Forensic anthropology and the concept of race: if races don't exist, why are forensic anthropologists so good at identifying them? *Social Science and Medicine*, **34**(2), 107–11.

Sayles, E. B. and Antevs, E. (1941). *The Cochise Culture*. Medallion Papers 29. Gila Pueblo, AZ: Globe.

Schanfield, M. S. (1992). Immunoglobulin allotypes GM and KM indicate multiple founding populations of Native Americans: evidence of at least four migrations to the New World. *Human Biology*, **64**, 381–402.

Schanfield, M. S., Crawford, M. H., Dossetor, J. B., and Gershowitz, H. (1990). Immunoglobulin allotypes in several North American Eskimo populations. *Human Biology*, **62**, 773–89.

Schindler, D. L. (1985). Anthropology in the Arctic: a critique of racial typology and normative theory. *Current Anthropology*, **26**, 475–99.

Schmitz, P. I. (1984). *Caçadores e Coletores da Pré-História do Brasil*. São Leopoldo: Instituto Anchietano de Pesquisas.

Schmitz, P. I. (1987). Prehistoric hunters and gatherers of Brazil. *Journal of World Prehistory*, **11**, 53–125.

Schurr, T. G. (2002). Tracking genes through time and space: changing perspectives on Pleistocene migration to the New World. Paper presented at the 2002 American Quaternary Association Meeting (AMQUA), University of Alaska, Anchorage, AK, August 9–12.

Schurr, T. G. and Wallace, D. C. (1999). MtDNA variation in Native Americans and Siberians and its implications for the peopling of the New World. In *Who Were the First Americans?*, ed. R. Bonnichsen. Proceedings of the 58th Annual Biology Colloquium, Oregon State University. Corvallis, OR: Center for the Study of the First Americans, Oregon State Univeristy, pp. 41–77.

Schurr, T. G., Sukernik, R. I., Starikovskaya, Y. B., and Wallace, D. C. (1999). Mitochondrial DNA variation in Koryaks and Itel'men: population replacement in the Okhotsk Sea–Bering region during the Neolithic. *American Journal of Physical Anthropology*, **108**, 1–39.

Sciulli, P. W. (1979). Size and morphology of the permanent dentition in prehistoric Ohio Valley Amerindians. *American Journal of Physical Anthropology*, **50**, 615–28.

Sciulli, P. W. (1990a). Deciduous dentition of a Late Archaic population of Ohio. *Human Biology*, **62**, 221–45.

Sciulli, P. W. (1990b). Cranial metric and discrete trait variation and biological differentiation in the terminal Late Archaic of Ohio: the Duff site cemetery. *American Journal of Physical Anthropology*, **82**, 19–29.

Sciulli, P. W. and Mahaney, M. C. (1991). Phenotypic evolution in prehistoric Ohio Amerindians: natural selection versus random genetic drift in tooth size reduction. *Human Biology*, **63**, 499–511.

Sciulli, P. W., Janini, C., and Giesen, M. (1988). Phenotypic selection on the dentition in a Late Archaic population of Ohio. *American Journal of Physical Anthropology*, **76**, 527–33.

Scott, G. R. (1973). Dental morphology: a genetic study of American white families and variation in living Southwest Indians. Ph.D. thesis, Arizona State University.

Scott, G. R. (1979). Increase in tooth size in prehistoric coastal Peru, 10 000–1000 BC. *American Journal of Physical Anthropology*, **50**, 251–8.

Scott, G. R. and Dahlberg, A. A. (1982). Microdifferentiation in tooth crown morphology among Indians of the American southwest. In *Teeth: Form, Function, and Evolution*, ed. B. Kurtén. New York, NY: Columbia University Press, pp. 259–91.

Scott, G. R. and Turner, C. G. II (1988). Dental anthropology. *Annual Review of Anthropology*, **17**, 99–126.

Scott G. R. and Turner C. G. II (2000)

Scott, G. R., Street, S., and Dahlberg, A. A. (1988). The dental variation in Yuman speaking groups in an American Southwest context. In *Teeth Revisited: Proceedings of the VIIth International Symposium on Dental Morphology, Paris 1986*, ed. D. E. Russell, J. Santoro and D. Sigogneau. Paris: Muséum National D'Histoire Naturelle.

Shafer, D. and Stang, J. (1996). Anthropologists fight to study Kennewick bones. *City Herald, Kennewick Interpretive Center*. Available at http://www.kennewick.com/story/09-97/.

Shaffer, H. A. (1986). *Ancient Texans*. Austin, TX: Texas Monthly Press.

Simons, E. L. (1971). A current review of the interrelationships of Oligocene and Miocene Catarrhini. In *Dental Morphology and Evolution*, ed. A. A. Dahlberg. Chicago, IL: University of Chicago Press, pp. 193–208.

Sjøvold, T. (1973). The occurrence of minor non-metrical variants in the skeleton and their quantitative treatment for population comparisons. *Homo*, **24**, 204–33.

Smith, F. H. and Spencer, F., ed. (1984). *The Origins of Modern Humans: A World Survey of the Fossil Evidence*. New York, NY: Alan R. Liss.

Smith, M. O. (1995). Bioarchaeological inquiry into Archaic Period populations of the Southeast: trauma and occupational stress. In *Archaeology of the Mid-Holocene Southeast*, ed. K. E. Sassaman and D. G. Anderson. Gainesville, FL: University of Florida Press.

Sofaer, J. A., Niswander, J. D., and MacClean, C. J. (1972). Population studies on southwestern Indian tribes, V. Tooth morphology as an indicator of biological distance. *American Journal of Physical Anthropology*, **37**, 357–66.

Sokal, R. R., Oden, N. J., and Wilson, C. (1991). Genetic evidence for the spread of agriculture in Europe by demic diffusion. *Nature*, **351**, 143–5.

Spencer, F. (1982). Introduction. In *A History of American Physical Anthropology 1930–1980*, ed. F. Spencer. London, Academic Press.

Spuhler, J. N. (1979). Genetic distances, trees, and maps of North American Indians. In *The First Americans: Origin, Affinities, and Adaptations*, ed. W. S. Laughlin and A. B. Harper. New York, NY: Gustav Fischer, pp. 1–12.

Stafford, M. (1990). The Powars II site (48PL330): a Paleoindian red ocher mine in eastern Wyoming. Unpublished M.A. thesis, University of Wyoming.

Stanford, D. J. (1999). Paleoindian archeology and late Pleistocene environments in the plains and southwestern United States. In *Ice Age Peoples of North*

America, ed. R. Bonnichsen. Center for the Study of the First Americans. Corvallis, OR: Oregon University Press, pp. 281–339.

Stanford, D. J. and Bradley, B. (1999). The Solutrean solution: did some ancient Americans come from Europe? Paper presentation at the *Clovis and Beyond* Conference, Santa Fe, NM.

Stanford, D. J. and Bradley, B. (2002). Ocean trails and prairie paths? Thoughts about Clovis origins. In *The First Americans: The Pleistocene Colonization of the New World*, ed. N. G. Jablonski. San Francisco, CA: Memoirs of the California Academy of Sciences, No. 27, pp. 255–72.

Starikovskaya, Y. B., Sukernik, R. I., Schurr, T. G., Kogelnik, A. M., and Wallace, D. C. (1998). MtDNA diversity in Chukchi and Siberian Eskimos: implications for the genetic history of ancient Beringia and the peopling of the New World. *American Journal of Human Genetics*, **63**, 1473–91.

Steele, D. G. and Powell, J. F. (1992). Peopling of the Americas: paleobiological evidence. *Human Biology*, **64**(3), 303–36.

Steele, D. G. and Powell, J. F. (1993). Paleobiology of the first Americans. *Evolutionary Anthropology*, **2**(4), 138–46.

Steele, D. G. and Powell, J. F. (1994). Paleobiological evidence of the peopling of the Americas: a morphometric view. In *Method and Theory for Investigating the Peopling of the Americas*, ed. R. Bonnichsen and D. G. Steele. Corvallis, OR: Center for the Study of the First Americans, pp. 141–63.

Steele, D. G. and Powell, J. F. (1998). Historical review of the skeletal evidence for the peopling of the Americas. Paper presented at the Annual Meeting of the Society for American Archaeology, March 13, 1998, Seattle, WA.

Steele, D. G. and Powell, J. F. (1999). Peopling of the Americas: a historical comparative perspective. In *Who Were the First Americans?*, ed. R. Bonnichsen. Corvallis, OR: Center for the Study of the First Americans, Oregon State University, pp. 97–126.

Steele, D. G. and Powell, J. F. (2002). Facing the past: a view of the North American human fossil record. In *The First Americans: The Pleistocene Colonization of the New World*, ed. N. G. Jablonski. San Francisco, CA: Memoirs of the California Academy of Sciences, No. 27, pp. 93–122.

Steele, D. G., Martin, L. D., Dort, W. Jr., and Powell, J. F. (1991). Human remains from Bonner Spring, Kansas: a late Pleistocene/Holocene locality. Paper presented at the 56th Annual Meeting of the Society for American Archaeology, New Orleans, LA.

Steele, J., Adams, J., and Sluctin, T. (1998). Modeling Paleoindian dispersals. *World Archaeology*, **30**, 286–305.

Stewart, T. D. (1960). A physical anthropologist's view of the peopling of the New World. *Southwest Journal of Anthropology*, **16**, 259–73.

Stewart, T. D. and Newman, M. T. (1951). An historical resumé of the concept of differences in Indian types. *American Anthropology*, **53**, 19–36.

Stone, A. C. (1996). Genetic mortuary analysis of a prehistoric Native American community. Unpublished Ph.D. thesis, Pennsylvania State University.

Stone, A. C. (1999). Reconstructing human societies with ancient molecules. In *Who Were the First Americans?*, ed. R. Bonnichsen. Proceedings of the 58th Annual Biology Colloquium, Oregon State University. Corvallis, OR: Center for the Study of the First Americans, Oregon State University, pp. 25–39.

Stone, A. C. and Stoneking, M. (1996). Genetic analyses of an 8000-year-old Native American skeleton. *Ancient Biomolecules*, **1**(1), 83–7.

Stoneking, M. and Stone, A. C. (1998). MtDNA analysis of a prehistoric Oneota population: implications for the peopling of the New World. *American Journal of Human Genetics*, **62**, 1153–70.

Storm, P. (1995). The evolutionary significance of the Wajak skulls. *Scripta geologica*, **110**, 1–247.

Straus, L. G., ed. (1996). *Humans at the End of the Ice Age: The Archaeology of the Pleistocene–Holocene Transition.* New York, NY: Plenum Press.

Straus, L. G. (2000). Solutrean settlement of North America? A review of reality. *American Antiquity*, **65**(2), 209–26.

Stringer, C. B. (1985). Middle Pleistocene hominid variability and the origin of late Pleistocene humans. In *Ancestors: The Hard Evidence*, ed. E. Delson. New York, NY: Alan R. Liss, pp. 289–95.

Stringer, C. B. (1988). The dates of Eden. *Nature*, **331**, 565–6.

Stringer, C. B. (1998). Chronological and biogeographic perspectives on later human evolution. In *Neandertals in Western Asia*, ed. T. Akazawa, K. Aoki and O. Bar-Yosef. New York, NY: Plenum Press, pp. 29–37.

Sutter, R. C. (1997a). Dental variation and biocultural affinities among prehistoric populations from the coastal valleys of Moquegua, Peru. Unpublished Ph.D. thesis, University of Missouri–Columbia.

Sutter, R. C. (1997b). Verticality or horizontal complementarity? A bioarchaeological search for Pre-Incaic altiplan colonies in the coastal valleys of Moquegua, Peru and Azapa, Chile. *Latin American Antiquity*, **11**(1), 43–70.

Suzuki, H. (1969). Microevolutional changes in the Japanese population from the prehistoric age to the present-day. *Journal of the Faculty of Sciences, University of Tokyo Section V*, **3**, 279–308.

Suzuki H. (1981). Racial history of the Japanese. In *Rassengeschichichte der Memschheit*, ed. J. Schwidetzley. Hong Kong: Asian Research Sercice.

Suzuki, H. and Tanabe, G. (1982). Skulls of Minatogawa Man. In *The Minatogawa Man: The Upper Pleistocene Man from the Island of Okinawa*, ed. H. Suzuki and K. Hanihara. Bulletin of the University of Tokyo Museum, No. 19, University of Tokyo, pp. 7–49.

Swedlund, A. and Anderson, D. (1999). Gordon Creek Woman meets Kennewick Man: new interpretations and protocols regarding the peopling of the Americas. *American Antiquity*, **64**, 569–76.

Szathmary, E. J. E. (1986). Comment on "The settlement of the Americas: a comparison of the linguistic, dental, and genetic evidence." *Current Anthropology*, **27**, 490–1.

Szathmary, E. J. E. (1993a). Genetics of aboriginal North Americans. *Evolutionary Anthropology*, **1**, 202–20.

Szathmary, E. J. E. (1993b). MtDNA and the peopling of the Americas. *American Journal of Human Genetics*, **53**, 793–9.

Szathmary, E. J. E. (1994). Modelling ancient population relationships from modern population genetics. In *Method and Theory for Investigating the Peopling of the Americas*, ed. R. Bonnichsen and D. G. Steele. Corvallis, OR: Oregon State University, pp. 117–130.

Tankersley, K. B. (1998). Investigating a possible Clovis–Solutrean link: the Crook County Clovis cache. *Current Research in the Pleistocene*, **15**, 11–17.

Tanner, J. M. (1990) *Fetus into Man*. Cambridge, MA: Harvard University Press.

Taylor, R. E. (1987). *Radiocarbon Dating. An Archaeological Perspective*. New York, NY: Academic Press.

Taylor, R. E. (1991). Frameworks for dating the Late Pleistocene peopling of the Americas. In *The First Americans: Search and Research*, ed. T. D. Dillehay and D. J. Meltzer. Boca Raton, FL: CRC Press Inc, pp. 77–111.

Taylor, R. E. (1992). Radiocarbon dating of bone: to collagen and beyond. In *Radiocarbon Dating after Four Decades: An Interdisciplinary Perspective*, ed. R. E. Taylor, A. Long and R. Kra. New York, NY: Springer-Verlag, pp. 375–402.

Taylor, R. E. (1994). Radiocarbon dating of bone using accelerator mass spectrometry: current discussions and future directions. In *Method and Theory for Investigating the Peopling of the Americas*, ed. R. Bonnichsen and D. G. Steele. Corvallis, OR: Oregon State University, pp. 27–44.

Taylor, R. E., Payen, L. A., Prior, C. A. *et al.* (1985). Major revisions in the Pleistocene age assessments for North American human skeletons by C-14 accelerator mass spectrometry: none older than 11 000 C-14 years BP. *American Antiquity*, **50**, 136–40.

Templeton, A. R. (1998a). Nested clade analyses of phylogeographic data: testing hypotheses about gene flow and population history. *Molecular Ecology*, **7**, 381–97.

Templeton, A. R. (1998b). Human races: a genetic and evolutionary perspective. *American Anthropology*, **100**, 632–50.

Templeton, A. R., Routman, E., and Phillips, C. A. (1995). Separating population structure from population history: a cladistic analysis of the geographical distribution of mitochondrial DNA haplotypes in the tiger salamander, *Ambystoma tigrinum*. *Genetics*, **140**, 767–82.

Thomas, D. H. (2000). *Skull Wars*. New York, NY: Basic Books.

Thomas, D. H. and Buxton (1923)

Thorne, A. G. (1971). Mungo and Kow Swamp: morphological variation in Pleistocene Australians. *Mankind*, **8**, 85–9.

Thorne, A. G. (1975). Kow Swamp and Lake Mungo. Unpublished Ph.D. thesis, University of Sydney.

Thorne, A. G. (1976). Morphological contrasts in Pleistocene Australians. In *The Origin of the Australians*, ed. R. L. Kirk and A. G. Thorne. Canberra: Australian Institute of Aboriginal Studies, pp. 95–112.

Thorne, A. G. (1977). Separation or reconciliation? Biological clues to the development of Australian society. In *Sunda and Sahul: Prehistoric Studies in Southeast Asia, Melanesia and Australia*, ed. J. Allen, J. Golson and R. Jones. London: Academic Press, pp. 187–204.

Thorne, A. G. (1984). Australia's human origins – how many sources? *American Journal of Physical Anthropology*, **63**, 227.

Thorne, A. G. and Macumber, P. G. (1972). Discoveries of Late Pleistocene man at Kow Swamp. *Nature*, **238**, 316–19.

Thorne, A. G. and Wolpoff, M. H. (1981). Regional continuity in Australasian Pleistocene hominid evolution. *American Journal of Physical Anthropology*, **55**, 337–49.

Torroni, A., Schurr, T. G., Yang, C. C. *et al.* (1992). Native American mitochondrial DNA analysis indicated that the Amerind and the Nadene populations were founded by independent migrations. *Genetics*, **130**, 153–62.

Torroni, A., Chen, Y. S., Semino, O. *et al.* (1994a). MtDNA and Y-chromosome polymorphisms in four Native American populations from southern Mexico. *American Journal of Human Genetics*, **54**, 303–18.

Torroni, A., Lott, M. T., Cabell, M. F., Chen, Y. S., Lavergne, L., and Wallace, D. C. (1994b). MtDNA and the origin of Caucasians: identification of ancient Caucasian-specific haplogroups, one of which is prone to a recurrent somatic duplication in the D-loop region. *American Journal of Human Genetics*, **55**, 760–76.

Torroni, A., Neel, J. V, Barrantes, R., Schurr, T. G., and Wallace, D. C. (1994c). Mitochondrial DNA "clock" for the Amerinds and its implications for timing their entry into North America. *Proceedings of the National Academy of Sciences USA*, **91**, 1158–62.

Turelli, M. (1988) Population genetic models for polygenic variation and evolution. In *Proceedings of the Second International Conference on Quantitative Genetics*, ed. B. S. Weir, E. J. Eisen, M. M. Goodman and G. Namkoong. Sunderland, MA: Sinauer Associates, pp. 601–18.

Turner, C. G. II (1969). Microevolutionary interpretations from the dentition. *American Journal of Anthropology*, **30**, 421–6.

Turner, C. G. II (1971). Three-rooted mandibular first permanent molars and the question of American Indian origins. *American Journal of Physical Anthropology*, **34**, 229–41.

Turner, C. G. II (1979). Dental anthropological indications of agriculture among the Jomon people of central Japan. X. Peopling of the Pacific. *American Journal of Physical Anthropology*, **51**, 619–36.

Turner, C. G. II (1983a). Dental evidence for the peopling of the Americas. In *Early Man in the New World*, ed. R. Schutler Jr. Beverly Hills, CA: Sage Publications, pp. 147–57.

Turner, C. G. II (1983b). Sinodonty and sundadonty: a dental anthropological view of Mongoloid microevolution origin and dispersal into the Pacific Basin Siberia and the Americas. In *Late Pleistocene and Early Holocene Cultural Connections of Asia and America*, ed. R. S. Vasilievsky. Novosibirsk: USSR Academy of Sciences Siberian Branch, pp. 72–6.

Turner, C. G. II (1985a). Dental evidence for the peopling of the Americas. *National Geographic Research Reports*, **19**, 573–96.

Turner, C. G. II (1985b). The dental search for Native American origins. In *Out of Asia: Peopling the Americas and the Pacific*, ed. R. Kirk and E. Szathmary. Canberra: *Journal of Pacific History*, pp. 31–78.

Turner, C. G. II (1986a). Dentochronological separation estimates for Pacific Rim populations. *Science*, **23**, 1140–2.

Turner, C. G. II (1986b). The first Americans: the dental evidence. *National Geographic Research Reports*, **2**, 37–46.

Turner, C. G. II (1989). Late Pleistocene and Holocene population history of east Asia based on dental variation. *American Journal of Anthropology*, **73**, 305–21.

Turner, C. G. II (1990). The major features of sundadonty and sinodonty including suggestions about east Asian microevolution population history and Late Pleistocene relationships with Australian aboriginals. *American Journal of Anthropology*, **82**, 295–317.

Turner, C. G. II (1992a). New World origins: new research from the Americas and the Soviet Union. In *Ice Age Hunter of the Rockies*, ed. D. J. Stanford and J. S. Day. Niwot, CO: University Press of Colorado, pp. 1–50.

Turner, C. G. II (1992b). Microevolution of east Asian and European populations: a dental perspective. In *The Evolution and Dispersal of Modern Humans in Asia*, ed. T. Akazawa, A. Kenichi, and T. Kimura. Tokyo: Hokusen-sha, pp. 415–38.

Turner, C. G. II (1994). Relating Eurasian and Native American populations through dental morphology. In *Method and Theory for Investigating the Peopling of the Americas*, ed. R. Bonnichsen and D. G. Steele. Corvallis, OR: Oregon State University, pp. 131–40.

Turner, C. G. II (2002). Teeth, needles, dogs, and Siberia: bioarchaeological evidence for the colonization of the New World. In *The First Americans: The Pleistocene Colonization of the New World*, ed. N. G. Jablonski. San Francisco, CA: Memoirs of the California Academy of Sciences, No. 27, pp. 123–58.

Turner, C. G. II and Bird, J. (1981). Dentition of Chilean Paleo-Indians and the peopling of the Americas. *Science*, **212**, 1053–5.

Turner, C. G. II, Nichol, C. R., and Scott, G. R. (1991). Scoring procedures for key morphological traits of the permanent dentition: the Arizona State University dental anthropology system. In *Advances in Dental Anthropology*, ed. M. A. Kelley and C. S. Larsen. New York, NY: Wiley-Liss, pp. 13–31.

Tuross, N., Fogel, M. L., Newsom, L., and Doran, G. (1994). Subsistence in the Florida Archaic: the stable isotope and archaeobotanical evidence from the Windover site. *American Antiquity*, **59**, 288–303.

Turpin, S. A., ed. (1991). *Papers on Lower Pecos Prehistory. Studies in Archaeology 8*. Texas Archaeological Research Laboratory, University of Texas at Austin.

Ubelaker, D. H. (1989). *Human Skeletal Remains: Excavation, Analysis, and Interpretation*. Washington, DC: Taraxacum.

Ulloa, A. (1944). *Noticias Americanas: Entretenimiento Físico-Histórico sobre la America Meridional y la Septentrional Oriental*. Madrid: Consejo Superior de Investigaciones Cientificas, Instituto Gonzalo Fernandez de Oviedo.

Virchow, R. (1888). La craniologie américain. *Proceedings of the International Congress of Americanists*, **7**, 250–62.

von Humboldt, A. (1811). *Political Essay on the Kingdom of New Spain, Containing Researchers Relative to the Military Defense of New Spain* (translation). New York, NY: I. Riley.

Wallace, D. C. and Torroni, A. (1992). American Indian prehistory as written in the mitochondrial DNA: a review. *Human Biology*, **64**(3), 403–16.

Ward, R. H., Redd, A., Valencia, D., Frazier, B., and Pääbo, S. (1993). Genetic and linguistic differentiation in the Americas. *Proceedings of the National Academy of Sciences USA*, **90**, 10663–7.

Waters, M. R. (1985). Early man in the New World: an evaluation of the radio-carbon dated pre-Clovis sites in the Americas. In *Environments and Extinctions: Man in Late Glacial North America*, ed. J. I. Mead and D. J. Meltzer. Orono, ME: Center for the Study of Early Man, pp. 125–42.

Waters, M. R. (1986). Sulphur Springs woman: an early human skeleton from south-eastern Arizona. *American Antiquity*, **51**, 361–5.

Webb, S. D. (1981). Cultural resources survey of the continental shelf from Cape Hatteras to Key West, Vol. I: Introduction and physical environments. Report submitted to the Bureau of Land Management, pp. 71–113.

Weidenreich, F. (1943). The skull of *Sinanthropus pekinensis*: a comparative study on a primitive hominid skull. *Paleonologia sinica, New Series D*, **5**, 1–485.

Weidenreich, F. (1945a). Giant early man from Java and south China. *American Museum of Natural History Anthropological Papers*, **40**, 1–134.

Weidenreich, F. (1945b). The brachycephalization of recent mankind. *Southwestern Journal of Anthropology*, **1**, 1–54.

Weidenreich, F. (1947). The trend of human evolution. *Evolution*, **1**, 221–36.

Weiss, K. M. (1973). *Demographic Models for Anthropology*. Society for American Archaeology Memoir No. 27. Washington, DC: Society for American Archaeology.

Weiss, K. M. (1994). Commentary: American origins. *Proceedings of the National Academy of Sciences USA*, **91**, 833–5.

Wendorf, F., ed. (1968). *The Prehistory of Nubia*. Dallas, TX: Fort Burgwin Research Center and Southern Methodist University Press.

Wendorf, F. and Schild, R. (1986). *The Prehistory of Wadi Kubbaniya. The Wadi Kubbaniya Skeleton: A Late Paleolithic Burial from Southern Egypt*, Vol. 1. Dallas, TX: Southern Methodist University Press.

Wendorf, F. and Schild, R. (1996). The middle Paleolithic settlement system in the eastern Sahara. Proceedings of the Congress of the International Union of Prehistoric and Protohistoric Sciences, Forli, Italy, pp. 305–12.

Wharton, B. R., Ballo, G. R., and Hope, M. E. (1981). The Republic Grove site, Hardee County, Florida. *Florida Anthropologist*, **34**, 59–80.

Wiessner, P. (1977). Hxaro: a regional system of reciprocity for reducing risk among the !Kung San. Ph.D. thesis, University of Michigan, Ann Arbor, MI.

Wilkie, A. O. M. and Morris-Kay, G. M. (2001). Genetics of craniofacial development and malformation. *Nature Reviews of Genetics*, **2**, 458–68.

Wilkie, A. O. M., Tang, Z., Elanko, N. *et al.* (2000). Functional insufficiency of the human homeobox gene MSX2 causes defects in skull ossification. *Nature Genetics*, **24**, 287–390.

Williams-Blangero, S. and Blangero, J. (1989). Anthropometric variation and the genetic structure of the Jirels of Nepal. *Human Biology*, **61**, 1–12.

Williams-Blangero, S. and Blangero, J. (1992). Quantitative genetic analysis of skin reflectance: a multivariate approach. *Human Biology*, **64**, 35–49.

Williams, R. C., Steinberg, A. G., Gershowitz, H. *et al.* (1985). Gm allotypes in Native Americans: evidence for three distinct migrations across the Bering Land Bridge. *American Journal of Physical Anthropology*, **66**, 1–19.

Wilson, D. (1857). On the supposed uniformity of cranial type, throughout all varieties of the American race. *Proceedings of the American Association for the Advancement of Science*, **11**, 109–27.

Wolpoff, H. E. (1980). *Paleoanthropology*. New York, NY: Knopf.

Wolpoff, (1997). *Race and Human Evolution*. New York, NY: Simon and Schuster.

Wolpoff, M. H. and Caspari, R. (2000)

Woo, J. (1959). Human fossils found in Liukiang, Kwangsi, China. *Gu Jizhuidongwu yu Gu Renlei*, **1**, 97–104.

Wright, H. E. (1991). Environmental conditions for Paleoindian migration. In *The First Americans Search and Research*, ed. T. D. Dillehay and D. J. Meltzer. Boca Raton, FL: CRC Press, Inc, pp. 113–35.

Wright, R. V. S. (1995). The Zhoukoudian upper cave skull 101 and multiregionalism. *Journal of Human Evolution*, **29**, 181–3.

Wright, S. (1943). Isolation by distance. *Genetics*, **28**: 114–38.

Wright, S. (1951). The genetical structure of populations. *Annals of Eugenics*, **15**, 323–54.

Wright, S. (1978). *Evolution and the Genetics of Populations*, Vol. 4: *Variability Within and Among Natural Populations*. Chicago, IL: University of Chicago Press.

Wu, R. and Lin, S. (1983). Peking Man. *Scientific American*, **248**, 78–86.

Yamaguchi, B. (1982). A comparative study of the skulls of the Ontario Iroquoians and of Asiatic populations. *Bulletin of the National Science Museum, Tokyo, Series D (Anthropology)*, **3**, 23–35.

Index

AAA statement on race, 52
Abbott, C. C., 21
Acosta, J. 18, 188
adaptation, 35, 36, 50, 171, 200, 206
ad-hoc models, 234
Afalou, 170
Ainu, 232
Aleuts, 189, 207
Allen's rule, 50
altitude, 50
American Paleolithic, 21
Amerind languages, 189
Amerindians, 189, 207
amino acids, 59
Amur, 207
Anzick (Willsall), 137
Archaic period, 116
artificial cranial modification, 179
Australasia, 176, 200
auxology, 37
Aztecs, 18

barbarians, 29
Bergmann's rule, 50
Beringia, 115
Bering Land Bridge, 8, 118, 229
Biblical Flood, 32
bioarchaeology, 23
biological species, 31
Blummenbach, J., 19, 20, 31
blunt trauma, 164
Boas, F., 27, 35, 36, 53, 214
Brace, C. L., 79, 205, 216
brachycranic (brachycephalic), 188,
   189, 190
Browns Valley Man, 136
Buhl, 152

canalized, 51
Chamberlin, T. C., 22
Chatters, J. C., 46

Chinese, 34
Ciencia, 19
civilized, 29
clinal distribution, 69
Clovis, 20, 128, 149, 169, 218,
   226, 231
   complex, 86, 115
   drought, 109, 116, 147
   -first, 115
   tools, 116
coastal refugia, 103
Cohuna, 178
Congoids, 40
Cook, H., 22
Coon, C. S., 38
Crania egyptica, 34
Crania americana, 25, 33
cranial (cephalic) index, 37
   brachycranic (brachycephalic),
      188, 189, 190
   dolichocranic (dolichocephalic),
      147, 188, 190
   mesocranic (mesocephalic), 190
Cro-Magnon, 172
cultural affiliation, 2
cultural patrimony, 2

Dahlberg, A. A., 208
Darwin, C., 21, 68
generis humani nativa, De, 20, 31
de Ulloa, A., 24
demography, 91
   survivorship, 68
   population growth, 214
dental
   anthropology, 190
   attrition (wear), 73
   calculus, 73
   homogeneity, 193
   Mongoloid dental complex, 194, 215
   morphological traits, 190

dental (cont.)
    deflecting wrinkle, 194
    dentochronology, 202
    distosagittal ridge (UP3), 216
    enamel hypoplasia, 51
    entoconulid, 194
    incisor (UI1) shoveling, 194, 211,
        215, 228
    protostylid, 194
descriptive historicism, 31, 36
diet, 200
diffusionism, 188
DNA, 59
    ancient DNA (aDNA), 62, 91, 92, 93, 95
    mitochondrial (mtDNA), 59, 85, 87,
        88, 92, 96
    nuclear DNA (nDNA), 59, 85, 216
    nucleotides, 59
    polymerase chain reaction (PCR),
        61, 91
    restriction fragment length
        polymorphism (RFLP), 61
Dryas, 103
    Older, 103
    Younger, 103
Dubois, E., 177

Early Archaic period, 128
eide, concept of, 31
Eskimo (Inuit), 189, 207
Esquimaux (Eskimos), 34
essentialism, 31, 36, 37, 53
Ethiopians, 32
Eurasian, 166
European contact, 222
evolution, forces of, 62
    genetic drift, 34, 62, 188, 202, 214,
        225, 235
        founder effect, 85, 214, 216, 225,
          235
        genetic bottleneck, 216
    gene flow (migration), 49, 70, 80,
        188, 214, 218, 229
    mutation, 62, 80, 214
    selection, 48, 62
        balancing, 68, 69
        natural, 48, 49, 68, 69
        fecundity, 68
        fitness, 68
        sexual, 48, 49, 68, 69
evolutionary approach, 58
extinction, 165

Fe divina, 19
Figgins, J., 22
First view point, 166
Folsom, 128, 149, 156, 166, 218
    Culture, 116

    Points, 116
foragers, sedentary, 171
fracture, 150
Franciscus, R., 50
F_{st}, 216, 223, 224, 234

Garcia, J., 19
genetics, 59
    alleles, 60, 63
    admixture, 90, 172
    fixation, 63
    genes, 60
        human leukocyte antigen (HLA),
          62, 85, 87, 88, 95
        GM alleles, 86
        KM alleles, 87
    genotype(s), 60, 85
    heterozygote advantage (hybrid
        vigor), 49
    phenotype, 30, 64
giant ground sloth, 147, 165
Gilder Mound, 138
Gloger, W., 48
Gloger's rule, 48
Goodall, J., 29
Gould, S. J., 33
Greenberg, J., 27

Harpending, H., 44
Heirakanopolis, 171
Historia natural y moral de las Indias, 18, 19
historical events, 215
Hoabinhian, 176
Holmes, W. H., 21, 22
Holocene, 59, 128
Homo erectus, 179
Homo sapiens sapiens, 169, 180
homogeneity, 214
Hooton, E. A., 4, 5, 26, 35, 36
Hrdlička, A., 22, 23, 25, 188, 189, 215,
    230, 235
Huddleston, L., 17
humidity, 50
hyper-diffusionism, 188

ice age (*see also* Pleistocene), 83
    interstadials, 111
    stadials, 109
        Nebraskan, 110
        Kansan, 110
        Illinoisan, 110
        Wisconsinan, 110
ice sheets
    Cordillerian, 8, 103, 104, 120
    Laurentide, 8, 103, 104, 120
Ice-Free Corridor, 103, 122
Indies, 19
insolation, 105

Jantz, R., 9
Jebel Qafzeh, 172
Jebel Sahaba, 171
Jews, 35, 36
Jomon, 221

Keith, Sir A., 35, 36
Kennewick Man, 6, 7, 8, 21, 46, 71, 83, 91, 153, 198, 200, 227, 234
Kerma, 170
Khoi, 41, 42
Konigsberg, L. W., 70
Kow Swamp, 178
!Kung San, 42

Late Pleistocene, 59, 115, 202
Linnaeus (Karl von Linne), 30, 147
Liukang, 174, 180
Livingston, F. B., 44
local races, 38, 188
Lothagam, 169

Malays, 32
mammoth, 147
mastodon, 147
megafauna, 165
metaconulid, 194
metric variation, 193
micro-races, 38
Midland point, 166
Midland site, 139
Milankovich cycle, 105, 108
    eccentricity, 105
    obliquity, 108
    seasonal precession, 108
Minatogawa, 174, 175, 180, 190, 221
Mixtecs, 18
model-free, 59, 187, 196
Moh Kiew Cave, 176
monstrous, 30
Monte Verde, 161
Morton, S. G., 20, 25, 33, 189
multiple analysis of variance (MANOVA), 196

Na-Dene (Athabaskan), 189, 207
NAGPRA (Native American Grave Protection Act), 2, 3, 8, 12
narrow sense heritability, 70
Native Americans, 2, 5, 17, 20, 24, 32, 229
    founding mtDNA haplogroups (A, B, C, D), of, 90
Neumann, G. K., 188
neurocranium (braincase), 32
New World migration models, 115
    coastal, 122, 123
    4-wave migration, 97, 117

tripartite model (3 wave), 37, 97, 189
Solutrean 123
Norris Farm, 93

Odd-male model, 49
Origen de los Indios de el Nuevo Mundo y Indias occidentales, 19
Origin of Species, 21
ossification, 74
overkill model, 226
Oviedo, V. G. F., de, 19
Owsley, D. W., 4, 9, 11, 166

Paleoamerican, 12
Paleoindian remains,
    North America
        Arlington Springs, 93
        Cutler fossil site, 133
        Gordon Creek, 151
        Grimes Burial Shelter, 149
        Horn Rockshelter, 142
        Hourglass Cave, 92, 141
        Little Salt Spring, 129
        Midland Woman, 166
        Natchez pelvis, 129
        Pelican Rapids ("Minnesota Man"), 135
        Prince of Wales Island Man (49-PET-408), 154
        Rancho La Brea ("La Brea tar pits"), 147, 188, 200, 227
        Sauk Valley, 137
        Shifting Sands, 140, 166
        Spirit Cave, 149, 200
        Stick Man, 153
        Sulphur Springs, 145
        Warm Mineral Spring (WMS), 131
    South America
        Cerca Grande VI, 200
        Cerca Grande VII, 161, 164, 165, 199, 200, 217
        Cerro Sota Cave No. 2, 162
        Fells Cave, 46, 162
        Luzia (Lapa Vermelha), 158, 159, 198, 234
        Paiján, 156
        Palli Aike Cave, 204
        Penon III, 151, 154
        Punin, 157
        Otovahalo, 157
Paleolithic, Upper, 175
Paleoliths, 21, 22
pathologies, stress-related, 164
Peru, atiplano, 51
phenomelanin, 54
Plainview, 143
Plato, 31
Pleistocene peoples, 169, 180

Pleistocene, 1, 8, 12, 21, 103, 128, 147, 169
  cultures, 114
  environment, 111
  North America, 103, 107, 109, 111, 112, 113, 229
  peoples, 169, 180
Plinius (Pliny the Elder), 29
population structure, 69
  effective population size (Ne), 81, 219, 234
  Hardy–Weinberg equilibrium, 62
  heritability, 70
  inbreeding (f), 64, 234
  island migration model, 64, 68
  isolation by distance (I by D) model, 49, 64, 70, 218
  spatio-temporal gene flow, 70
  stepping-stone model, 65, 66, 67
  survivorship, 68
post-hoc models, 78, 187
pre-Clovis, 117
Predmosti, 173
probable mutation effect, 79, 203
Putnam, F. W., 21, 22

quantitative traits, 46, 46
  gene–gene interaction (epistasis), 46
  polygenic trait, 71
Quechua, 51
Quirihuac, 156

race, 30, 44, 196
  Australoid(s), 42, 174, 187
  Capoids, 42
  Caucasoid, 6, 7, 9, 10, 11, 20, 32, 124
  Mongolian types, 189, 221
  Mongoloid(s), 20, 38, 175, 190
  Negroids, 20
  Nigritos, 43, 44
  non-Mongoloid, 212
  proto-Australoid, 177
  proto-Caucasoid, 166, 221
  proto-Mongoloid, 180, 190
  racial types, 188
  Racial–typological methods, 11, 187, 190, 214, 221, 231
radiocarbon (^{14}C), 7
Rastell, J., 17
red ocher, 180
  red ocher burial, 180
Relethford, J., 223

secular trend, 51
Seminole Sink, 140
Sewall Wright, 63
sex, 1
sexual dimorphism, 72, 196

sharp trauma, 164
Siberia, 188, 189
single tandem repeat (STR), 61
sinkhole, 129, 141
size correction, 196
skin color, 48
slaves, 34
Smith, E., 188
Smithsonian Institution, 21, 22
Stadial, 103
statistical methods
  Penrose shape coefficient, 81
  principal components analysis (PCA), 195, 198
  R-matrix analysis, 223, 224
Steele, D. G., 9
subspecies, 30, 31
Sudanese Nubians, 171
Sulphur Springs stage, 145
Systema naturae, 30

temperature, 50
Tepexpan, 155
Thailand, 176
Origin of Races, The, 38
Tlapacoya XVIII, 155
trade, exchange networks, 218
Trenton Gravels, 21, 22, 128
Turner, C. G., 99, 194, 202, 203, 207, 215
typicality probability, 200

Upper Cave (Shandingdong), 174, 190, 221
Ushki Lake level, 179

variety, 31
variation
  additive variation, 71
  dominance variation, 71
  environmental variation, 72
  epistatic variation, 46, 71, 75
  nonmetric (discrete) variation, 193
Vietnam, 176
violence, interpersonal, 164

Wadi Kubbaniya, 171
Wadjak 1, 176
Weidenreich, F., 177, 234
Whitewater Draw (Sulphur Springs) site, 144
Wilson–Leonard, 143, 166, 227
Windover, 133
Wizards Beach, 200, 202
WMS "Brown" skull, 132, 221

Y-chromosome DNA (Y-DNA), 93, 97

Zhoukoudien, I., 174